The Textual History of
KING LEAR

The Textual History of
KING LEAR

P. W. K. STONE

Scolar Press London

First published by
Scolar Press 90/91 Great Russell Street
London WC1B 3PY

Scolar Press is an imprint of Bemrose UK Limited

BRITISH LIBRARY CATALOGUING IN PUBLICATION DATA
Stone, P W K
The textual history of King Lear.
1. Shakespeare, William. King Lear
2. Shakespeare, William — criticism, textual
I. Title
822.3'3 PR2819
ISBN 0 85967 536 x

Phototypeset in V.I.P. Garamond by
Western Printing Services Ltd, Bristol

Printed in Great Britain
at The Pitman Press, Bath

Designed by Brian Dunce

CONTENTS

REFERENCES

Line numbers in Shakespeare's plays are cited throughout from the Globe edition of 1864.

The titles of secondary sources most frequently referred to appear in the footnotes and appendices in the following abbreviated forms:

Abbott   E. A. Abbott, *A Shakespearian Grammar*, 3rd edition (London, 1870)

Bentley, *Profession*   G. E. Bentley, *The Profession of Dramatist in Shakespeare's Time 1590–1642* (Princeton, 1971)

Chambers, *Stage*   E. K. Chambers, *The Elizabethan Stage* (Oxford, 1923), 4 vols.

Chambers, *Wm. Sh.*   E. K. Chambers, *William Shakespeare, A Study of Facts and Problems* (Oxford, 1930), 2 vols.

Dobson   E. J. Dobson, *English Pronunciation 1500–1700*, 2nd edition (Oxford, 1968), 2 vols.

Doran, *Text*   Madeleine Doran, *The Text of 'King Lear'* (Oxford, 1931)

Duthie, *Shorthand*   G. I. Duthie, *Elizabethan Shorthand and the First Quarto of 'King Lear'* (Oxford, 1949)

Gaskell, *New Introduction*   Philip Gaskell, *A New Introduction to Bibliography* (Oxford, 1972)

Greg, *EPS*   Sir W. W. Greg, *The Editorial Problem in Shakespeare*, 3rd edition (Oxford, 1954)

Greg, *Folio*   Sir W. W. Greg, *The Shakespeare First Folio* (Oxford, 1955)

Greg, *Publishing*   Sir W. W. Greg, *Some Aspects of London Publishing between 1550 and 1650* (Oxford, 1956)

Greg, *Variants*   W. W. Greg, *The Variants in the First Quarto of 'King Lear'* (London, 1940)

Harsnett   Samuel Harsnett, *A Declaration of Egregious Popish Impostures* (London, 1603). Readings cited from G. Bullough, *Narrative and Dramatic Sources of Shakespeare*, vol. VII (London, 1973), pp. 414–20

Hinman, *Printing*   Charlton Hinman, *The Printing and Proof-Reading of the First Folio of Shakespeare* (Oxford, 1963), 2 vols.

Kirschbaum, *Stationers*   Leo Kirschbaum, *Shakespeare and the Stationers* (Columbus, Ohio, 1955)

Kökeritz   Helge Kökeritz, *Shakespeare's Pronunciation* (Yale, 1953)

Onions, *Glossary*   C. T. Onions, *A Shakespeare Glossary*, 2nd edition, reprinted with corrections and enlarged addenda (Oxford, 1958)

PREFACE

The text of *King Lear* presents the critic with a fascinating but complex and difficult problem. Of the play as Shakespeare wrote it we have no evidence but that of the early printed editions, and of these the first three offer conflicting testimony. The third, especially, differs from the first two not, perhaps, on any single point of major importance, but in a multitude of particulars, which amount in sum to a disparity of major proportions.

Each of these early prints is manifestly defective, so that the critic must attempt to discover not only why they differ from each other, but also how and why it is they have suffered so much corruption. His task is further complicated by the fact that, in spite of the marked differences between them, they have clearly been derived in large part one from the other, the later from the earlier. The second and the third, in other words, are reprints, but reprints of no ordinary kind.

Until the relationships between the early texts have been accurately traced, and the origin of each clearly understood, the critic has no hope at all of sifting the mass of evidence they supply, ambiguous or contradictory as it so frequently is; and no hope, consequently, of reaching any conclusion about what Shakespeare's true intentions may have been in respect of a very large number of details which make up no inconsiderable portion of the play. He needs, in other words, a complete and coherent historical explanation of the genesis of the texts: if he can trace the processes by which they came into being, he is in a much better position to appraise the value of their testimony to the author's original.

The attempt to supply an explanation has, of course, often been made, and not entirely without success. Some, at least, of the perplexities have been, by general agreement, satisfactorily unravelled. In the main, however, scholars have reached what might be called a tentative and uneasy consensus: no one appears fully satisfied with the hypothesis which is now, for lack of a better, generally accepted, and there are indeed good reasons why it has commanded an allegiance sometimes more nominal than real among recent editors of the play.

There is every inducement, therefore, to tackle the problem afresh. Since the difficulties to be met are not only numerous, but often complex, and since, in my opinion, they have not yet been resolved very largely because they have not yet been thoroughly enough considered, it seemed advisable to cast this fresh attempt to deal with them in the form of an extended essay, with supplementary appendices containing the relevant textual data, rather than in the form of a new edition of the play, the text of which would inevitably appear to occupy an viii incongruously unimportant place beside the necessary volume of introduction and commentary.

A book of this kind must necessarily address itself to the specialist. It is not designed, however, to exclude the reader whose interest in Shakespeare is more general. It assumes no prior knowledge of the textual problem in *King Lear*, or of the literature devoted to it; neither does it assume a familiarity with the disciplines of bibliography and textual criticism in general beyond an acquaintance with their not very extensive technical vocabulary. One special demand only is made upon the reader: he should have at his disposal a scholarly edition of the play, such as the Arden, which records the variant readings of the early printed texts. Quotations in the chapters which follow should be found in most instances full enough to illustrate the arguments to which they apply; but the commentaries in the appendices will not in most cases be intelligible without reference to the surrounding context of the key word or phrase to which, for reasons of space, citations in that part of the book have been confined.

The theory developed here is in many respects new, in so far as it incorporates fresh interpretations of the evidence, and to some extent, too, inferences from evidence hitherto unnoticed. I should not care to claim that the main conclusions reached are original – there can be scarcely a speculation possible about the origin of the Shakespearean texts which has not occurred to someone in the course of the last two and a half centuries – but they have not, I believe, been advanced before in precisely the form they take here, or on precisely the same grounds. I have, on the other hand, made use very freely of the findings of previous investigators. Some of this knowledge is now familiar common property, but the reader will, I hope, find all my particular debts duly acknowledged.

Since I do not provide a complete list of the books and articles I have referred to or consulted, I should mention here that a classified and fully annotated bibliography of the subject is available in T. H. Howard-Hill, *Shakespearian Bibliography and Textual Criticism: A Bibliography* (Oxford, 1971). A few relevant publications too recent to be listed in this volume are noticed in my footnotes.

In common, I imagine, with every other contemporary student of Shakespeare's text I owe more to one previous scholar in the field than to all the others combined: I refer, of course, to Sir Walter Greg. If I seem more than once to emphasise my disagreement with him, that is only because his authority extends over so wide an area of the subject: it would be impossible to propose independent views on any one of a large number of questions without attempting at the same time to justify them against his own invariably well-informed and well-argued case.

CHAPTER ONE
THE TEXTUAL PROBLEM

Only the three earliest known editions of Shakespeare's *King Lear* have any possible claim to authority. All later editions of the play derive directly or indirectly from one or more of these three.

The earliest of them, a quarto (Q1), was entered in the Stationers' Register to Nathaniel Butter and John Busby on 26 November 1607. The entry refers to the play as 'Master William Shakespeare his historye of Kinge Lear, as yt was played before the Kinges maiestie at Whitehall vppon Sainct Stephens night at Christmas Last, by his maiesties seruantes playinge vsually at the Globe on the Banksyde'.

The book was published the following year. We find repeated on its title-page the information about a Court performance at Christmastide. The publisher's imprint reads: 'London, Printed for Nathaniel Butter, and are to be sold at his shop in Pauls Church-yard at the signe of the Pide Bull neere St. Austins Gate. 1608'. It has been surmised, from the use of a printer's ornament on the title-page which is known to have been used by Nicholas Okes, that he was responsible for printing the book.

A second quarto (Q2) followed the first. Its title-page reproduces that of Q1 exactly except for a few changes of spelling and punctuation and a much abbreviated imprint, *viz*: 'Printed for Nathaniel Butter. 1608'. The order in which the two quartos appeared long remained doubtful, and indeed it was thought that the evidence of the extant copies might point to more than two separate editions. It was not until 1866 that the editors of the Cambridge Shakespeare, W. G. Clark and W. Aldis Wright, settled both issues, proving the priority of the 'Pied Bull' edition by demonstrating that it had been corrected during printing and that some of its uncorrected readings had been inherited by its successor.[1] At this time Q2 was still regarded, on the *prima facie* evidence of the imprints, as a more or less immediate re-edition of Q1. Between 1908 and 1910, however, one of the most interesting investigations yet conducted in the field of Shakespearean textual studies revealed that Q2 was not, in fact, published in the same year as its predecessor. Bibliographical

---

1 Curiously, they refer to the 'Pied Bull' edition throughout their text as the *later* of the two.

2 evidence was brought forward to establish its true pedigree as one of a series of
nine plays printed by William Jaggard for Thomas Pavier in 1619. All of these
plays were reissues. Some of them Pavier frankly acknowledged as such, but on
others, such as the *Lear* reprint, he reproduced the date of their first edition. His
motive for so doing remains something of a mystery.[2]

Four years later *King Lear* was printed for the third time, again by William
Jaggard. It appears in the first collected edition of Shakespeare's plays, the First
Folio of 1623 (F). The Folio was published, as the colophon indicates, by a
syndicate consisting of the Jaggards, William and his son Isaac, Edward
Blount, John Smethwick and William Aspley. It is generally assumed that they
received the assistance, in an editorial or perhaps only entrepreneurial capacity,
of John Heminges and Henry Condell, two of Shakespeare's associates in the
King's Men. The names of these actors are found appended to a prefatory
'Address to the Reader' — which suggests that they were responsible for
collecting the plays, if not also seeing them through the press.

A cursory inspection of the three texts would undoubtedly give rise to an
impression that Q1 was the least satisfactory. It prints long tracts of verse as
prose; and, in places, what is obviously prose as crippled verse. Passages rightly
printed as verse are sometimes badly misaligned. The punctuation, which
consists largely of commas, often fails altogether to serve its purpose. Questionable readings meet the eye on nearly every page, many of them obviously wrong,
and some of them egregious nonsense (e.g. *accent teares*; *flechuent*; *Mobing, &
Mobing*).

Most editors seem to have agreed that, when Q1 differs from F (which is very
frequently), F more often than not preserves the better reading, even when — as
sufficiently often happens — both readings make acceptable sense. Compared
with the text of F, that of Q1 appears distinctly less satisfactory.

About one hundred lines, including a large number of scattered words,
phrases and part-lines, appear in F which are absent from Q1. Q1, on the other
hand, contains roughly three hundred lines that are missing from F.

The text of Q1 was corrected in the course of printing. The process has been
exhaustively investigated by Sir Walter Greg, who based his study on a collation
of the twelve surviving copies.[3] These copies show five sheets of the quarto (D,
E, F, G and H) in two states, uncorrected and corrected. Two further sheets (C,

---

2 The relevant facts are conveniently
   summarised in Chambers, *Wm.
   Sh.*, I. 133–7.

3 Greg, *Variants*.

K) exist in three states: uncorrected, partly corrected and corrected. The 3
remaining sheets (B, I and L) show no variation in the existing copies. The
variants in the corrected sheets amount in all, on Greg's reckoning, to 146.

An important part of Greg's purpose was, of course, to distinguish, with
respect to each variant sheet, the original from the 'corrected' state of the text.
The reader is referred to his conclusions, which have commanded universal
assent and which are scarcely, indeed, open to question.[4] Q1 readings may safely
be identified as 'corrected' or 'uncorrected' on Greg's authority.

In the pages that follow it will be convenient, wherever relevant, to distinguish the uncorrected version of Q1 as 'Q1a' from the corrected version, 'Q1b'.[5]
It will be important to remember, however, that although any given sheet of the
quarto may be described as 'corrected' or 'uncorrected', the sheets were bound
up in an apparently random fashion to form complete copies of the book. Thus
no known copy of the book is composed exclusively of corrected or of uncorrected sheets, and if such a copy or copies ever existed, they must have been the
product entirely of chance. 'Q1a', therefore, must be taken to refer not to an
uncorrected *copy* or *copies* of the First Quarto, but to an uncorrected *state of the
text*.

In seven out of the twelve extant copies of Q1 there appear manuscript
corrections in seventeenth-century hands, a list of which is given in Appendix
IV of Greg's book. None of these corrections has any textual authority, but they
have a value in indicating the readings contemporaries recognised as erroneous,
and in illustrating the kind of emendation they found appropriate. The copy
known as 'BM2', much more lavishly corrected than the others, is particularly
interesting in this respect.[6]

The peculiar features of the Q1 text — its faulty lineation and poor punctuation, its passages of nonsense, some of them clearly traceable to errors of
hearing, its haphazard stage directions — early suggested to editors that it was
printed from a report of a theatrical performance. It was natural to assume
further that the report must have been taken in shorthand which was later
transcribed for the printer.[7]

---

4 Greg, *Variants*, ch. III, esp. pp.
    38–9.

5 The partly-corrected states of
    sheets C and K, containing, as
    they do, very minor corrections,
    may be discounted for the purpose
    here.

6 See Greg, *Variants*, pp. 106–7 and
    115ff. The British Library
    shelfmark of BM2 is C.34.k.17.

7 There is contemporary testimony
    to the fact that plays were pirated
    with the help of stenographers.
    Thomas Heywood twice refers to
    the practice (see Chambers, *Wm.
    Sh.*, I. 147).

4   This theory, though it did not go uncontested, was widely accepted until the publication in 1949 of G. I. Duthie's *Elizabethan Shorthand and the First Quarto of 'King Lear'*. Duthie maintained that, of the three systems of shorthand known to exist in the early 1600s, the two earlier and more primitive methods would have been incapable of producing a text as full and accurate as that of the *Lear* Quarto. The third system, John Willis's 'stenographie', might conceivably, he argued, have proved adequate. On the other hand, it could not satisfactorily account for the errors in Q1, few of which are of the kind one would expect to see generated by such a system. This last point Duthie elaborated with a wealth of illustration.

Duthie's demonstration carried conviction, and the shorthand hypothesis was abandoned. Critics were subsequently obliged to suppose a different origin for the report which apparently underlies the text. Duthie himself, in his edition of 1949, suggested that the report emanated not from a theatrical performance but from a collective effort on the part of the King's Men to reconstruct a missing prompt-book, the company dictating their parts from memory to a scribe. A new version of this theory was put forward in 1953 by Alice Walker, who concluded that only one member of the company was responsible for dictating while another wrote, and that the evidence pointed to the boy actors playing the roles of Goneril and Regan. Their aim was not to reproduce a missing prompt-book, but to dispose of the copy surreptitiously for profit. Moreover, they did not rely on their memories but called in aid a manuscript: Shakespeare's rough draft of the play, purloined for the purpose from the archives of the company. The accuracy with which they performed this task must have been impaired by interference from their imperfect recollections of previous performances: the scenes in which Goneril and Regan appear are, Miss Walker argued, more seriously garbled than any others in the text.

In a later edition of the play Duthie abandoned his previously held views in favour of Miss Walker's, though with some reservations, notably about the restriction of the enterprise to two actors.[8]

These may be taken to represent the latest developments in critical orthodoxy on the subject of Q1. Greg, at all events, accepted them as representative in his survey of the situation some years ago.[9] He, too, favoured Miss Walker, but with more serious reservations, concluding on a note of dissatisfaction: 'It is to be feared that a consideration of the various theories so far advanced can only lead

8   Alice Walker, *Textual Problems of the First Folio* (Cambridge, 1953); G. I. Duthie, editions of 1949 and ('New Cambridge Shakespeare') 1960.

9   Greg, *Folio*, pp. 375ff.

to the conclusion that it remains as true to-day as it was twenty-five years ago that *King Lear* still offers a problem for investigation'.[10]

Most recent critics have inclined to the view that the text of Q1 was by one means or another aurally transmitted. Not all, however. In the 1930s a theory was advanced that the Q1 text was printed from a prompt-book. The same decade saw yet another proposal: that it was Shakespeare's original manuscript which served as copy for the printer.[11]

The arguments for and against these theories will be examined in the next chapter.

It has long been recognised that Q2 is a reprint of Q1. It can, indeed, easily be demonstrated that it reproduces a copy of Q1 of which sheets D, G and H remained in the uncorrected state. The repetition of Q1's errors (especially on these sheets, which we know to have been contemporaneously corrected) is the clearest evidence that no authoritative source of copy was available to the publishers.

Some attempt, however, was made in the printing house to remedy the confusions of Q1. Spelling and punctuation were revised, though far from thoroughly, lineation here and there modified and a large number of new readings introduced (together, of course, as is usual in reprints, with a fresh crop of mistakes). Of the deliberate changes of reading most are trivial: they bear witness to a persistent, though not by any means unremitting, attempt to 'polish' the details of the style; many are corrections of obvious misprints, while a handful reveal themselves as more or less luckless attempts at emendation. These patent sophistications offer by themselves strong evidence of the wholly derivative status of Q2.

Curiously, a number of Q2 variants re-appear in F, and it is a surprising number at first sight. This has led some scholars to believe that Q2, if it lacks authority, must nevertheless possess some importance as an influence on F.

The F text of *King Lear* differs from that of Q1 in several important respects. It is, on the immediate view, clearly a 'better' text. In spelling and punctuation it is far more regular and consistent. Most of the verse is correctly aligned. It provides all but a few of the necessary stage directions, in contrast to Q's numerous omissions. And, whereas Q presents a continuous text, F's is carefully divided into acts and scenes.

10   Greg, *Folio*, p. 383.

11   Doran, *Text*; B. A. P. van Dam,
      The Text of Shakespeare's 'Lear'
      (Louvain, 1935).

6   F is characterised as well by a large number of verbal variants. The bulk of these alternative readings are 'indifferent', neither obviously superior nor obviously inferior to their counterparts in Q. And of these 'indifferent' variants most are relatively unimportant: connectives, contractions and the like. But a substantial minority of the variants in F may be seen as clear improvements on Q. They make better sense and often better metre, and not infrequently it is obvious that they supply correct versions of the Q compositor's misreadings. One or two instances of this are especially interesting since they show that F may provide the right reading even when the Q proof-corrector has gone astray:

	Q1a	Q1b	F
II.ii.133	ausrent	miscreant	ancient
	[misreading of *ansient?*]		
III.iv.6	crulentious	tempestious	contentious

F possesses the additional asset of about a hundred lines of text which are absent from Q. None of this additional matter could be described as essential to the play, and one part of it at least has been condemned by various scholars as spurious (III.ii.79–96). This passage apart, however, the fresh material is not noticeably different in style or in quality from the rest of the play, and there is no *prima facie* case for suspecting it.

As against these improvements, F lacks about three hundred lines which are to be found in Q. But none of the omitted passages is necessary to an understanding of the action, and none of the omissions, with two exceptions to be discussed later in more detail, results in discontinuity. F is not without further blemishes, however. Mechanical misprints apart, the text is by no means free from errors and problematical readings, some echoing the mistakes of Q1, others diverging with doubtful accuracy, others again arising strangely where Q1 is manifestly correct. It could not, in other words, be said that F presents a wholly satisfactory version of the text.

Despite the anomalies, however, scholars have almost unanimously agreed that F is the more authentic text of the two, and that where it diverges from Q it does so in the vast majority of instances on good authority. Editors of the play have, almost without exception, used F as the basis of their editions.

It was P. A. Daniel who, in the last century, was the first to argue that F was printed from a copy of Q1.[12] The case rests on a number of errors common to the

---

12   Introduction to the Praetorius
     facsimile (1885).

two texts, more particularly a few readings in which F agrees (erroneously) with
Q1a. The argument as further developed by Greg[13] is now very generally
accepted as conclusive.

It follows, of course, if Q1 served as copy for F, and if F is the more authentic
text, that the Q1 'copy' for F must have been compared with an authoritative
manuscript and very extensively corrected. An editor, naturally, must have
been employed about this laborious task: it could not have been left to compositors in the printing-house. It is usually assumed, for reasons which I shall
discuss later, that the manuscript he consulted was a prompt-book on loan from
the playhouse.

On these assumptions two sorts of explanation are available for the errors
discoverable in F: they may be compositorial mishaps, or they may be oversights
or aberrations on the part of the editor in his work of collation and correction.
Where F is not obviously mistaken, its divergence from Q must reflect upon the
unreliable transmission of the earlier text, mutilated as that was twice over, first
by the imperfect memories of actors and then by the carelessness of a scribe,
before being submitted to a not overly conscientious or competent printer.
Nearly all recent editors have accepted these inferences, and prepared their texts
accordingly.[14]

13 *Variants*, pp. 139–42.

14 They may subscribe, however, to
    different views of the origin of Q.
    Kenneth Muir based his 'Arden'
    text (London, 1952) on Duthie's
    1949 hypothesis, but later inclined
    to Alice Walker's (prefatory note
    to reprint of 1953, later incor-
    porated into the Introduction).
    G. K. Hunter (New Penguin
    Shakespeare, Harmondsworth,
    1972) appears also to favour Alice
    Walker ('An Account of the Text',
    p. 315). J. L. Halio (The
    Fountainwell Drama Texts,
    Edinburgh, 1973) reverts, by
    contrast, to Madeleine Doran's
    theory (see above) of an authorial
    manuscript as 'copy' for Q. He
    therefore bases his edition on Q,
    but with liberal importations from
    F, of which he takes the accepted
    view that it contains authoritative
    corrections from a playhouse

manuscript (*op. cit.*, 'A Note on
the Text', pp. 13–14). Among
recent commentators who share the
general understanding of F's
derivation, E. A. J. Honigmann
accepts the Walker–Duthie theory
about Q, but with the reservation
that Q–F variants do not
necessarily imply Q errors: they
may, sometimes at least, indicate
authorial revision in F (*The
Stability of Shakespeare's Text*
(London, 1965), ch. VIII); while
J. K. Walton returns to preferring
Duthie's theory of 1949 (*The
Quarto Copy for the First Folio of
Shakespeare* (Dublin, 1971), pp.
269–72).

8   One critic has in the past adopted a different explanation of F's relation to Q. Madeleine Doran, who believed Q1 to represent the author's original draft, was not persuaded that F derived in any way from the printed version of Q. She detected a manuscript source: not the same manuscript that had served for Q1, but a copy of it cast in the form of a prompt-book which, after transcription, had been thoroughly revised.[15] Her argument has since been neglected rather than refuted: the evidence she cites of manuscript 'copy' for F has never been otherwise explained. We shall in due course consider this question in detail.

It may now have become evident that, despite individual differences in the interpretation of evidence, recent scholars have by and large agreed about the status, relative to each other, of the *Lear* texts. F has the greatest authority, but, where it fails, Q1 is not a hopeless resource. For Q1 presents what is largely an authentic text, one, however, which has suffered from serious defects in the transmission. Q2 may be dismissed as derivative, though it may retain some interest as the source of a few readings in F.

So much is generally agreed. Yet difficulties remain and most critics have been uneasily aware of them. Duthie and Alice Walker have offered their theories rather tentatively, and Greg, as we have seen, after reviewing these theories, stated firmly that *King Lear* still offered 'a problem for investigation'.

The problem arises out of the complexity of the evidence, a complexity apparently unsusceptible to any simple and uncompromising explanation. At all events, none of the theories so far propounded is capable of accounting satisfactorily for all the facts. To see that this is so, the reader would require much more than the synoptic view of the evidence so far provided. The chapters that follow will, in fact, explore the difficulties piecemeal and in detail, at the same time as they attempt to develop, step by step, a coherent solution to the problem as a whole.

Nevertheless some of the issues – not necessarily the most important – can be exemplified at once. The reader may find it helpful to be given at the outset some indication why the proponents of what I have called the 'orthodox' theories fail to satisfy.

The text in the Folio is held to have been printed from a copy of Q1 after its correction by reference to a manuscript. If this is so, if all the variants in the F text derive from this manuscript source, the task must have been very thoroughly, in fact fastidiously, performed. Hundreds upon hundreds of changes are involved, a large number of them affecting matters of small detail. Plurals are substituted for singulars, and singulars for plurals where, from the

15 Doran, *Text*, pp. 39–40.

viewpoint of sense, either would do equally well; *that* is often carefully altered to *which*; *betwixt, you, oh* become *between, ye, ah*; elsewhere *between, ye, ah* become *twixt, you, oh*. Let us assume, however, what is occasionally suggested, that many, most, or all of these 'indifferent' changes were the result not of the collation itself but of editorial officiousness, or even of compositorial caprice — although it is difficult to imagine the motives of a copy-editor who alters *that* to *which*, while, as for the compositors, all the evidence goes to show that, if they were allowed to regularise spelling and punctuation, they were otherwise expected to reproduce their copy as they found it. But, however that may be, the F text abounds in minor alterations of another, less 'indifferent' kind — the substitution, addition or omission of pronouns, conjunctions, and the like, changes of tense, of word order and so on, which do not leave the meaning unaffected. These small but significant alterations must be, and always are, presumed to derive from the authoritative manuscript copy. If they do, they bear witness to a fairly high degree of care and accuracy in the collation.

It is all the more extraordinary, then, to find the collator committing so many oversights and blunders. The number of errors in F, in fact, errors which cannot be ascribed to compositorial mishaps, puts the collation theory to considerable strain, and places the editors who espouse it in a difficult position. They may occasionally, in emending an error which F has taken over from Q, explain that the collator must have overlooked the mistake in the printed copy; or, when restoring a Q reading from which F has wrongly diverged, argue that the master manuscript, being perhaps less than totally legible at this point, must have led the collator astray. But, in view of the reliance which must in general be placed on the collator's efficiency, carelessness of this kind cannot be too frequently attributed to him. The choice, then, must eventually lie between, on the one hand, an expedient but illogical willingness to distrust the collator and, on the other, a stubborn but (as it must prove) misguided faith in his conscientiousness and accuracy.

A similar difficulty is presented by the numerous synonymous or quasi-synonymous equivalents in F for readings in Q. It is generally agreed about these that the collator has in each case restored the original where Q has recorded an actor's improvised substitution. But we meet exceptions. Recent editors have decided, for example, that in the two instances following Q is to be preferred to F:

	Q	F
III.vii.58	*rash* borish phangs	*sticke* boarish phangs
III.vii.63	that *dearne* time	that *sterne* time

10 Evidently Q offers in both cases more difficult readings, words which are most unlikely to have occurred spontaneously to an actor. So that their equivalents in F are seen to be the spurious substitutions of an editor wishing to replace an out-of-the-way vocabulary with a more familiar one.

Yet if there is reason to detect such motives at work in two cases, why not in others? And if a collator or editor went so far in interference, might he not have gone still further in the interests of an easier and smoother text? In redeeming clumsiness of syntax or metre, for example, or in supplying fancied hiatuses or pruning fancied superfluities? His handiwork might be present on every page.

Once a source is acknowledged of spurious alterations to the text, the collation hypothesis is much weakened. The collator's authority comes in question: how often did he exceed it, or how often was it over-ridden by editorial 'improvements'? An even more serious problem is posed by his apparent blunders, which cast doubt upon the very aptness of the hypothesis. How can we reconcile so many obvious and damaging oversights with a minute attention to relatively unimportant particulars?

Examples could be multiplied of the dilemmas with which a supporter of the orthodox theory must inevitably be faced. But I have said enough, perhaps, to show by way of preliminary that the theory does not very comfortably accommodate the facts.

Less orthodox critics, such as Madeleine Doran, have found themselves in little better case. Miss Doran supposes, for example, that F was printed throughout from a manuscript copy. She thus gets rid of the collator and the perplexities that follow in his train. She does not on the other hand confront the problem of obvious bibliographical links between F and the printed quarto, a problem which cannot be disposed of on her theory without postulating a series of extraordinary coincidences in the printing history of the two texts.

There is, I think, a reason why these theories fall short of the mark. It reflects not upon the capacities of their inventors but upon the principles which they have adopted. I do not wish to embroil the reader at this point in a purely theoretical argument, but it will be useful if, before I present the whole problem to him afresh, I am able to explain what I consider to be the unfortunate consequences in the case of *Lear* of applying methods which, in my view, must be defective in all cases of the kind.

16 The most thorough consideration so far of the *Lear* problem, Miss Doran's, reaches the following conclusion on p. 14: 'on the whole F is a much superior text'. Thereafter, throughout the course of a long book, F's 'superiority' is assumed, without argument, to have established its superior *authority*.

With one or two exceptions, all recent investigations into, or reviews of, the *Lear* problem have incorporated the assumption that the F text is 'better' than that of Q. By 'better' is meant 'more authentic', but no reasons are put forward why one judgement should entail the other.[16] This looks like a plain blunder which no critic of experience could possibly perpetrate. But indeed the matter is not quite so simple.

The fact is, I believe, that a strong intellectual prejudice is at work. It has become an established rule of editorial practice, one that is universally (as far as I can judge) subscribed to, that all the details of a text must be treated in strict conformity with a pre-formulated hypothesis about its provenance and the circumstances of its printing. It is less clearly established how much, and what kind of, evidence is needed to suggest the hypothesis, but in practice the field is restricted to what is clearest and least controversial: strictly bibliographical data of various kinds, stage directions and prefixes, variants, obvious misprints, self-evident and easily emended corruptions. When such features of the *Lear* texts are passed under review it is hard to separate the impression one receives that F is a 'better' text from the impression one is likely to receive at the same time that it is a 'more authentic' one. Two only of its salient features suggest authenticity – a series of 'corrections' of Q which could probably not have been arrived at by conjecture, and a mass of additional matter which, if it does not prove itself genuine, may well be so – but these suggestions are powerfully reinforced. The greater regularity and polish of the text and its presentation, by themselves of no significance, confer great additional authority where a likelihood of authenticity has already been discovered. It may then be only sensible to decide that the 'better' text – given one or two striking indications of its independent derivation – is *ipso facto* the more authentic one.

Yet the decision has been ill prepared. As we have seen, it has led to the formulation of insufficient working hypotheses. How could it be otherwise? We would not, in any other context, hope to arrive at a convincing historical explanation of a body of facts until *all* the facts had been examined, compared and weighed. We would, of course, be prepared to entertain any number of preliminary, partial or interim hypotheses as a necessary aid to our researches, but we should immediately notice the fallacious reasoning in a suggestion that it would be more 'objective' or 'scientific' to found a complete hypothesis on *some* only of the facts (those which appear easiest to interpret), allowing that hypothesis thereafter to determine our judgement of the mass of more problematical detail. As historians we would reject the suggestion. As textual critics, I believe, we should be equally cautious.

12   It is, I can only suppose, because this false conception of critical method has so long prevailed that the *Lear* texts have not yet been fully investigated. The Quarto, in particular, has been neglected. Mistrusted, if not dismissed, as the 'inferior' text, it has perhaps been considered unlikely to repay any very detailed study. In consequence its relationship to the Folio text has never, in my opinion, been fully understood. It need scarcely now be said that the present study sets out to remedy the deficiency. If it cannot pretend to finality, it may at least succeed in formulating the problems afresh and in recommending a more promising method of approach to future investigators.

The method, it must be confessed, is not exactly reflected in the plan of the book. It would much tire the reader's attention and burden his memory if he were presented at the start with large collections of data, from which a large number of provisional inferences were drawn to be progressively developed, eliminated or combined, a comprehensive *dénouement* being reserved for the last chapter. I have instead cast my argument throughout in its final form, arranging the exposition of evidence in an order which, it seems to me, would best assist a clear comprehension of the problems and their attempted solution. So as to avoid lengthy interruptions, no more detail will be cited in the text than is necessary to illustrate the matter under discussion, or support a line of reasoning. The reader will be referred, where further information may be called for, to the lists of data in the appendices.

This strategy is not without its drawbacks. Where the evidence touched upon is both extensive and debatable the relevant appendices must and do contain not only supplementary citations, but commentaries upon them, extending, so to speak, the discussion in the text. The reader is asked to bear in mind that, whereas evidence adduced in the course of the argument on such occasions can only be explained to him in terms of the theory *as put before him so far*, the remaining evidence in an appendix, less obvious perhaps in its implications, may require to be discussed in terms of the theory *as finally developed.* This will not, I hope, cause him too much uneasiness. Evidence detailed in the text will generally be offered as strong enough for the time being to justify the hypothesis suggested, or at least to exclude alternative hypotheses. In spite of this he may prefer, very properly, to reserve judgement. The remaining evidence will not be concealed from him. The exposition once completed, he will have the opportunity to measure the theory as a whole against the comprehensive collection of data which the appendices supply. He may then judge, too, singly and collectively, the arguments there presented to show that the facts not so far explained are, at best, consistent only with the theory proposed, or, at worst, not inconsistent with it.

CHAPTER TWO
THE FIRST QUARTO

It cannot but be concluded, upon any thorough examination of the evidence, that the text of Q1 derives from a theatrical report: from *verbatim* notes, that is, taken down at an actual performance or performances in the theatre. The motive of the reporter, of course, could only have been the sale of this copy to a piratical publisher. We have seen that precisely this conclusion was arrived at in the last century. Although it does not seem to have been publicly endorsed in England until E. K. Chambers gave it his tentative support in 1930,[1] it was not altogether rejected until the publication in 1949 of G. I. Duthie's book on Elizabethan shorthand. Subsequent speculation about the origins of the Q1 text has carried little conviction, for which the reason will presently appear. It may, in fact, be shown without much difficulty that the evidence, considered as a whole, overwhelmingly favours the hypothesis of a theatrical report.

Leaving aside, for the moment, the theatrical origins of the copy for Q1, it may be as well, first, to show why it must be regarded at all as a report (or the transcript of a report) rather than as an authorial manuscript or prompt-book, or transcript of some such document.

There may be some significance in the fact that the punctuation in Q1 is both primitive (it is virtually confined to periods, question marks and commas, with the latter predominating) and often inaccurate, even by the rather imprecise criteria of the age. It might be argued that a reporter would, as he wrote, have little, if any, leisure for punctuating his notes, and in transcribing them might not find it worthwhile to expend much time and thought on the matter.

A much stronger argument in favour of reporting rests on the management, or mismanagement, of line-division revealed throughout the text of Q. Misline-ation, of varying degrees of faultiness, occurs on nearly every page, and sometimes persists through entire speeches. Prose is occasionally printed as verse; more frequently, and more persistently, verse is printed as prose (e.g. the last 150 lines, approximately, of I.iv, and the first hundred lines of II.i).

The grossness and frequency of these errors prove that, in the matter of line-division at least, the copy offered the compositor imperfect assistance or none at all. He must either have reproduced the errors of a badly misaligned copy; or, if the copy itself were undivided, the errors resulted from his own clumsy attempts to set it in order. In either case, it is highly unlikely that he was

---

1 *Wm. Sh.*, I. 465.

14 working from a prompt-book or even the transcription of a prompt-book. A number of contemporary theatrical manuscripts have survived, many of them demonstrably book-keeper's copies. Though they are not all absolutely free from irregularities of lineation, only those of the most dubious ancestry show anything like the persistent and radical misarrangements of Q1.[2] The theatrical 'book' of a new play, recently introduced into the repertory of the author's own company, could not possibly have degenerated into this condition.

It may, on the other hand, appear possible, though only barely possible, that an authorial rough draft would show such irregularities. Shakespeare may have left the work of line-division for a later fair copy, or he may, as Miss Doran maintains, have so covered the manuscript with revisions and interlineations as to obscure the line-division over large parts of it.

This hypothesis would have much to recommend it if we were able to recognise that, by and large, mislineated passages offer a well-marked contrast to the correctly-lineated ones, so that, for example, we could see them frequently enough as insertions into a context which would be complete without them. But such is not the case. The transitions in the text from erroneous lineation to regularity and back again appear for the most part quite arbitrary. There is, besides, nothing else in the text to suggest that it derives from authorial 'copy'. Such further evidence as we find strongly corroborates the hypothesis of a report.

As was long ago recognised, many of the corruptions of the Q text originate in errors of the ear. I give a short list below of the more obvious of these errors, including neither those which, though ostensible mishearings, may possibly be explained as misreadings or sophistications of the compositor, nor those which may be construed as aberrant spellings (e.g. *obrayds* for *upbraids*). I exclude many, too, which have hitherto (in my opinion) gone undetected, confining myself to those generally acknowledged in modern editions. Naturally, the admission of even a singly incontrovertibly phonetic error creates a strong presumption that the text will contain others, and lends colour to the doubtful instances. A limit must, in any case, be set to the number of coincidences we allow in maintaining that apparent mishearings are actually misreadings. It is remarkable that one only of the many errors in F, when we exclude those

---

2 A good example is *John of Bordeaux*, most of which is unlined. It contains what appears to be an abridged version of the play. Marking omitted passages are notes to indicate what is missing. W. L. Renwick, the editor of the Malone Society reprint, concludes from the signs of hasty writing and from the phonetic spellings and errors that the manuscript was probably taken down from dictation.

inherited from Q, could possibly be mistaken for an error of the ear.[3]

A full list of the phonetic errors in Q, both probable and possible, may be found in Appendix A3. In the brief list which follows, Q readings are entered in the left-hand column, their accepted emendations on the right.

1. *Homonymous substitutions*
I.iv.369	ought	oft (F)
II.iv.248	chanc'st	chanc'd (F)
III.iv.23	one	own (F) .

2. *Near-homonymous substitutions*
I.i.112	mistresse	mysteries (F: miseries)
II.ii.115	dialogue	dialect (F)

3. *Errors involving a dropped initial aspirate*
I.iv.363	after[4] (Qa)	hasten (Qb)
II.iv.213	owle	howl[5]
III.iv.79	a lo	Hollo (F: alow)
IV.i.62	Obidicut	Hoberdicut
V.iii.306	a rat of life	a rat have life (F)

4. *Errors involving misapprehensions of word-division*
I.iv.236	beit[6]	by it (F)
II.ii.153	hee's so	he, so
III.iv.127	O light	alight (F)
III.vii.62	holpt the	holpe the (F)
IV.iv.27	in sight	incite (F)
IV.vi.163	a dogge, so bade[7]	a dog's obey'd (F)

3 At I.i.308: *let vs sit together* for *lets hit together* (Q).

4 This can only be a misreading of *asten*. It is highly unlikely that the compositor would have overlooked or ignored an initial 'h'.

5 Not always accepted by modern editors, though a verb is absolutely required by the context at this point, and *howl* is obviously the right one.

6 'By' was pronounced not very differently from 'be'.

7 *O light*, *in sight*, and *a dogge, so bade* are, just conceivably, misreadings. Misdivision of words in the copy is evident elsewhere. If so, the two latter errors depend as well on irregular phonetic spellings (*insight* for *incite*; *obade* for *obey'd*). Phonetic spellings, too, are a feature of the copy. Yet likelihood surely favours the simpler hypothesis of mishearing. *Bade*, it should be noted, was pronounced to rhyme with 'made'.

16   5. *Errors resulting in nonsense or the garbling of names*

I.ii.99	aurigular	auricular (F)
I.iv.305	thourt[8]	thwart (F)
III.vi.32	Hoppedance	Hoberdidance[9]
IV.i.62	Hobbididence	Hoberdidance
IV.i.64	Mohing	mowing

It will be seen that even a small part of the evidence available in this category strongly reinforces the assumption that the Q text was 'copied by the ear'. It is impossible to suppose that Shakespeare wrote *Obidicut* or *Mohing*, and extremely difficult to believe that such corruptions were copied into, or out of, a theatrical manuscript: they are obviously not misreadings. It has been suggested that the Q compositor may himself have been guilty of these and all other such blunders. A compositor, in committing a line or so to memory before setting it, is undeniably subject to aural confusions. Such errors, however, are generally trivial. It may be doubted whether a compositor's tricks of memory would mislead him into setting gibberish: he would surely, when in any danger of doing so, permit himself a second look at the copy, particularly – paradoxical though it may sound – if he were scrupulous enough to set gibberish when that was what the copy appeared to show (*cf. a nellthu night more*, Qa, for *he met the night mare*, Qb, at III.iv.126). It is certain that the misprinting of *after* for *hasten*, at least, derived from a deception of the compositor's eye, not of his ear. The aural error stood in the copy.

This evidence is persuasive testimony that the text of Q1 was based on a report. It might suffice by itself to demonstrate that any other hypothesis would scarcely be tenable. That being so, we may examine the remaining evidence of reporting not primarily as a confirmation of the preceding argument – though it would serve as such – but with a view to establishing the *theatrical* origin of the copy for Q.

There is little doubt that plays of the time were pirated by means of theatrical reports. Thomas Heywood twice complains of the practice, in terms which do

---

8   Possibly an irregular spelling of *thwart*, which was pronounced, and sometimes spelt, *thort* (also *thought*, *thaught*; see *OED*).

9   This is the form of the name as it appears in Samuel Harsnett's *A Declaration of Egregious Popishe Impostures*, the source of many names, as well apparently as of words and phrases, in the play. See Appendix 7 to the New Arden edition (ed. K. Muir, London, 1952), pp. 253ff. *Hoppedance* is unknown to Harsnett, and is obviously a corruption, although modern editors tend to reproduce it. *Cf.* the closer approach to the correct form at IV.i.62.

not suggest that he was in any way exceptionally its victim.[10] We have, besides, evidence of the results. To look no further than contemporary editions of Shakespeare, the earliest quartos of *Romeo and Juliet, Henry V* and *Hamlet* could hardly have been produced by any other means. There is reason to believe, however, that these texts were founded (or for the most part founded) on *memorial* reports, i.e. on a reporter's recollections of what he had heard in the theatre. A much more reliable method of reporting would necessarily have been used to produce the text of *Lear*, which is self-evidently more complete and more accurate as to substance than the 'bad' quartos of the other plays. The reporter, if a reporter is responsible, must have attempted a *verbatim* record of the play: he must have taken notes in the theatre, possibly in shorthand.

Contemporary critics no longer admit this possibility, for reasons that were explained in the preceding chapter. Retaining the hypothesis of a report, they have re-formulated it: the text was dictated to a scribe (who may also have been an actor), either by a member or members of the company reading from the prompt-book or by the company at large rehearsing the play from memory.[11] Dictation from the prompt-book would imply surreptitious proceedings of some kind undertaken with a view to providing a pirate with copy. Dictation from memory, in which the whole company would necessarily have partici-pated, could only have been motivated by a need to reconstruct the prompt-book. Speculation has proceeded further to specify the precise circumstances in which such transactions may be supposed to have taken place, but I must stop short of exploring the details to claim the reader's attention for the dictation hypothesis itself. The evidence does not, I believe, bear it out.

It is, of course, very nearly, if not perfectly, consistent with the evidence already examined; less than perfectly so since it is a little puzzling why the scribe did not ask for repetitions when he found himself writing nonsense, as from time to time he clearly must have done. But perhaps for some reason time was

---

10   In the epistle to *The Rape of Lucrece* (1608) he states: 'some of my plaies haue (unknown to me, and without any of my direction) accidentally come into the Printers handes and therfore so corrupt and mangled (copied onely by the eare) that I haue bene as vnable to knowe them, as ashamde to challenge them'; and in a prologue first published in 1637 and intended apparently for a revival of an early play, *If You Know Not Me, You Know Nobody* (1605), he protests that the printed version has been obtained by stenography, 'scarce one word trew'.

11   The possibility of dictation directly to the compositor has also been raised, only to be dismissed. There is no evidence of the practice in English printing houses of the time, and no reason to believe that it would ever have recommended itself. See Gaskell, *New Introduction*, p. 49.

18 short; which would explain, too, if necessary, why he received no help with punctuation and lineation.

With another part of the evidence, however, the hypothesis of dictation, or dictation at least from a prompt-book, does not square. It is a generally acknowledged fact that the Q1 text abounds in what is known as 'gag': words or phrases improvised by actors to accompany a movement or gesture, to emphasise an effect, or simply to cover a lapse of memory. Such interpolations in Q are all, as far as we can tell, very brief. They betray themselves, firstly, in being devoid of any real substance; secondly, in disrupting the metrical pattern of the verse. There are probably dozens of them scattered through the text, but, since the likely instances are frequently embedded in passages of which the scansion is in any case problematical, no more than a score or so may be identified with any certainty. A few examples follow. The hyper-metrical line in each case is preceded and followed in the text by lines of regular length.[12]

> *Reg.* [Sir] I am made of the selfe same mettall that my sister is,
> I.i.70

> *Kent.* Now by *Appollo* [King] thou swearest thy Gods in vaine.
> I.i.163

> [*Cord.*]   . . . such a tongue,
> As I am glad I haue not, though not to haue it,
> Hath lost me in your liking.
> *Leir.* [Goe to, goe to] better thou / hadst not bin borne,
> Then not to haue pleas'd me better.
> I.i.234–7

> [*Leir.*] . . . let it . . . / turne all her mothers paines and benefits / to laughter and contempt, that shee may feele, [that she may feele,] / how sharper then a serpents tooth it is,
> I.iv.308–10

---

12   See also I.iv.332 and 333,
II.iv.239, III.vii.55, IV.i.19,
V.iii.78 and 309 for redundant
words and phrases omitted in F.
Several, however, are retained, e.g.
Sir (II.ii.144), *Sirra* (III.iv.184),
Madam (IV.ii.28), *So fare you well*
(IV.v.36 – the farewell is repeated
in l.40), *Euen so* (V.iii.242) and
heere (V.iii.295).

If twenty or so examples of 'gag' can be detected with some certainty, at least
as many more may plausibly be suspected. The appearance in such quantity of
actors' interpolations makes it very unlikely that the Q text was read aloud from
a prompt-book. Although it is, indeed, still open to question whether one
should expect to find extra-metrical words and phrases in authoritative texts of
the period, the most reliable evidence suggests that it was not the practice of
dramatic authors to divagate from a strict metrical pattern without reason. In
the authorised printed editions of dramatists such as Jonson or Webster we find
little metrical irregularity. Vocatives, exclamations, rhetorical repetitions and
the like are incorporated into the normal rhythm of blank verse. The surviving
theatrical manuscripts, those at least which appear to be either originals or
accurate copies of originals, offer like evidence.[13] It is therefore most unlikely
that the amount of extra-metrical 'padding' which appears in *Lear* could have
been discovered in the prompt-book.[14]

It is, besides, not very plausible that it would have been added in the process
of dictation. It is interesting that the parts of Edmund and Edgar, though they
may reveal corruption of other kinds, show no traces of 'gag', certain, probable
or even possible. Regan's part contains, relatively, a great deal, Goneril's
scarcely any. Of the rest (the doubtful examples included), by far the major
portion is associated with Kent, Gloucester and, especially, Lear. Were the
actor or actors engaged in dictating the text from a prompt-book to have
embroidered upon it at will, we should not expect so clear a pattern to appear.
As it is, improvisation is clearly associated with certain roles, and dissociated
from others, and we cannot suppose that reading from the text, unless the book
changed hands with every speech, would naturally have brought about this state
of affairs.

The entire company, dictating from memory, might well, of course, have
produced such results. We must now, however, notice another piece of evidence
which is scarcely consistent even with that possibility. The stage directions in Q
are very defective: a comparatively large number of entrances and exits are not

---

13 For example, *The Second Maiden's
Tragedy, The Two Noble Ladies, The
Captives* (Heywood), *Bonduca*
(Fletcher), *The Parliament of Love*
and *Believe as You List* (Massinger).
Most of these date from the 1620s,
but there is no reason to think that
had better manuscripts survived
from an earlier period they would
have showed greater irregularity.

14 It should be remembered that a
recently prepared prompt-book is
in question which we cannot
suppose to have been submitted as
yet to the ravages of theatrical
revision or the hazards of
recopying.

20 marked at all, and of those marked several are unclear or faulty.[15] This is further evidence against the dictation hypothesis. It needs no arguing that a prompt-book is unlikely to have been the source of such errors and, especially, omissions. Entrances in a prompt-book were customarily written in a bold, italic hand across the centre of the page and would scarcely have been overlooked in such numbers. But it is unlikely, too, on the memorial hypothesis, that the company as a whole would have failed so often to apprise the scribe of their movements on to and off the stage, particularly if, as the hypothesis assumes, they were engaged in reconstructing a prompt-book. It is, in fact, only by supposing a reporter at work in the theatre that we can satisfactorily account for the mistakes and the lacunae. We should naturally not expect him to achieve, or even attempt, a full complement of stage directions as he took his notes. And we might easily suppose him less than meticulous or accurate in supplying the gaps at a later stage.

The character of the stage directions, too, indicates that they originated with a spectator rather than with the author or the book-keeper or any professional member of a theatrical company. Such evidence, considered piecemeal, is usually difficult of interpretation, but taken in the mass its significance may become quite obvious. It is so with the stage directions in Q. They show a consistent preoccupation with striking details of production and stage business of the sort that a book-keeper of the period would have thought it superfluous to record, since they might well be altered from one performance, or at least production, to another. For example, at III.vii.80: *Shee takes a sword and runs at him behind* (where the Folio has simply: *Killes him*); again at IV.vi.208: *Exit King running* (F: *Exit*); and at V.ii.1: *Enter . . . Cordelia with her father in her hand* (F: *Enter . . . Lear, Cordelia . . .*). Q's omissions of incidental directions are equally indicative since they show the reporter overlooking details of great practical importance to a book-keeper. He pays little attention to sound-effects, and allows the storm in Acts II and III to pass unremarked. He fails to mention essential props, notably the stocks in II.ii. His directions, furthermore, tend to be vague or diffuse where a book-keeper would aim at succinctness and accuracy. A good example of his imprecision occurs at V.iii.40: *Enter Duke, the two Ladies, and others* (F: *Flourish. Enter Albany, Gonerill, Regan, Soldiers*).

15 E.g. II.iv.i: *Enter King* (F: *Enter Lear, Foole, and Gentleman*); II.iv.129: *Enter Duke and Regan* (F: *Enter Cornewall, Regan, Gloster,* *Seruants*). According to Greg (*Folio*, p. 378), 'some sixteen entrances and twice that number of exits are unmarked'.

The 'two Ladies' introduce us to another aspect of Q, the most informative of all in this connection: whoever produced the copy was very unclear about the characters' names. It is perhaps not very significant that he consistently notes Edmund as 'Bastard', and Oswald (most of the time) as 'Steward'; nor even that, in speech-prefixes, as also once or twice in stage directions, he calls both Cornwall and Albany 'Duke', though this latter failure to distinguish clearly between two important characters neither argues his familiarity with the play nor suggests any close co-operation with its cast. Much more significantly, he appears not to know what to call the characters unless they are named in the text.

We fully expect, of course, to meet in any play of the period a number of anonymous functional characters: servants, messengers, soldiers, citizens and the like. *Lear*, however, contains an exceptionally large array. Over and above the usual supernumeraries, which include an Old Man, a Herald, a Doctor and a Captain, more courtier-like personages, referred to as 'Gentlemen', frequently appear to speak a few lines, but on occasion as many as twenty or thirty. They appear, indeed, so often that it is difficult to believe that each successive appearance betokens a different Gentleman. Yet none is identified.[16] This is suspicious in view of the fact that an entirely insignificant character appears briefly at the beginning of II.i, and *is* identified – apparently because his name (Curan) occurs in the text.

Suspicion is strengthened when we notice the treatment of Oswald. He first appears (I.iii) as one of the nameless 'Gentlemen'. At his next entrance (I.iv.49) he merely passes across the stage with a brief remark but, presumably since he must have identified his office at this point with a personal prop or some piece of 'business', he is now referred to as 'Steward'. (There is no doubt that the 'Steward' of I.iv is the 'Gentleman' of I.iii, who has been presented as a retainer of Goneril's, instructed by her to use the King 'with what weary negligence you please', and who now proceeds to carry out her commands.) Oswald remains 'Steward' throughout the rest of the play, except – and this is most illuminating – on the single occasion when he is referred to in the text by name. At this point, his re-entrance at the end of I.iv, he is recognised in two speech-prefixes as 'Oswald'.

---

16 Is it one and the same Gentleman who appears in II.i, IV.iii, IV.vi (with two companions) and IV.vii, and who may also be the 'Knight' of II.iv? One might imagine a courtier in Lear's retinue who, like Kent, having accompanied his wanderings for a time, precedes him to Dover. But there is little to go on, and the loose strands of plot in III.i and IV.iii baffle conjecture.

22   It would be difficult to avoid the inference from such evidence that the person responsible for preparing the text of Q relied entirely for his knowledge of the characters' names on the text itself. Only a reporter in the theatre could have found himself in this position, reduced as he necessarily was in the absence of theatre programmes to the evidence of his ear. He was able, of course, to devise generic descriptions for some of the characters, going by the context in some cases (the Doctor), in others (the Old Man) by their visible characteristics, but for the rest was obliged to fall back upon unidentified 'Gentlemen'.[17]

All the ascertainable evidence, then, points in the direction of a reporter, and a reporter who obtained his copy as a member of the audience in the theatre. Yet one may not feel entirely comfortable with this conclusion. As Greg once wrote, though he later felt obliged to abandon the conviction he expresses here:

> I have no doubt in my own mind that the 1608 *Lear* was reported and in view of the fact that it is far more accurate than any of the texts recognized as memorial reconstructions, I see no escape from the conclusion that it was based on a shorthand report. If I could imagine how otherwise such a text could have been obtained, I would gladly dispense with the stenographic theory, for . . . it introduces quite considerable difficulties.[18]

There are difficulties, but some that have been raised prove on examination to be more imagined than real. It may be as well to look first in brief at the objections set forth in Miss Doran's study.[19]

1. The Quarto is regularly entered in the Stationers' Register and therefore cannot have been pirated. (Since Miss Doran wrote it has been demonstrated conclusively that an entry in the Register is no guarantee whatever of authorised publication.)[20]

17 The text of F reproduces the generic character-designations (except for the Doctor who is dropped from the list of characters) and the anonymous 'Gentlemen'. We should beware, however, of taking this as a confirmation of Q's correctness — in respect, at least, of the 'Gentlemen', since the other characters were probably never, in any case, individually named. The entire question of F's authority must be settled on other, less ambiguous, grounds. Meanwhile it may be observed that, if the naming of characters in Q is so clearly and consistently dependent on a single condition (the appearance of their names in the dialogue), a similar helplessness in F should perhaps rather raise doubts about F than allay them about Q.

18 'King Lear — Mislineation and Stenography', *The Library*, 4th series, XVII (1936–7), p. 180.

19 Doran, *Text*, pp. 122ff.

20 In Leo Kirschbaum, *Shakespeare and the Stationers* (Columbus, Ohio, 1955).

2. The text is too accurate and complete to be categorised along with the 'bad' quartos as a product of reporting. (But standards of reporting must surely have varied with the skill and assiduity of the reporters and the efficiency of the methods they adopted. It is not necessary to assume that the Shakespearean 'bad' quartos set a standard of inaccuracy to which all other reported texts invariably sank. They do not, in any case, set a uniform standard: the best of *Hamlet* Q1 is not inferior to the best of *Lear*.)

3. The text contains 'relatively few errors of mishearing', and those may all be attributed to the compositor. (We have already considered this misinterpretation of the evidence.)[21]

4. Had Q been derived from a performance, it would show some variation in the frequency of error, according as a more or less competent actor were being reported. We notice variation, however, not between the parts of different actors but between different sections of the play. (This objection rests on an unargued presupposition about the distribution of error in Q. Miss Doran takes for granted that on the report hypothesis Q must be assumed erroneous, for the most part, wherever it differs from F. But the objection is in any case weak. A reporter might well reproduce different parts of a play with varying accuracy according to the rapidity with which they were played, the proximity or remoteness from him of the action on a large Elizabethan stage, the noisy excitement or quiet attentiveness of the audience, and so on. As for the actors, it is a strange presumption that some would betray faulty memories, others not. All actors forget their lines from time to time; few, probably, are word-perfect at every performance. But a weak memory is no qualification for the professional stage, and it could not have been otherwise in Shakespeare's day. It is, therefore, absurd to look for chronic misremembering in certain of the parts as a guarantee that the play was copied in the theatre.)

5. No stenographer capable of aligning correctly two-thirds of the verse in the play would have failed so disastrously with the rest. There is nothing about the misaligned passages to suggest that they presented special problems. (Here is indeed an interesting puzzle – to which a solution will presently be offered. As an objection to the report hypothesis, however, it is not particularly telling: if it

21 Patricia Ingham ('A Note on the Aural Errors in the First Quarto of King Lear', *Shakespeare Studies*, III (1967), pp. 81–4) has more recently maintained that the aural errors in Q are 'fewer than generally supposed'. Her brief list of genuine mishearings is drawn, however, from a very limited selection of evidence – a handful of the errors, namely, which Miss Doran and others had previously cited as possibly or probably aural in origin.

24   is difficult to imagine reporter or compositor behaving so inconsistently, how much more difficult would it be to ascribe the confusion to some more responsible person. For confusion it is: as we have observed, the misaligned passages are not neatly separable from the rest so that we may suppose them second-thought additions interlineated in the author's rough draft.)

Further objections have been voiced by G. I. Duthie, whose work has already been cited in this and the previous chapter. They may be summed up in two propositions: one, that none of the systems of shorthand known to the first decade of the seventeenth century can have played any part in the transmission of the Q text, since none of them could have given rise to the kind of errors observable in Q; the other, that, in any case, no shorthand system of the time would be adequate to the task of reporting a play with any accuracy. Duthie stresses as well the *a priori* unlikelihood of successful shorthand reporting. How would the reporter conceal his surreptitious activities from the watchful eyes of playhouse employees? Would he hear well enough above the rumour and doubtless occasional din of a large audience? How would he manage to identify speakers on the stage, and then in his speech-prefixes, at the same time catching and noting the first lines of their speeches?

These arguments have succeeded in discrediting the theory that Q originates in a theatrical report. Yet, as we have seen, the alternative hypotheses to which subsequent critics (including Duthie himself) have turned cannot be reconciled with the evidence. It may, therefore, be worth our while to consider the problem afresh.

There is certainly no cause to demur at Duthie's description of the three Elizabethan shorthand systems, Timothy Bright's 'Characterie', Peter Bales's 'Brachygraphie' and John Willis's 'Stenographie', and his demonstration of their capabilities. Nor can one doubt his contention that John Willis's system is the only one of the three likely to have been used for the text of *Lear*. Doubts do arise, however, when he sets out to show that the errors in Q could not have been produced by this system. Everything depends on the chosen criterion of error. In Duthie's 1949 edition of the play we find his criterion: F being a generally superior text, any QF variant creates a presumption of error in Q at that point (except when F is manifestly wrong).[22] To the extent that we baulk at this assumption, we remain less than fully convinced by the general drift of his argument.

A further weakness appears when he concedes that, in testing the shorthand theory against the capacities and limitations of contemporary systems, he may

22 *King Lear*, ed. G. I. Duthie
(Oxford, 1949), p. 18.

not have examined all the possibilities. In considering, and dismissing as irrelevant, a fourth system of the time (Edmond Willis's *An Abreuiation of Writing by Character*, 1618), he quotes the author as saying that he has studied shorthand 'for these fourteene yeeres past', that during that time he has consulted several teachers and that, *besides* Bright, Bales and John Willis, there are 'others who have *Laboured* to shew their skill, and with their *Bills* haue besprinkled the posts and walls of this Citie'. 'If', however, says Duthie, 'in 1608 there were shorthand systems in existence other than those of Bright, Bales, and John Willis, we do not know what they were like.'[23] This effectively restores us to the state of ignorance in which we began.

By way of conclusion, however, Duthie falls back on the *a priori* arguments: 'As regards other systems which may have existed, I can only re-emphasize the considerable objections to the theory of shorthand transmission for Q *Lear* by any system'.[24] These objections do deserve consideration, but seeing that in the nature of the case they amount merely to a speculative assessment of probabilities, they can be matched by equally strong counter-objections of the same kind. Is it unlikely that shorthand of the primitive type we must suppose could have been written fast enough to report a long play with accuracy? Not necessarily: the reporter might have attended several performances. A new play (such as *Lear* was two or three years before its publication) would certainly have been given sufficiently frequently. Would a reporter have been noticed and ejected? A new play would attract large audiences: at capacity the theatre would hold, it has been estimated, between two and three thousand people. We cannot suppose that the playhouse staff were numerous enough to keep so many under surveillance, even if they attempted to do so, which we may reasonably doubt. Would the reporter have found it impossible to watch the stage, as he would have to, while taking his notes? He might have an assistant to note entrances, exits, the distribution of speeches and so forth; or he might rely on repeated attendances at the play to get these details right. And so on. In spite of which, there is no doubt that on one of the main issues Duthie is correct: shorthand can have played no part in the preparation of 'copy' for Q. We are directed to this conclusion by the evidence of the text itself.

It was Miss Doran, as we have noticed, who first pointed out the strange inconsistency of the mislineation in Q. Aside from one or two extended passages, and several scattered speeches, the verse of which is printed throughout as prose, the misalignments do not fall into any immediately recognisable pattern: a single speech will contain correct lines, others only speciously correct

---

23 Duthie, *Shorthand*, p. 82. 24 *Ibid.*, p. 82.

26 and others much too long to have deceived anyone capable of recognising a pentameter. There seems as little reason, at first sight, for the divagations into metrical nonsense as for the reversions to accuracy.[25]

Since this curious phenomenon has received very little notice, it may be worth examining it in some detail. Three main types of anomaly are distinguishable:

1. Verse is printed as prose; for example:

> *Cord.* Vnhappie that I am, I cannot heaue / my heart into my
> mouth, I loue your Maiestie / according to my bond, nor more nor
> lesse.
>
> I.i.93–5

2. Verse is printed in unscannable lines of unusual length. These 'overloaded' lines may take up the major portion of a speech, but are nearly always to be found together (within the confines of a single speech) with lines of more regular length and pattern. For example:

> *Fran.* Is it no more but this, a tardines in nature, /
> That often leaues the historie vnspoke / that it intends to do,
> My lord of *Burgundie*, / what say you to the Lady?
> Loue is not loue / when it is mingled with respects that stāds /
> Aloofe from the intire point wil you haue her?
>
> I.i.238–43

25 Greg's article, '*King Lear* – Mislineation and Stenography' (*The Library*, 4th series, XVII (1936–7), pp. 172–83), written at a time when he still subscribed to the shorthand-report hypothesis, attributes the mislining entirely to the compositor. He argues, firstly, that the compositor must have been setting from, and at the same time attempting to correct, 'copy' which showed no line-division at all. (An unlikely assumption *a priori*, one might think; and see pp. 27–8 below for evidence against it.) Secondly (he suggests), since it is clear that the compositor used two measures throughout the text, a narrower one for verse, and a wider one for prose, he may when setting verse have occasionally forced a short piece of prose into the narrower measure, disguising it as verse 'rather than transfer what he [had] already set to the galley and start afresh with a longer composing stick' (*op. cit.*, p. 182). This argument is plausible, though it accounts (and is intended to account) for a very limited amount of the evidence. The mislineations, it should be added, are not located in the text in such a way as to suggest the (in any case very remote) possibility of setting by formes. They are as likely, that is to say, to be found at the beginning of a page or opening as at, or towards, the end, so that it is scarcely possible to see them as an occasional response to shortage, or excess, of space.

3. Very frequently a speech is mislined because a short line at its opening has been misinterpreted as the first half of a line of regular length. (Less frequently we find the opposite error, whereby a first line of regular length is split in two, so that the speech opens wrongly with a short line.) The resulting mislineation may persist throughout the speech, or it may be corrected after the intervention of one or more extra-long lines. The following instance represents a large number:

> *Lear.* My L. of *Burgŭdie*, / we first addres towards you,
> Who with a King / hath riuald for our daughter,
> What in the least / will you require in present
> Dower with her, / or cease your quest of loue?
>
> I.i.192–6

(This plausible mislineation continues for several further lines.)

The first type of error is easily enough explained. The compositor must on these occasions have found verse-lines written as prose in his 'copy', or set out there in such a way as to be indistinguishable from prose. (Compositors would sometimes set verse as prose when obliged to save space, but there is no sign that the Q compositor was ever under any such necessity.)

If we may be reasonably certain that when we find verse printed as prose the source of the error must lie in the 'copy', a presumption is created that other sorts of error derive from the 'copy' as well. It is, of course, just possible that, if the 'copy' were written as prose throughout, the compositor himself may have made intermittent efforts to turn it into verse where appropriate, with the results we have noticed. Possible, but, on a closer inspection of the evidence, not really credible.

The second type of metrical disturbance we have noted (the presence among regular or quasi-regular lines of one or more of extraordinary length) cannot be reconciled with the idea of a compositor deliberately attempting to set the verse to rights. How could we possibly believe, for example, that if the compositor were capable of arranging the whole of Kent's speech at II.ii.78–90 otherwise correctly, he would perpetrate the following blunder in the middle of it?

> [such smiling roges as these] . . .
> Reneag, affirme, and turne their halcion beakes
> With euery gale and varie of their maisters,   (epeliptick
> Knowing nought like dayes but following,a plague vpon your
> Visage, smoyle you my speeches, as I were a foole?
>
> II.ii.84–8

28 It will be seen that a regular and very easily identifiable line (from *a plague* to *Visage*) has been, so to speak, squeezed in between two others equally regular and equally obvious. One can only conclude that the compositor here was naively reproducing his 'copy'; and that, if he were willing to pass over so glaring and so readily rectifiable a mistake, he can have had no interest in diverging from the 'copy' elsewhere.

We are led to assume, then, that the mislineations were a feature of the 'copy' and that the reporter must have been responsible for them. Why should the reporter, though, any more than the compositor, have so often proved incompetent where not the slightest difficulty confronted him? There is, I believe, a good explanation, though it does not turn entirely on the question of his competence. The evidence, in fact, goes so far to suggest that the copy was badly mislined not because the reporter was incapable of doing better – it is plain from the substantial amount of correctly lined verse that he knew what he was about – but because his method of producing the copy set limits to the accuracy he could achieve.

To explain: let us assume that the reporter paid several visits to the theatre, building up his copy piecemeal by taking down on each occasion as much as he could, while leaving spaces on the page to be filled in on later visits. Where the last remaining spaces were not ample enough, the line or lines still missing would have to be crowded into them without attention to the proper divisions. The misplacement of II.ii.87 in the passage quoted above might well have resulted from its interpolation in this way (together, perhaps with the succeeding line) into a copy which already contained the surrounding context. This might be the best way to explain, too, the numerous occasions on which two or more lines of anomalous length are interposed, with an effect of crowding, between regular lines, or lines, at least, of regular appearance. To the extent, however, that such 'runs' of long lines continue beyond two or three the explanation becomes more strained. We may find as many as five or six long lines together: is it at all likely that the reporter would grasp so much material at once, foreseeing before he began taking it down that the space available for it was too restricted?

Other questions arise, too, which cannot be satisfactorily answered without modifying the simple explanation I have suggested. How does it happen that the reporter, so often correct in his division of lines, quite frequently loses his way even where we cannot suppose him to have run short of space (where, that is to say, since the printed text shows lines of the normal length, we cannot assume that the 'copy' was at all crowded)? And why is it that he sometimes, apparently, abandons his attempt to divide the verse into lines – as we are inclined to think when we find not merely isolated speeches but entire pages of verse set by the compositor as prose?

Let us begin with the first question. We may notice, for a start, that the reporter was entirely dependent on pauses in delivery for judging the points of division between lines of verse. This holds true, almost without exception, for the first lines of speeches. Where an opening line of regular length is more or less strongly end-stopped he almost invariably gets it right:

> *Burg.* I am sory then you haue so lost a father,
> That you must loose a husband.
>
> I.i.249–50

> *Gent.* Contending with the fretfull element,
> Bids the wind blow the earth into the sea, . . .
>
> III.i.4–5

> *Edg.* A most poore man made lame by Fortunes blowes,
> Who by the Art of knowne and feeling sorrowes . . .
>
> IV.vi.225–6

He is equally successful when the speech begins with a firmly end-stopped short line, followed by an unambiguously regular second line:[26]

> *Bast.* I doe serue you in this busines:
> A credulous Father, and a brother noble, . . .
>
> I.ii.194–5

> *Lear.* No *Regan*,
> She hath abated me of halfe my traine, . . .
>
> II.iv.160–1

> *Reg.* That's as we list to grace him,
> Me thinkes our pleasure should haue beene demanded . . .
>
> V.iii.61–2

---

26 Some notable exceptions occur in the first scene of the play (because the reporter was not at the beginning fully alert to the possibility of short lines commencing a speech?). In the latter scenes short lines are frequently combined with the full line immediately succeeding, but this is tantamount to evidence that one and a half lines were correctly recognised as such.

30 Where these conditions are not fulfilled, the reporter goes wrong. He finds it difficult to identify a short line at the start of a speech if it happens to be 'run on' to the next:

> *Duke.* This is a fellow / who hauing beene praysd
> For bluntnes doth affect / a sawcy ruffines, . . .
>
> II.ii.101–3

> *Alb.* This shewes you are aboue / you Iustisers,
> That these our nether crimes / so speedely can venge . . .
>
> IV.ii.78–80

Elsewhere he is deceived by a pause into marking a short line where none should be:

> *Gon.* By day and night he wrongs me,
> Euery houre / he flashes into one grosse crime or other . . .
>
> I.iii.3–4

> *Kent.* Alas sir, sit you here?
> Things that loue night, / loue not such nights as these, . . .
>
> III.ii.42–3

Occasionally a more complex difficulty is responsible for his failure:

> *Reg.* Not altogether so sir, / I looke not for you yet,
> Nor am prouided / for your fit welcome, . . .
>
> II.iv.234–6

(The reporter may no doubt have noticed the short line here had he not been tricked by the pause after *yet* and the absence of any after *prouided*.)

These examples have been selected with very little search by opening the text more or less at random. The reader may find many more in each category with as little effort. This remarkably consistent evidence points clearly to the conclusion that the reporter's efforts at lineation were guided primarily by the ear; it suggests indeed that he tried to divide the lines of verse as best he could even as he heard them and copied them down.

This conclusion is borne out by the fact that errors are liable to occur even in the middle of a speech which is otherwise correctly lineated throughout. Even, that is, when the reporter has got off to a good start, and is proceeding correctly, his ear is liable to fail him, or positively to deceive him, over details. The following errors occur in otherwise perfectly aligned speeches:

> Commanded me to follow, and attend / the leasure
> Of their answere, gaue me cold lookes, . . .
>
> II.iv.36–7

> They traueled hard to night, meare Iustice,
> I (=Aye) / the Images of reuolt and flying off, . . .
>
> II.iv.90–1

> Why the hot bloud in *France*, that dowerles
> Tooke / our yongest borne, I could as well be brought . . .
>
> II.iv.215–16

Before we consider the significance of these facts, it will be worth noting another point of interest. The longer speeches, whether or not they are misaligned from the beginning, or whether or not, beginning correctly, their lineation is then disturbed by a patch of excessively long lines, frequently revert to correctness before they close with the appearance of a regular line. Once again, one is led to conclude that the reporter's ear has determined the result: these 'corrective' lines are always rhythmically obvious and fairly clearly end-stopped, as the following examples show:

> My iudgement, / thy yongest daughter does not loue thee least, /
> Nor are those empty harted . . .
>
> I.i.153–5

> To bandy hasty words, to scant my sizes,
> And in conclusion, . . .
>
> II.iv.178–9

> Now to you, / if on my credit you dare build so farre, /
> To make your speed to Douer, . . .
>
> III.i.34–6

(These lines are drawn from speeches the first two of which are misaligned from the beginning, while the third, beginning correctly, lapses into over-long lines just prior to the passage quoted. All three speeches continue and conclude without further error.)

32   There is, I think, only one possible inference to draw from this evidence. The reporter began his work by attempting, as far as possible, to set down the opening lines of all the speeches in the play, and, where he could catch more than one line at a time, as no doubt he often could, to align them correctly. It is a very striking fact that, whereas lines in the middle of a speech will sometimes appear as merely random arrangements of words, opening lines, though they may be mistakenly arranged, show almost without exception the effect of conscious care. The reporter would, of course, leave spaces between each pair or group of opening lines to be filled in at a second or further hearing.

    It is at this stage, necessarily, that he would have sought to identify the speakers. At this stage, too, he would have the opportunity, during the longer speeches, of copying rather more than the opening lines – perhaps a few lines from the body of the speech, which again he would attempt to arrange correctly. (I am assuming, for the moment, that even if he were a stenographer, he would not be capable of writing fast enough to take down the whole *seriatim*.) When he came, on a second hearing, to fill in the gaps he would be able to proceed faster, but not fast enough, presumably, to complete the work: shorter and more frequent gaps would show in the copy. As he wrote, he would presumably listen for a complete line to jump to next. Where he was able to record a sufficient number of complete lines correctly in the course of a speech, he would have no difficulty in reconstituting the entire speech without error, or almost so. But where his ear deceived him oddities such as the following might result:

> *Glost.* Good friend I prithy take him in thy armes,
> I haue or'e heard a plot of death vpon him,
> Ther is a Litter ready lay him in't, / & driue towards Douer frend,
> Where thou shalt meet / both welcome & protection, take vp thy
>   master,
> If thou should'st dally halfe an houre, his life / with thine
> And all that offer to defend him / stand in assured losse,
> Take vp the King / and followe me, that will to some prouision /
> Giue thee quicke conduct.
>
>   III.vi.95–104

It will be observed that, although only the first two lines and the last line of the speech are correctly aligned, each of the lines as printed might be construed as beginning with a regular pentameter. The fourth would lend itself especially well to misconception, and the seventh, though it meets a stop after the fourth foot, opens deceptively with the trochaic rhythm which so often announces a new line after an emphatic pause. It is easy to see that if these two false pentameters — or, for that matter, any two more or less separated from each other in the latter part of the speech — were written before the rest, the remaining matter would inevitably come to be disposed in an irregular pattern of the kind we observe.

Most of the anomalous lineation in Q may be readily explained on the same or similar assumptions. The reporter's procedure must obviously have varied somewhat with circumstances, but it remained throughout, I believe, essentially the same. I shall not, therefore, further elaborate the analysis through a variety of examples. There were, naturally, occasions on which he met with little or no success. The irregular rhythms of Lear's speech at the beginning of III.ii, for instance, defeated him completely, although he managed to get the first line right. One may still, however, observe at least one weak attempt in the middle of the speech to rediscover the metrical pattern:

> And thou all shaking thunder, smite flat
> The thicke Rotunditie of the world, . . .

This failure, and others like it, are almost as good an indication as his successes or near-successes of the principles on which the reporter worked.

It may be worth adding that occasionally it does indeed seem to be lack of space rather than metrical misunderstanding which produces a faulty line. In the following example the line beginning *Is boūd* was clearly not heard as separated metrically from the preceding words: it is more reasonable to suppose that the whole of the matter from *where to* to *oprest* was interlined between a correctly grasped pentameter (*Infirmitie . . . office*) and a spurious one (*Cōmand . . . bodie*).

> Infirmitie doth still neglect all office, / where to our health
> Is boūd, we are not our selues, / when nature being oprest
> Cōmand the mind / to suffer with the bodie, ile forbeare . . .
>
> II.iv.107–10

Before we turn to consider the more interesting implications of these findings, it remains to enquire why so many extended passages of verse were set by the Q compositor not in faulty or irregular arrangements but straightforwardly as prose. This is a more puzzling question — to which, however, a not altogether implausible answer may be found.

The reporter must have been capable — on the whole, if not invariably — of recognising from the tone and style of an actor's utterance whether he were

34   speaking verse or prose. Even, however, when he was conscious of taking down a
speech in prose, he would not, one must suppose, proceed upon different
principles. He would attempt to find key-lines in the speech to serve as a
skeleton for filling out on a subsequent hearing or hearings. That he did follow
this procedure seems to be confirmed by the only passage in the text which we
can feel virtually certain was intended as prose, though it is set by the
compositor as verse. This speech, which must have been set out by the reporter
exactly as it appears in print, shows us how prose lines were arranged in the
'copy':

> *Glost.* Go toe say you nothing, ther's a diuisiō betwixt the Dukes,
> *And a worse matter then that, I haue receiued
> A letter this night, tis dangerous to be spoken,
> *I haue lockt the letter in my closet, these iniuries
> The King now beares, will be reuenged home
> *Ther's part of a power already landed,
> *We must incline to the King, I will seeke him, and
> Priuily releeue him, goe you and maintaine talke
> With the Duke, that my charity be not of him
> Perceiued, if hee aske for me, I am ill, and gon
> To bed, though I die for't, as no lesse is threatned me,
> *The King my old master must be releeued, there is
> Some strāge thing toward, *Edmund* pray you be careful.

> III.iii.8–21

Though several of these lines, or the initial portions of them, might be counted
on the fingers as pentameters, none could conceivably have been heard as such: it
is highly improbable that the reporter believed he was copying verse. It is
strikingly evident, on the other hand, that the lines are not merely run on in a
random way. On several occasions a new line begins after a more or less marked
pause. If this were deliberately effected, as it must have been, one can only
assume that some or all of these lines (marked above with asterisks) served as an
initial framework for the recording of the rest of the speech.

      If it was the compositor who on this occasion failed to recognise prose, it must
have been the compositor who frequently elsewhere failed to recognise verse,
printing it as prose. Given that he was obviously quite unable to distinguish
acceptable lines of verse from unacceptable, the decision whether to cast a speech
in verse or in prose must always have been a difficult one for him to make. The
'copy' produced by the reporter would give him no indication beyond the
repetition, in a verse speech, of lines of moderate length and, in a prose speech,

the lack of any such pattern. Naturally he must often have drawn the wrong conclusion, and naturally he was more apt to be deceived by the absence of moderately long lines, hence to print verse as prose, than to be misled by a fortuitous repetition of moderately long lines in a passage of prose, hence to print it as verse. For several pages towards the beginning of the text (the last 150 lines or so of I.iv, I.v and the first hundred of II.i) he apparently abandoned the ungrateful task, setting everything as prose. It is impossible to tell why, unless it was that the 'copy', the earlier part of which may have been comparatively clear, began at about this stage to present him with more serious dilemmas. We should feel more surprised, perhaps, that he eventually resumed his efforts, and carried them through to the end.

If the evidence in general provided by Q demonstrates the origin of its text in a theatrical report, the particular evidence of mislineation strongly suggests that the report was obtained by a process of piecemeal accumulation, the reporter attending repeated performances of the play, acquiring more of the text on each occasion until, presumably, he judged it complete, or as nearly so as he could make it.

The reader is doubtless quite aware by now that the reporter's methods as I have described them could scarcely be thought natural to a stenographer, or even practicable by the use of stenography, and I shall not stress the point. Could we, on the other hand, possibly suppose a slow and laborious process of copying by longhand? If the reporter were incapable of anything more efficient, his visits to the theatre, it might seem, would have to be multiplied beyond endurance, not to mention considerations of economic profit.

This, however, is not so, as the reader may prove by experiment. If he writes a reasonably fluent and legible hand, let him attempt to take down, neatly and clearly, a passage of prose or verse dictated to him – as many times over as need be – at an unhurried pace. (We should have in mind, I take it, the somewhat deliberate pace of a speaker addressing a large audience: actors, however skilfully they may, at need, produce an impression of excitement and haste, cannot speak more rapidly than the physical conditions allow.) It will be found that four repetitions are quite enough to produce readable 'copy': practice might undoubtedly reduce the number necessary to three.

The 'copy' will not be perfect. Pauses in delivery will easily enough be noted, and suitable (if not very nicely discriminated) marks of punctuation introduced without special effort. By the same token, lines of verse may be correctly divided wherever metrical units coincide with units of syntax (but otherwise it will be a matter of chance). Extraordinary mistakes will, however, occur because the method imposed on the writer makes it almost continuously necessary to be

36   copying one line mechanically while listening to and memorising another quite unconnected with it. Under the circumstances, it is nearly impossible to attend to sense or grammar; and it is nearly impossible, even on the third hearing, to check what has been written on the first or second, since the attention must almost entirely be concentrated on identifying and filling in the remaining gaps. Consequently even a relatively short passage reproduced in this way, however carefully and completely it is done, will reveal one or two small errors as to verbal endings, particles, conjunctions or pronouns, very probably at least one minor omission and almost certainly one major phonetic error which makes nonsense of its context. It is, interestingly, in mistakes precisely of this kind that the text of Q abounds.

There is no need at all, therefore, to reject the hypothesis that the reporter's copy was written *ab initio* in longhand. If it requires any further substantiation we need not look very far. It would be difficult to suppose that the 'copy' for Q was transcribed from a preliminary draft of any kind: the 'copy', as we find it adumbrated in print, is full of obvious mislineations (not to mention other glaring errors) of a kind which must surely have been eliminated in a transcription. There can be little doubt that the original report with all its imperfections was submitted to the printer as it stood: if so, it goes without saying, it cannot have been written in shorthand.

Additional confirmation is supplied by such inferences as we can make about the nature of the handwriting on this 'copy', and about other features of its appearance. It was, not surprisingly, written in the secretary hand, as is proved by many obvious misreadings in Q. To have served its purpose in the printing house it must have been quite legible. The writer, however, seems habitually to have distorted certain letter-forms, or rather to have delineated them very carelessly. Judging from the misreadings which result ('k', for example, is frequently read as 'b'), these eccentricities all show a tendency towards greater simplicity and speed.[27] Yet another of the writer's habits suggests haste. He frequently joined two words together, by means (one supposes) of the sweeping ligature one sometimes finds in secretary, or for that matter in modern, hands. On occasions he did not, apparently, produce this stroke far enough, since we find the compositor deceived into printing two words as one. The opposite error – that of printing one word as two – occurs even more frequently and suggests

27   For further details, see
introductory note to Appendix A1,
p. 177 below.

that when the reporter did lift his pen, or pencil,[28] he sometimes (and very possibly through haste) carried it too far forward, leaving too large a gap within a word. The following instances of misdivided words in Q are recognised by all modern editors: *my rackles* (= miracles); *A'Iax* (= Ajax); *so phisticated*; *ma hu* (= Mahu); *a nellthu night more* (Qa: corrected in Qb to *he met the night mare*); *Per du* (= perdu). Others, though not strictly classifiable as errors, reflect this peculiarity of the 'copy' equally clearly: *many fould, where so ere, or'e heard*, etc.[29]

The 'copy' cannot have contained any large amount of cramped interlineation, interpolation in the margins or other abnormalities of layout beyond the highly idiosyncratic line-arrangement we have supposed it to display in the first place. But there is bound to have been some untidiness of this kind, and we do in fact find a few errors apparently due to the resultant obscurities. At V.iii.47 Qa omits a phrase from the end of an unusually long line, possibly because it was tucked into the margin of the 'copy': it is retrieved in Qb. Some irregularity in the 'copy' must be responsible, too, for the puzzle presented by IV.vi.230, where Qa prints *to saue thee*, and Qb substitutes, surprisingly, *to boot, to boot*. Again, II.iv.103 contains a phrase which probably belongs in the succeeding line, and which may have been misplaced because it was squeezed into a margin.[30]

Thus what we are able to deduce about the physical characteristics of the 'copy' is not inconsistent with the hypothesis that the original report, written in longhand, was submitted to the printer.

Its punctuation and orthography conform equally well to the hypothesis. One would, in normal circumstances, assume that the compositor re-punctuated the 'copy' and imposed his own spellings on it: that was, it is now agreed, the customary practice of the time. But we have here to do, as we shall presently see, with an especially naive and probably inexperienced compositor. We have already found that he made no attempt to regularise the lineation of the 'copy', apparently because he did not know how to. It is probably safer, therefore, to suppose that he contributed nothing very material to the details of its presentation. We find, at any rate, in the general run of punctuation, very much what we should expect from the reporter's 'copy'. It presents a very poor appearance since it consists mainly of commas. But if we regard the commas as marking off

28 No doubt the latter. Graphite pencils were in use by the end of the sixteenth century. We find the first recorded reference to a pencil of the modern type (black-lead in a wooden holder) in a German publication of 1565.

29 Further, more problematical, examples are discussed in Appendix A2, p. 187 below.

30 See pp. 87–8 below and Appendix A2, p. 188 below.

38 units of speech, we find that in the overwhelming majority of instances they are correctly placed. From this point of view the principal errors, as we might expect, are mistakes of omission. And it is therefore not unreasonable to conclude that the few errors of misplacement (e.g. *Is practise, only giue me* for . . . *is practice only. Give me* . . . , II.iv.116) must have resulted from attempts by the compositor or press-corrector to repair the more obvious of such mistakes.

About spelling it is more hazardous to speculate. It is well known that Elizabethan custom allowed considerable latitude, and that eccentricity was not taken as proof of illiteracy. We cannot judge, therefore, what significance should be attached to the large number of extraordinary spellings in Q. But it is perhaps a sign of the nature of the 'copy' that it abounds in phonetic spellings: *obrayds* (= upbraids), *flea* (= flay), *thourt* (= thwart), *bile* (= boil), *ceaze* (= seize), among many others not much less strange. And on occasions we may be certain that the reporter is responsible since what we find is less a form of spelling than a naive (and no doubt only half conscious) representation of what he must have heard (e.g. *asten*, misprinted *after*, for 'hasten'; *Mohing* for 'mowing').

It is a fair presumption that the reporter must freely have used the contractions familiar to writers of secretary hand. He certainly used abbreviations, especially of names, since some of them found their way into the printed text. At I.i.78, for example, we find:

> *Cord.* Then poore *Cord.* & yet not so, since I am sure

The line is, comparatively, a long one; and yet, the measure in use on this page, which permitted appreciably longer lines both above and below this one, would certainly have allowed the full spelling-out of *Cordelia*. At II.iv.312 it is even more obvious that the compositor is not saving space but, in all probability, reproducing the abbreviation in his copy:

> My *Reg* counsails well, come out at'h storme.   *Exeūt.*

At IV.ii.15 Q has *Edgar* in error for *Edmund*, and at IV.vi.1 (stage direction) *Edmund* in error for *Edgar*. It seems very likely that on both occasions the compositor was expanding an ambiguous *Ed*. At IV.v.4, faced no doubt with a similar dilemma, he opted for *Lady* instead of, as the context makes necessary, *Lord*.

Thus, in the 'accidentals' of Q, in its punctuation, spelling and in its repetition or misrepresentation of abbreviations, we find further slight, though not altogether insignificant, corroboration of our hypothesis.

Perhaps enough has been said on the subject now to show that the theory of a theatrical report is sufficient to explain the major anomalies of the Q text, and that it is consistent with a variety of other evidence. The theory of memorial reconstruction does not square with all the facts, even if we share the groundless belief that an Elizabethan theatrical company, when faced with the loss of a prompt-book, would gather together to dictate it to a scribe.[31] Still less satisfactory, however, is the theory of dictation from a prompt-book; and much less satisfactory still the theory of transcription from the author's rough draft. The evidence scarcely tallies with the postulates of dictation or transcription. The possibility of an immediate connection between the text of Q and a manuscript of dependable origin it flatly disallows.

Having considered in detail the reporter's role in the transmission of Q it will be as well, before turning from the subject of Q to consider the character and relations of the F text, to look briefly at the part played by two other people concerned in its production, namely the compositor[32] and the press-corrector.

We have learnt something already of the compositor's dealings with his copy: he aimed, so far as we can judge, exactly to reproduce its extraordinary lineation, except for a brief spell during which he printed everything as prose; he does not seem to have interfered much with punctuation or spelling; he reproduces other characteristics of the 'copy' with the same literal-mindedness, misdividing words and failing to expand abbreviations. It is above all, however, in the large number of his misreadings that we find him revealed as a man quite remarkably devoid of initiative. Seeing that he was perfectly content to tolerate nonsense (printing *kill*, for example, as *bitt*) and even on numerous occasions to

31 If they were concerned about an immediate production would they not risk a performance without the book rather than waste an inordinate amount of rehearsal time dictating it? And if they were concerned about a future production would they not appeal to the author to recopy his rough draft?

32 It has been demonstrated, by means of the usual spelling-tests, that a single compositor set the text of Q. (Philip Williams, 'The Compositor of the "Pied Bull" *Lear*', *Studies in Bibliography*, I (1948–9), pp. 61–8). This conclusion has been questioned by E. A. J. Honigmann who, applying more elaborate tests, found some evidence to suggest that Acts IV and V may have been set by a second compositor ('Spelling Tests and the First Quarto of King Lear', *The Library*, 5th series, XX (1965)). Honigmann acknowledges, none the less, that 'one might still argue that the *King Lear* Quarto was set by a single compositor – because Acts I–III and IV–V resemble each other so closely in typographical and other features determined, in some instances, quite unconsciously' (*op. cit.*, p. 314). I see no reason to disagree.

40 reproduce gibberish, if that is what he saw (*a nellthu*, for instance, for *a mett the*, i.e. *he met the*), we can safely assume that he rarely, if ever, made any conscious attempt to divagate from the 'copy'. Though his inexperience (or, as it may be, lack of interest) resulted as well in a fairly large crop of accidental errors – the text is full of minor omissions and transpositions, dropped, added or substituted letters and the like – this incompetence is, on the whole, a great boon to the textual critic, who, for obvious reasons, would far rather deal with helplessness in a compositor than an untrustworthy disposition to ingenuity and enterprise.

It is just such a disposition, unfortunately, which characterises the press-corrector. The compositor's work was reviewed, as we noticed earlier, by a proof-reader who in the course of printing introduced a substantial number of corrections into the text. Greg first drew attention to the fact that this corrector is not entirely to be relied upon.[33] He clearly did on occasion consult the copy before marking up the proof-sheet: at III.iv.126, for example, he was able to reconstruct *a nellthu night more* correctly as *he met the night mare*. Elsewhere, on the other hand, he as clearly either ignored the copy or else (as seems more likely) gave it up as illegible. At III.iv.6 he changed *crulentious storme* to *tempestious storme*, whereas the correct reading is self-evidently the one we find in F: *contentious storme*. The corrector was thus sometimes more resourceful than the compositor in deciphering the manuscript, but sometimes not, and he was evidently quite willing to fabricate a reading if necessary. Our trust, therefore, in the compositor's fidelity to his copy must often be tempered by a wariness of possible interference from the corrector. We must assume, of course, that the corrector's emendations, whether reliable or not, invariably made sense of a kind. Not even in Jacobean times would a proof-reader think it worth converting nonsense into further nonsense. Hence when we find gibberish in a 'corrected' reading of Q, this can only mean that the compositor failed to make out the hand-written correction. An example occurs at III.vii.60. Qa has *layd*; Qb *bod* – which cannot represent the corrector's intention. He doubtless wanted *boyd* (for *buoy'd*), but was careless in marking the deletion of *la*, thus inducing the compositor to remove three letters instead of two.

33 *Variants*, p. 136.

CHAPTER THREE
THE DERIVATION OF THE FOLIO TEXT

We have seen that Q has some claim to be regarded as a true reflection of the original text, though not, in view of the vagaries of its transmission, by a long way the truest possible. We noted earlier that F appears, at least, superior to it, and that it is generally indeed accepted by editors as the 'better' (hence the more authoritative) text. It is now time to examine the arguments for and against this preference.

Anyone coming fresh to the problem would discover a contradiction in the evidence which first met his eye. On the one hand F is obviously *derived* from Q. A number of common errors make this clear. I give a list below of Folio readings which all editors recognise as wrong, citing the Quarto counterparts in parentheses where they differ in spelling or vary slightly in form.

> . . . *Edmond* the base
Shall to'th'Legitimate: (Q: tooth'legitimate:)
> I.ii.21; usually emended to *top the legitimate*

Your are much more at task (Qb: attaskt) for want of wisedome,
> I.iv.366; a crux

Historica passio, downe thou climing sorrow,
> II.iv.57; *Hysterica passio*

Hound or Spaniell, Brache, or Hym: (Q: him,)
> III.vi.72; *lym*

Crown'd with ranke Fenitar (Q: femiter), and furrow weeds,
> IV.iv.3; *fumiter*

To this list might be added (though the mistake is not generally noticed in modern editions):

The Prince of Darkenesse is a Gentleman. *Modo* he's call'd, and *Mahu*. (Q: ma hu - - -)
> III.iv.149; the names come from Harsnett,
> who gives them as *Modu* and *Maho*

42   Further instances, only slightly less certain, might be accumulated, but there is no need of more to settle the point that, unless the mistakes were transmitted to both by a common ancestor, one text must have inherited them from the other. The relevant dates make it impossible that Q received them from F, and it is most unlikely that a common ancestor was responsible. We should have to suppose that this ancestral text, the source of the 'copy' for F, was also used for the performance reported in Q, and that, amid a host of divagations and corruptions, these half-dozen small errors were reproduced unchanged in the actors' parts, in the actors' utterances and in the reporter's notes – while by another route they reached the text of F.

If this were not sufficiently incredible, a further piece of evidence would resolve our doubts. The mislineations in Q are on occasion exactly reproduced in F.[1] Mistakes of this kind can only be transferred by a process of copying, and it is obvious that the Q text was not copied from F, however else it may have been produced. We are obliged to assume instead that F was copied from Q.

On the other hand it appears equally evident that F is in many respects an independent text. Its lines of additional matter have already been referred to. Incidental additions of a word or a phrase are also very frequent. Numerous corrupt readings in Q are successfully emended, and some of these corrections it would be difficult to consider as merely conjectural. They bear the stamp of authenticity. Metre, too, is emended, and the erratic line-arrangement of Q largely, though not entirely, set to rights.

F, therefore, although it depends on Q, appears to derive as well from some independent source. How is this apparently conflicting evidence to be interpreted?

A neat, and immediately persuasive, solution to the problem is now generally accepted. It is based on two assumptions: first, that the publishers of the Folio had at their disposal an authoritative manuscript of the play, perhaps the prompt-book currently in use at the theatre; secondly, that they were unwilling or unable to print their text from this manuscript (for fear of spoiling it, perhaps, or because it was not allowed into their hands for long enough), but instead printed from a copy of Q which had been revised and corrected by reference to the manuscript. On these suppositions, the difficulty can be

1   Obvious mistakes in Q at
    I.i.286–8 (prose printed as verse),
    III.vii.44–5 (verse printed as
    prose), IV.iv.24–5 and V.iii.46–7
    (one and a half lines printed as
    one) recur in F.

resolved. F is a generally superior text because it draws on an authoritative source; its dependence, however, on the inferior Q is occasionally betrayed, because the reviser was occasionally careless enough to overlook the mistakes of the printed copy.

The theory has the merits of simplicity and plausibility, and it has provided a convenient working hypothesis for editors. It cannot, however, survive a detailed examination of the evidence. In an earlier chapter we noticed one or two of the difficulties in which it is bound to implicate the critics who espouse it. We must now examine in more detail the two assumptions upon which it rests, and we may start by considering the first: that an authoritative manuscript was available to the publishers of the Folio, who consulted it, or caused it to be consulted, in the preparation of their text.

If, in comparing the texts of F and Q, we look somewhat further than the obvious signs of F's superiority (the corrected readings, the accurate lineation, the additional lines), we must soon notice a substantial body of evidence which points another way. F's inadequacies are many and serious. They are serious enough individually to create embarrassing difficulties for the champions of the F text, who are obliged repeatedly to suppose that the collator has been careless when it would most have rewarded him to consult his authority. What is not generally noticed is that such errors are numerous enough, too, *en masse* to cast very serious doubt on the theory that F stems largely from an authoritative source independent of Q. Indeed the weight and quantity of the negative evidence makes any such view untenable upon a reasonable balancing of the probabilities.

An examination of the readings compared in Appendices A1–A7 will enable the reader to estimate from a wide range of evidence the frequency with which F either fails to deal satisfactorily with the errors of Q or gratuitously introduces errors of its own. No more is perhaps necessary here than to provide a representative selection of instances which by themselves would, I think, go far to substantiate the case against the orthodox theory.

I present the evidence under three heads: (a) serious obscurities, or obvious corruptions, in Q which have either been transferred without change into F, or undergone a merely specious 'tidying up'; (b) errors in Q which have either been wrongly emended in F or the problem evaded by inappropriate substitutions; (c) gratuitous – and erroneous – alterations in F. We may then consider whether this evidence can, on any plausible hypothesis, be presumed consistent with the use of a reliable manuscript in the preparation of F.

44   (a) CORRUPTIONS IN Q REPEATED, OR GLOSSED OVER, IN F

1   F: I finde she names my very deede of loue:
              Onely she comes too short, that I professe
              My selfe an enemy to all other ioyes,
              Which the most precious square of sense professes,

      Q: . . . onely she came short . . . square of sence possesses,

I.i.73–6

Various ingenious, but always strained and implausible, explanations have been offered for *square of sense*, all of them designating to the word 'square' a function it cannot well perform.

2   F: Well, my Legittimate, if this Letter speed,
              And my inuention thriue, *Edmond* the base
              Shall to'th'Legitimate: I grow, I prosper:

      Q: . . . tooth'legitimate . . .

I.ii.19–21

Editors usually accept Capell's emendation *top the legitimate*.

3   F: *Foole.* Truth's a dog must to kennell, hee must bee whipt out, when the Lady Brach may stand by'th'fire and stinke.

      Q: . . . Ladie oth'e brach . . .

I.iv.124–6

There seems no point to the contrast between Truth the dog and 'the Lady Brach', and editors remain puzzled, a few conjecturing *Lie the brach* or *Liar the brach*.

4   F: Approach thou Beacon to this vnder Globe,   45
                 That by thy comfortable Beames I may
                 Peruse this Letter. Nothing almost sees miracles
                 But miserie. I know 'tis from *Cordelia*,
                 Who hath most fortunately beene inform'd
                 Of my obscured course. And shall finde time
                 From this enormous State, seeking to giue
                 Losses their remedies.

       Qa: . . . my rackles . . .
       Qb: . . . my wracke . . .

                                  II.ii.170–7

One of the most baffling in the play, this passage presents editors with two apparently intractable problems in its second and fourth sentences.

5   F: . . . poore *Turlygod*, poore *Tom*,
                 That's something yet: *Edgar* I nothing am.

       Qa: . . . *Tuelygod* . . .
       Qb: . . . *Turlygod* . . .

                                  II.iii.20–1

No one has yet identified *Turlygod*.

6   F: *Lear.* The King would speake with *Cornwall*,
                 The deere Father
                 Would with his Daughter speake, commands, tends,
                   seruice,

       Qa: . . . deare fate . . . come and tends seruise
       Qb: . . . deare father . . . commands her seruice

                               II.iv.102–3

A well-known crux.

46 7   F: *Edg.* This is the foule Flibbertigibbet; hee begins at Curfew,
                and walkes at first Cocke: Hee giues the Web and the Pin,
                squints the eye, and makes the Hare-lippe;

        Qb: *Edg.* This is the foule fiend *fliberdegibek*, hee begins
                at curphew, and walks till the first cocke, he giues the web,
                & the pin, squemes the eye, and makes the hare lip,
        Qa: . . . the web, the pin-queues the eye . . .

III.iv.120–3

F's *squints* can scarcely be the word intended by Q's *squemes*, which is generally supposed to represent *squinies*. Both words bear the same meaning, but neither fits the context very happily. If Flibbertigibbet is said to 'squiny the eye', it is implied that he squinies his own eye. The *OED* records no transitive usage of the verb except in this quasi-reflexive sense.

     8   F: *Swithold* footed thrice the old,
                  He met the Night-Mare, and her nine-fold;

        Q: . . . nine fold

III.iv.125–6

Editors are agreed that *nine-fold* is wrong. Some restore the Q reading *nine fold*, but without satisfactory explanation.

     9   FQ: *Edg.* Yet better thus, and knowne to be contemn'd,
                  Then still contemn'd and flatter'd,

IV.i.1–2

These lines are unintelligible as they stand, since there is no reason why Edgar should connect his present condition (*better thus*) with his reputation (*knowne to be contemn'd*). He is disguised as Tom o'Bedlam at this point, and no one knows his true identity, so that his dishonour as Edgar cannot be dogging him, as he appears to imply. One editor paradoxically glosses *knowne* as 'known to himself', thus admitting the difficulty without resolving it.

10   F: But who comes heere? My Father poorely led?

        Qb: Who's here, my father parti, eyd,
        Qa: . . . poorlie, leed,

IV.i.9–10

A crux.

11   FQ: Ten Masts at each, make not the altitude
            Which thou hast perpendicularly fell,

IV.vi.53–4

The phrase *at each* means neither what it should mean here ('set end to end') nor anything else.

12   F: *Edg.* But by your fauour:
            How neere's the other Army?
            Gent. Neere, and on speedy foot: the maine descry
            Stands on the hourely thought.

      Q: *Gent.* Neere and on speed fort the maine descryes,
            Standst on the howerly thoughts.

IV.vi.215–18

F is adopted by all editors. But the paraphrase they characteristically offer in explanation of the last sentence (e.g. 'sight of the main part of the army is hourly expected' – Duthie) depends on an entirely unwarrantable series of glosses. It would indeed be difficult to attribute a precise significance to *stands on, hourly* or *thought* on any such interpretation. And, if one could, it would be impossible to find support for one's definitions in any dictionary. This is not to mention the wrenching of syntax supposed to have been perpetrated in *the maine descry* (= 'the descry of the main'), a strange procedure for which no precedent or parallel has been found. The Q version of these lines is obvious nonsense: but the 'improvement' offered in F leaves us no less bewildered.

48 13   F: *Glou.* Heartie thankes:
                     The bountie, and the benizon of Heauen
                     To boot, and boot.

        Qb: . . . the bounty and the benizon of heauen, to boot, to
               boot.
        Qa: . . . the bornet and beniz of heauen to saue thee.

IV.vi.228–30

F's *and boot* is implausible, with all deference to those editors who claim that the first *boot* is a noun, the second a verb, and that the preposition *to* must be understood to apply to both, forming, with the first, an adverbial phrase and, with the second, an infinitive. Even supposing (what is doubtful) that Elizabethan English would have tolerated so illogical and awkward a construction, the sense it produces strikes one as an excessively slight return for the violation of idiom. It is worth noting, too, that both F and Qb ignore the phrase *to saue thee*, which appears in Qa, and which one is reluctant to believe sprang from the Q compositor's fancy.

14   F: The good yeares shall deuoure them, flesh and fell,
                 Ere they shall make vs weepe?

        Q: The good shall deuoure em, . . .

V.iii.24–5

Much care has been devoted to elucidating *good yeares*, and a variety of interpretations suggested, none of them entirely plausible.

(b) Q ERRORS WRONGLY EMENDED IN F   49
A *Graphic errors*

1   Q: *Lear.* Denie to speake with mee, th'are sicke, th'are weary,
            They traueled hard to night, meare Iustice,
            I the Images of reuolt and flying off,
            Fetch mee a better answere.

       F: *Lear.* Deny to speake with me?
            They are sicke, they are weary,
            They haue trauail'd all the night? meere fetches,
            The images of reuolt and flying off.
            Fetch me a better answer.

                                         II.iv.89–92

Q's *Iustice* is obviously nonsense. Yet we must assume that the word it displaced
did make sense; furthermore, that that word could not have been *fetches*, which
neither looks nor sounds at all similar. The original reading must have been
justles, the usual form in the seventeenth century of *jostles*. If the word were spelt
jusles in the copy, as was then acceptable, it would very easily be misread as
justis. (Compare a successful correction in F at II.iii.17, which reveals that the
reading in the copy for Q was *fermes* (= farms), misread by the Q compositor as
seruis, and printed by him as *seruice*.) The meaning of *justle*, 'a push or thrust that
shakes', is exactly appropriate. Calling them 'justles', which represent 'images
of reuolt and flying-off', Lear describes the excuses of Regan and Cornwall as
gross rebuffs. *Fetches* (i.e. 'tricks') does not fit the context nearly so aptly, and
one cannot help speculating that it has been suggested by *Fetch* two lines further
down. It is in any case quite certainly a substitution, not a correction.

2   Q: *Ken.* All the power of his wits haue giuen way to
            impatience, the Gods deserue your kindnes.

       F: *Kent.* All the powre of his wits, haue giuen way to his
            impatience: the Gods reward your kindnesse.

                                         III.vi.4–6

Deserue is clearly wrong. But equally clearly it represents a misreading of *discern*,
which was no doubt spelt in the copy *deserne*, a seventeenth-century form

50   recorded in the *OED*. (Compare IV.ii.52, where Q *deseruing* is rightly altered in F to *discerning*.) Again we may be quite certain that F's reading (*reward*) is not a restoration of the copy for Q, but a new reading; and we may note that, although not noticeably inferior, it is the less 'difficult' reading.

3   Q: Some fiue or sixe and thirtie of his Knights hot questrits
                after him, met him at gate, who with some other of the
                Lords dependants are gone with him towards Douer, . . .

        F: Some fiue or six and thirty of his Knights
                Hot Questrists after him, met him at gate,
                Who, with some other of the Lords, dependants,
                Are gone with him toward Douer; . . .

                                        III.vii.16–19

Questrists (in F) is a coinage that should never have deceived anyone, since it implies superfluous derivation from a noun, 'quester', of identical meaning. It is acknowledged in the *OED*, but, naturally, as a nonce-word. Quite plainly it is a sophistication, and an unhappy one, of Q's *questrits*, which should read *questrels*. ('Questrel' is a variant of 'custrel', an attendant on a knight or man-at-arms. In the copy of Q codified by Greg as BM2 the reading has been corrected to *coystrills*, another variant of the same word.)

     The meaning of the lines in Q is still not quite satisfactory since the passage contains another error, this time a phonetic one (*after him* for *after 'em*). Duly emended, the lines would read:

        Some five- or six-and-thirty of his knights,
        Hot (= *eager, excited*) questrels after 'em, met him at gate, . . .[2]

     It is evident that in this instance F presents not merely an inferior version of the text but an incorrect one.

---

2   The knights, in other words, are
     followed by squires. *Cf.* I.iv.262:
     'Here do you keep a hundred
     knights and squires'.

THE DERIVATION OF THE FOLIO TEXT

B *Phonetic errors*   51

4   Q: You haue obedience scanted,
                And well are worth the worth that you haue wanted.

           F: . . . you haue obedience scanted,
                And well are worth the want that you haue wanted.

                                                        I.i.281–2

This gibe against Cordelia (ascribed to Regan in Q and to Goneril in F) is hardly
very telling in either formulation, but F's is much the less intelligible. It seems
to me very probable that phonetic confusion corrupted an original version of the
second line which read:

           And well are worth the words that you have wanted.

It is, after all, Cordelia's refusal to 'speak and purpose not' which is the
mainspring of the action in this scene, and it is appropriate that Regan (or
Goneril) should at this point spitefully return the snub she holds Cordelia guilty
of in 'wanting words'. The sentence, it is true, comes perilously near to saying
the opposite of what it should. But it is characteristic of Shakespeare occasionally to lose control of logical structure when expressing negative ideas (*cf.*
Regan's speech, II.iv.140–2). One is reminded of the line that Jonson alleged
he had found, possibly in *Julius Caesar*: 'Caesar did never wrong, but with just
cause'.
     Whether, in any case, Q may be emended or not, F is again in this instance
manifestly yet further astray.

5   Q: . . . why brand they vs with base, base bastardie? who in
                the lusty stealth of nature, take more composition and feirce
                quality, then doth within a stale dull lyed bed, goe to the
                creating of a whole tribe of fops got tweene a sleepe and
                wake; well . . .

           F: Why brand they vs
                With Base? With basenes Barstadie? Base, Base?
                Who in the lustie stealth of Nature, take
                More composition and fierce qualitie,
                Then doth within a dull stale tyred bed
                Goe to th'creating a whole tribe of Fops
                Got 'tweene a sleepe, and wake? Well then, . . .

                                                        I.ii.9–15

52   It has been assumed, on the authority of F, that Q's *lyed* is a misreading of *tyred*. Were one, however, to examine Q without reference to F, it would appear much likelier that *dull lyed* was a phonetic mistake for *dull-eyed*. Corrected in that sense, the Q reading gives not only a vivid image, but one entirely appropriate to the state ''tween asleep and wake' which it is meant to suggest. F's *dull . . . tyred* seems apt rather to the state between wake and sleep. One might notice too, that if three separate adjectives are in question, they are unnaturally arranged in Q, with the least emphatic in the middle ('stale, dull, tired'): F's rearrangement, apparently dictated by the emendation, arouses suspicion.

    The F reading in this instance is not self-evidently wrong, but an easy emendation of Q casts doubt upon it, to say the least.

6   Q: . . . go sir seeke him, I apprehend him, abhominable villaine where is he?

           F: Go sirrah, seeke him: Ile apprehend him. Abhominable Villaine, where is he?

                                                    I.ii.82–4

It is obvious that the *I* in Q is intended (as it is frequently elsewhere) for *aye*,[3] and that F's *Ile* is a sophistication. It would be very odd if Gloucester were telling Edmund to search for Edgar so that he, Gloucester, could arrest him: he surely means Edmund both to seek out Edgar and to seize him, as in Q.

7   Q: *Kent.* That such a slaue as this should weare a sword,
                   That weares no honesty, such smiling roges as these,
                   Like Rats oft bite those cordes in twaine,
                   Which are to intrench, to inloose . . .

           F: *Kent.* That such a slaue as this should weare a Sword,
                   Who weares no honesty: such smiling rogues as these,
                   Like Rats oft bite the holy cords a twaine,
                   Which are t'intrince, t'unloose: . . .

                                             II.ii.78–81

A somewhat loose reference is apparently intended to the mouse in the fable who, out of gratitude to a lion for once saving his life, released him from the net

---

3   *I* for *aye* is indeed a phonetic mis-spelling rather than an error in the strict sense, and so common a mis-spelling that it should hardly, perhaps, be regarded even as an irregularity.

THE DERIVATION OF THE FOLIO TEXT

in which he lay entrapped by gnawing through the ropes. Still fresher possibly 53 in Shakespeare's mind than his recollection of Aesop would have been two lines from *The True Chronicle Historie of King Leir*, a play he very probably consulted before writing his own:

> The silly mouse, by vertue of her teeth,
> Releas'd the princely Lyon from the net

642–3

As applied to Oswald, the similitude seems to imply that 'smiling rogues' of his type will release their masters from trammels of conscience which their masters by themselves would be unable to break free of. That interpretation would, at any rate, be consistent with the gist of the ensuing lines, which is that servants like Oswald make a trade of pandering to their masters' whims and passions.

It is most unlikely on palaeographical grounds that *intrench* derived by misreading from *intrince*. We may note also (a) that the word *intrince* or *intrinse* (allegedly an abbreviated form of *intrinsicate*) is unknown outside this passage; what is more that *intrinsicate* (derived from the Italian *intrinsecato*, which means either 'intrinsic, essential', or 'inward' in the extended senses 'familiar [with], expert [in]') would not, in any case, supply an acceptable sense; (b) that the lines present an image of tightly-bound *cords* (which cannot be unloosed) rather than of entangled *knots* (which cannot be unravelled), so that *intrince*, even if it represents 'intrinsicate' as a mistake for 'intricate',[4] as is usually maintained, is scarcely apt to the context; (c) that *to intrench, to* may easily be supposed a mishearing of *too intrench'd to*, so that the line reads: *Which are too entrench'd to unloose*; and (d) that *entrenched* (literally 'placed in a trench') requires little metaphorical extension of meaning to convey the idea 'embedded'.

We may notice, too, though it is not here a strictly relevant consideration, that the word *holy* has been added to the F version of the third line. This might

4 *OED* quotes four examples of this erroneous usage of 'intrinsicate'. The earliest (from Whitehorne's translation of Machiavelli's *Art of War*) is certainly a mistake. Another is scarcely an example of usage at all, since the passage (from Marston) merely cites the word as a 'new-minted epithet'. I am not convinced that the remaining two (Jonson, *Cynthia's Revels*, V.ii.14; *Antony and Cleopatra*, V.ii.307) are evidence that the word has been misunderstood. It would indeed be astonishing if Jonson had naively misinterpreted a word of not-very-obscure Latin origin. Nevertheless, it does appear that the reading *intrince* in F may provide a further instance of the confusion with 'intricate'.

54 appear a satisfactory mending of the metre were it not for the fact that the metre does not need mending. The line should begin with the words *as these*, mistakenly attached to the previous line in both Q and (following Q) F.

8   Q: *Duke.* This is a fellow of the selfe same nature,
                 Our sister speake of, . . .

      F: *Cor.* This is a Fellow of the selfe same colour,
                 Our Sister speakes of.

II.ii.145–6

Cornwall's remark applies to Kent and refers, one must presume, to what Goneril has said about him in the letter brought by Oswald. In the circumstances one would expect to find 'speak' in the past tense. F's historic present strikes the ear as unidiomatic without the addition of 'in her letter' (or the presence of the letter in Cornwall's hand) to distinguish it from a present denoting frequent and continuing action. It solves the problem to assume that Q's *speake* represents *spake*, its homonym in sixteenth-century pronunciation (*cf.* the survival of this vowel in the modern 'break').

This list might be much extended by a series of less obvious errors in F, readings which have received more or less plausible explanation at the hands of editors, but which nevertheless strike one as less than happy in their context. Here are two by way of illustration:

      F: *Lear.* Ile tell thee:
          Life and death, I am asham'd
          That thou hast power to shake my manhood thus,
          That these hot teares, which breake from me perforce
          Should make thee worth them.

      [Q: should make the worst]
I.iv.318–21

      F: If Wolues had at thy Gate howl'd that sterne time,
          Thou should'st haue said, good Porter turne the Key:
          All Cruels else subscribe: but I shall see
          The winged Vengeance ouertake such Children.

      [Q: All cruels else subscrib'd]
III.vii.63–6

We very frequently discover the text of F to be obviously erroneous where that of Q is not. Many of these mistakes, including the evident misprints and all the errors of punctuation, may, of course, be attributed to the compositors. Others, and in particular the errors of lineation, may be due to the fact that the 'copy' was incorrectly or unclearly marked by the collator.[5] But we find a significant number which it would be difficult to explain on any such grounds.

A *Misreadings from manuscript*

Several of the readings in F which are clearly wrong can only be understood as misinterpretations of manuscript 'copy'. A good example is *strangenesse* for *strange newes* (Q) at II.i.89:

> *Corn.*   . . . since I came hither
> (Which I can call but now,) I haue heard strangenesse.

It is as obvious here that the Q reading is correct as that the error in F cannot have derived from it unless by some extraordinary aberration of the compositor's eyesight or memory. Certainly we cannot hold the collator responsible since he would have no reason for tampering with what in Q is clearly satisfactory. Such, furthermore, is the nature of the mistake – the substitution of an unacceptable, though not nonsensical, reading for another closely resembling it in ortho-graphical form – that we are irresistibly led to suppose not the miscopying of *strange newes* as it appears in Q, but as it appeared, perhaps erratically spelt, in some manuscript version of the text.

---

5 The evidence is briefly discussed below, p. 118, n. 10. Certain of the mislineations, however, are demonstrably also attributable to the compositors. I do not know whether it has been noticed that the compositor identified as 'B' never – never, at least in the course of this text – 'turns over' a word at the end of a full line of print, whereas compositor 'E' does so not infrequently. 'B' was evidently so averse to this practice that, when he found himself with more matter for a line than could be accommodated in his measure, he preferred to remove one or more words to the next line, adjusting the lineation from then onwards *tant bien que mal*. The results of this unconcern may be seen at III.vi.68–9; III.vii.30–1; IV.v.19–20; and IV.vi.25–7. Compositor E is once guilty of misplacing a word for the same reason (I.i.236–7). Once or twice the necessity to use up excess space caused the compositors to misarrange as faulty verse what is correctly given in Q as prose (e.g. at II.i.2–5 and IV.vii.79–80).

56 We find errors of this kind scattered throughout the text of F, e.g. at III.vi.73, *tight* (Q: *tike*, presumably read in manuscript as *tite*); IV.i.71, *slaues* (Q: *stands*, for *'stands*); IV.iv.4, *Hardokes* (Q: *hor-docks*).

B *Substitutions*

We have already noticed that on several occasions acceptable readings in Q are apparently arbitrarily altered, and (as nearly all editors agree) for the worse. For example, *I neuer got him* (II.i.80) is replaced by *said he?*; *rash* by *sticke* (III.vii.58); *dearne* by *sterne* (III.vii.63); *British* by *English* (IV.vi.256); and so on.

C *Errors in the ascription of speeches*

Of the many alterations of speech-prefix in F some are arguably correct. But it would be difficult to justify the following, and few editors attempt to do so:

1   Q: *Foole.* Sirra, you were best take my coxcombe.
            Kent. Why Foole?
            Foole. Why for taking on's part, that's out of fauour . . .

I.iv.109–11

F allots the question *Why my Boy?* to Lear — wrongly since the Fool's immediate answer, and most of the remainder of his speech with its reference to Lear as 'this fellow', is obviously addressed to Kent.

2   Q: *Reg.* My sister may receiue it much more worse,
            To haue her Gentlemen abus'd, assalted
            For following her affaires, put in his legges,
            Come my good Lord away?

II.ii.155–8

F omits the third line of Regan's speech, and attributes the last (as *Come my Lord, away*) to Cornwall. Since the line marks Cornwall's exit with Regan, it is most unlikely that we should find him ignoring Regan to summon Gloucester — who in fact is to remain on stage for a brief exchange with Kent.

3   Q: *Alb.* Stop your mouth dame, or with this paper shall I
            stople it, thou worse then any thing, reade thine owne
            euill, nay no tearing Lady, I perceiue you know't.

Gon. Say if I do, the lawes are mine not thine, who shall   57
arraine me for't.
Alb. Most monstrous know'st thou this paper?
Gon. Aske me not what I know.   *Exit. Gonorill.*
Alb. Go after her, shee's desperate, gouerne her.

V.iii.154–61

F places Goneril's exit two lines earlier, causing Albany's question to be addressed to, and answered by, Edmund. This arrangement is implausible to say the least since (a) Albany's *Go after her* now appears as an afterthought, (b) Goneril, without her second furious evasion of Albany's challenge, is left with scarcely enough to establish that she is 'desperate' and (c) Edmund's confession of guilt (which follows immediately the passage quoted) comes as a surprising *volte-face* after the refusal of *Aske me not what I know*.

4   Q: *Duke.* Runne, runne, O runne.
               Edg. To who my Lord, who hath the office, send
               Thy token of repreeue.
               Bast. Well thought on, take my sword the Captaine,
               Giue it the Captaine? *Duke.* Hast thee for thy life.

V.iii.247–51

Q marks no exit after these lines, but Edgar's lines make it clear that the other speeches are addressed to him, and that it is he who hurries off with the 'token of reprieve'. F, too, omits the stage-direction, but implies – surprisingly – the employment of a messenger, since Albany's speech (*Hast thee for they life*) is ascribed to Edgar. This is not logically impossible, but does not square at all with the drift of the earlier speeches. One would expect the Duke, if he had it in mind to despatch a soldier or officer, to issue a peremptory command rather than the urgent personal plea ('Run, run, oh run!') which is more appropriate to an equal; and one would expect the messenger, not Edgar, to enquire 'To who, my Lord?' if he were not clear where he were being sent.

We have here a fairly remarkable record of the insufficiencies of F: fourteen passages in which Q's errors have been either preserved or ineffectually tinkered with; eight passages, corrupt in Q, which have been emended, but demonstrably at a venture and without success; and (quite apart from the evidence of misreading from manuscript) eight instances of gratuitous and misguided alteration, four involving substitution and four affecting the ascription of

58 speeches. The most conservative editor would hesitate to sustain the authority of F at these points in the text, though naturally in several cases (e.g. *poorely led?*) he may be obliged to uphold the reading of F in default of anything better. On thirty several occasions the F text proves to be seriously problematical or obviously incorrect. A much longer list might be compiled of mistakes or corruptions only slightly less evident. These weaknesses in F are not confined to certain scenes of the play or pages of the text, but are scattered in an apparently random way throughout its full extent.

How are we to explain them on the hypothesis of an independent manuscript consulted by a collator? That F on many occasions reproduces the errors of Q might be accounted for by his carelessness. If he failed to correct *Turlygod*, for example, that might be because he failed to notice it: we should not be too surprised at such momentary lapses of attention. It is much less plausible, however, that he overlooked *Ladie oth'e brach* or *commands her seruice*, since he made some attempt to change these readings. And it is hardly credible at all that he would pass over Kent's speech at II.ii.167ff., parts of which are seriously defective in sense or metre, without noticing that it differed from the manuscript (as it surely must have done) in more than the one or two details he picked out for correction. Perhaps, however, the collator was not only negligent but occasionally lazy and indifferent.

If so, his laziness and indifference must have been accompanied by a certain over-confidence in his own judgement since, obviously without consulting his authority, he altered *deserue* to *reward* instead of *discern*, *questrits* to *questrists* instead of *questrels*, *I apprehend* to *Ile apprehend* instead of *aye, apprehend*. In fact, for someone in whom a great deal of faith must be placed the collator shows himself to be sadly unreliable.

Need we, however, suppose him guilty of such high-handedness? May we not attribute his lapses rather to the illegibility at crucial points of his authoritative copy, or assume that it had, at those points, suffered damage? Unfortunately, this would not help at all. We should find ourselves relying on a very weak *ad hoc* hypothesis (in assuming the collator's manuscript to be deficient when it was obvious that he had gone wrong but not otherwise); one, besides, which it would be very difficult to sustain in the light of other evidence.

It is clear, in the first place, that the independent manuscript, if it existed, must have been unusually legible. We have, in the hundred or so lines of the text that appear only in F, a representative sample of its quality. Plainly the collator had no difficulty whatever in reading and in copying (as presumably he did) these lines. They are free of corruption but for a single trivial misreading (*Place* for *Plate* at IV.vi.169) and a minor mishap of copying (*the walls is thine* for

the wall is thine at V.iii.76),[6] for both of which errors the compositor, reading
from the *collator's* copy, may well have been responsible. If these hundred-odd
lines, distributed piecemeal through the text, were manifestly derived from
'clean' copy, it is not very likely that this copy elsewhere contained frequent and
serious illegibilities. And it is in the highest degree implausible that its flaws
were so frequent that they happened to coincide not once or twice but repeatedly
with corruptions in Q, so that the collator could derive no help at these points
from either source. The odds against such a series of coincidences would, one
fancies, have to be calculated in millions.

It would be equally difficult to admit the possibility of damage. The errors in
F are not confined, nor even for the most part confined, to the beginning and
end of the text or to the beginnings and endings of verse-lines, as we should
expect if the manuscript in use had suffered damage of the kind most frequent.
We should have to suppose some more serious state of disrepair: missing or torn
leaves or even tattered fragments of leaves. Such speculations hardly recommend
themselves – and in any case do not dispose of the difficulties. If we assume
mutilation of the manuscript to explain the mistakes at II.iv.90 (*meere fetches*)
and II.iv.103 (*commands, tends, seruice*), how do we account for the origin of lines
99 and 100 which do not appear at all in Q? Similarly, if IV.i.10 was not
available to the collator, so that he was forced to make do with the unsatisfactory
reading *poorely led?*, where did he find IV.i.6–9, lines which he could not have
discovered in the printed quarto? In short, F's errors find themselves in such
close proximity to alterations of every kind (which cannot, *ex hypothesi*, be
rejected as spurious) that it would be impossible to define areas of unreliability
in the F text such as might correspond plausibly with areas of damage in a
manuscript exemplar.

The same considerations make it impossible to suppose that the authoritative
manuscript contained an abridged version of the play or that only a portion of it
survived to reach the collator. It would clearly be impossible on any principle to
distinguish 'genuine' parts of the text from those containing 'untrustworthy'
additions and alterations, so that faulty passages were associated only with the
latter. We have no recourse, then, but to accept that if the F text was prepared
by collating the quarto with an independent manuscript (as the more convincing corrections in F and its additional lines seem to suggest), the task was less
than conscientiously performed. Serious mistakes were overlooked, while others
were patched up or arbitrarily (and wrongly) corrected without reference to the
manuscript.

6   See Appendix B2, p. 246 below.

60   This is sufficiently unsatisfactory. But the evidence of misreadings from manuscript places us in difficulties still more awkward. What was this manuscript which for a part, or parts, at least, of the text seems to have served as the 'copy' for F? Was it a transcript of the collator's specimen of Q which he had already brought into line with the prompt-book? And, if so, is it not very strange that the prompt-book – the authoritative manuscript – was not itself transcribed? No purpose can possibly have been served by a preliminary transference of corrections from the manuscript to Q. Or was the manuscript itself, after all, submitted to the printer who used it in setting up a part of the text? But if that happened, how do we account for the pervasive traces of Q in the very passages of the F text which indicate manuscript 'copy'? In the following lines, for example, we notice in close proximity (a) an erroneous reading which must have been inherited from Q and (b) two further errors which were quite certainly not derived from Q, and which can best be explained as misreadings from manuscript:

> F: Hound or Spaniell, Brache, or Hym:
>   Or Bobtaile tight, or Troudle taile,
>
> Q: [grim-] houd or spaniel, brach or him, Bobtaile tike, or
>   trūdletaile,

III.vi.72–3

Hym, it is generally agreed, is an error for *lym*;[7] *tight* is only explicable as a mistaking of handwritten *tike* for *tite*; while *Troudle* apparently derives from *Trondle* (an alternative spelling of *trundle*), manuscript 'n' being misread as 'u'.

    The manuscript from which this passage was printed must, to contain the error *Hym*, have been copied from Q. Yet it is difficult to imagine why, if copying by hand were thought necessary here and elsewhere, the prompt-book itself was not taken for model. Since we start from the premise that the collation of Q with prompt-book was undertaken to provide printer's 'copy', we necessarily assume that at this stage the prompt-book was ready to hand.

    When we come to consider the remaining instances of what I have called gratuitous error in F – the substitutions and the unwarranted changes in speech-ascription – we find ourselves in still deeper uncertainties. There can be no doubt that these alterations offer evidence of deliberate editing: there can be no question of misunderstanding or confusion as their cause. We may doubtless

---

7   See Appendix A1, p. 182 below.

assume that they originated in the theatre, so that they will have appeared in the prompt-book handed to the collator. But whether we suppose that the book-keeper or a theatrical reviser tampered with the text, or whether we hold the collator himself responsible, the awkward question arises of how much un-authorised interference we should recognise – how far, in other words, over the great multiplicity of small changes we find in F, by no means all of them obvious improvements, we should allow the reliability of the 'authoritative' manuscript to extend.

Certainly, once we have admitted the possibility of more or less arbitrary editing, we do not have to look far in F for additional evidence of changes which decidedly *impair* the text. We should not, perhaps, attach too much importance to the fact that many variant readings in F, though acceptable in themselves, have repeatedly been judged inferior to their counterparts in Q. Such editorial preferences are generally in part subjective, and so, perhaps, controvertible. Oddly it is a less straightforward type of variant in F, rarely if ever rejected by the editors, which may on quite objective grounds be condemned as intrusive and erroneous. I refer to the many occasions on which an added word or phrase in F disrupts the metrical regularity we find in Q.

We have met one such addition ('*holy* cords') which the metre condemns as unwarrantable. Others can be cited:

(a)   Q: . . . and here I take *Cordelia*
        By the hand, / Dutches of *Burgundie*,
        Leir. Nothing, I haue sworne.

        F: And here I take *Cordelia* by the hand,
        Dutchesse of *Burgundie*.
        Lear. Nothing, I haue sworne, *I am firme*.

                                                    I.i.246–8

(b)

        Q: . . . ingratitude! thou marble harted fiend, / more hideous
        when thou shewest thee in a child, / then the Sea-monster,
        detested kite, thou list . . .

        F: Ingratitude! thou Marble-hearted Fiend,
        More hideous when thou shew'st thee in a Child,
        Then the Sea-monster.
        Alb. Pray Sir be patient.
        Lear. Detested Kite, thou lyest.

                                                    I.iv.281–4

62   (c)   Q: . . . you, we first seaze on.
                     Bast. I shall serue you truly, / how euer else.
                     Glost. For him I thanke your grace.

       F: You we first seize on.
            Bast. I shall serue you *Sir* truely, how euer else.
            Glo. For him I thanke your Grace.

                                                          II.i.118–19

(d)   Q: *Edg.* Poore *Toms* a cold, I cannot dance it farther.
                Glost. Come hither fellow.
                Edg. Blesse thy sweete eyes, they bleed.

       F: *Edg.* Poore Tom's a cold, I cannot daub it further.
            Glou. Come hither fellow.
            Edg. And yet I must:
            Blesse thy sweete eyes, they bleede.

                                                          IV.i.54–6

(e)   Q: For as I am a man, I thinke this Ladie
                To be my child *Cordelia. Cord.* And so I am.

       F: For (as I am a man) I thinke this Lady
            To be my childe *Cordelia.*
            Cor. And so I am: *I am.*

                                                          IV.vii.69–70

  None of these additions, it is true, impairs sense or violates logic: they are too
vacuous for that. But their very triviality betrays their spuriousness, destroying
as they do in each case the regularity of the metre for no necessary purpose. In (b)
and (d) they have evidently been motivated by the context. In (b) Albany has
just entered, and Q gives him nothing to say – improperly it may have been felt
– for fifteen lines or so after his entrance. In (d) Edgar, if he is to use the
expression 'daub it' rather than 'dance it', must retract his statement immediately. 'To daub it' means 'to put on a false show'. At this point, of course, he
has every intention of 'daubing it further'. In (a) and (c) short lines have been
unnecessarily extended into full ones, perhaps because in both cases the
arrangement of the lines in Q is faulty and confusing. In (e) Cordelia's half-line

has apparently been padded out to join with the succeeding half-line (Lear. *Be your teares wet?*). There then follows a further incomplete line (*Yes faith: I pray weepe not*). In Q this speech of Lear's begins correctly with a complete line: *Be your teares wet, yes faith, I pray weep not.*[8]

If we have been obliged to assume, in addition to the collator and his mistakes, an editor who deliberately interfered with the text, altering readings and the ascription of speeches for purely contingent purposes, it is not unreasonable to find his hand in these interpolations as well. Their intrusiveness is as obvious as the intention, 'reformatory' in each case, which prompted them. But if they are to be rejected as spurious, or at least treated as strongly suspect, then all the briefer additions in F, including those not clearly mistaken, fall under suspicion as well. We cannot refuse to entertain the possibility that the editor would be capable of intervening with a *plausible* word or phrase on the necessary occasion. We cannot assume that his efforts would invariably declare their own ineptitude.

This consideration, added to those we have already discussed, makes it well nigh hopeless to rely, for practical purposes, on the collation hypothesis. Where is the advantage in invoking the authority of an independent manuscript to sanction the variants in F if we can feel certain that the collator frequently omitted, whether accidentally or deliberately, to consult it, and that, in any case, it had already been contaminated by unauthorised alterations to an unknown and, in the nature of the case, unknowable extent? There are, besides, the problematical misreadings which suggest, most improbably, that the independent manuscript was first superimposed, by way of corrections and additions, on the text of Q before being recopied, at least in part, from *that* source — exactly as though an equally important contribution were required from Q to make up the final amalgam. Were it not, indeed, for the longer additions in F and the evidence it gives, in the successful emendation of Q errors, of access to some *bona fide* source, we should have little encouragement to regard the text of F as supported by any genuine authority.

Apart, however, from the general weakness and inexactitude of the hypothesis and the perplexities it must therefore inevitably introduce into the process of editing, it leads, when related to certain features of the evidence, to conclusions which one is bound to find extremely implausible. Can one believe,

8 For further examples of metrical disturbance in F resulting from interpolation or omission, see Appendix C2, p. 254 below.

64   for example, in a collator who would tax his own brains to miscorrect a difficulty when he had the answer at his elbow? Who would punctiliously change *she came short* to *she comes too short* (I.i.74), though it makes no whit of difference to the sense, but fail to alter *square of sence* (I.i.76) in the same sentence, which leaves the meaning totally obscure? Who, in tidying up Edmund's speech at the beginning of I.ii – by no means a straightforward task – would either be so foolhardy as to neglect the help at hand, or, seeking the aid of his manuscript in dividing lines, altering readings and supplying lacunae, would leave one line (15) short of a foot and another (21) meaningless? Who would look up *my wracke* (II.ii.172) and discover it to be *miracles*, but take no further interest in this and the succeeding lines which are, as they stand, baffling and must have read differently in the original? The more one reflects on his operations the more bizarre and illogical they seem, and the less faith one has that they ever took place.

We could, in fact, do very well without this collator and his manuscript if we could find some other means of extricating ourselves from the problem which they were invented to solve. In fact the evidence we have already considered itself indicates another possibility.

Instead of selecting as our principal clues the additional lines and the patently successful corrections in F, which lead us naturally to suppose the consultation of an independent manuscript and to embroil ourselves consequently in a tangle of inconsistencies, we might choose as our starting point the many deliberate alterations of the text which could not possibly stem from an authoritative source. We might, in other words, suppose an editor or reviser freely and extensively refurbishing the corrupt and muddled text of Q without reference to any other authority.

The facts that constituted awkward counter-evidence to the previous hypothesis now underprop the argument. It is not difficult to suppose that a reviser, working unaided at the long and exacting task of re-punctuating, re-aligning and thoroughly correcting an extremely badly produced printed text, would perpetrate the kind of mistakes we have noticed. We should not, at least, be at all surprised to find him guilty of guessing ineptly in correcting errors, of merely touching up on occasion what he could not hope to emend, or of abandoning a difficulty temporarily and forgetting to return to it. We should expect, too, that he would be highly suspicious, and justly so, of the line-arrangement and speech-prefixes in Q, and that he might well be misled at times into altering them without proper cause. When he had finished his work it is not at all unlikely that he would make a fair copy of it in manuscript, and that, therefore, such errors as he had overlooked in Q would be transcribed into this manuscript. A further curious feature of the F text which we have not yet noticed is also plausibly accounted for: the fact that of the passages in Q chosen for excision, a surprisingly large number contain serious corruption. Though there can be no doubt that the F text was curtailed intentionally by the omission of inessential matter, not all of it by any means obscure, yet it seems likely that whoever performed this task was especially ready to dispense with passages of textual difficulty.

In postulating a reviser we imagine necessarily a person of some literary expertise. Let us postpone until the hypothesis has been thoroughly tested all speculation as to who might have filled the role, how he carried out the work and in what circumstances. It is, all the same, not too unrealistic to suppose at the outset that the task was delegated not to a scribe or book-keeper but to another playwright (another, since we can hardly suppose the author himself capable of such helpless and frequent bungling). It is well known that contemporary dramatists were hired by theatrical companies or their impresarios to carry out recensions of precisely this kind.[9]

The Quarto text does not, on the face of it, inspire confidence. Its surreptitious origin is obvious to us, and would have been well known to Shakespeare's colleagues. It is easy to suppose that a writer, given a free hand in setting the text to rights, might feel justified in introducing a large number of minor verbal changes in the shape of corrections or substitutions, omissions or interpolations.

So far the evidence may be seen as satisfactorily of a piece. But the important facts on which the collation hypothesis has been based still remain to be considered. The problem has not been solved, merely turned about, and difficulties must now be admitted from the opposite quarter. How, on the hypothesis of revision, can we account for the longer additions in F, given that most of them show no obvious discrepancy with the rest of the text in point of style? And how do we explain the ingenious and 'difficult' emendations to be found in F, the accuracy of which it is impossible to doubt? They can scarcely be passed over as lucky accidents; still less can they be regarded as the fruit of care and application, in view of the reviser's obvious reluctance elsewhere to puzzle for long over the textual problems he encountered.

In investigating the further evidence which can be brought to bear on these questions it will be best to consider them separately. We shall begin by enquiring whether the additional passages in F can be held at all plausibly to originate elsewhere than in an authoritative manuscript version of the play.

9 Evidence for the practice of 'play-patching' is discussed in Chambers, *Wm. Sh.*, I. 211ff., and, much more thoroughly, in Bentley, *Profession*, Ch. IX.

CHAPTER FOUR
THE FOLIO ADDITIONS

It has proved till now convenient to describe as 'additional' the hundred or so lines of text which appear for the first time in F. They are, of course, additional to the text as given in Q; but we must not beg the question whether they are additional in respect of the original version of the play, and it is now time to ask: were the passages unique to F incorporated into the text at some date after the performances reported in Q; or do they represent portions of the original which were deleted prior to the production which Q records? To a large extent our estimate of their authenticity must depend on how we determine this question.

Unfortunately, the arguments which most readily present themselves as relevant to the issue are those we must place least faith in, since they can all too easily be turned inside out. Do certain passages in F appear to have been added because they serve a purpose – that of clarifying a point, for example, or of easing an awkward transition in sense or action? These very passages may have been omitted from Q because the clarification was judged unnecessarily explicit or the transition smooth enough without inessential padding. Do certain other lines in F seem to betray their extraneous origin by introducing irrelevancies or inconsistencies into the plot? The plot abounds in irrelevant and inconsistent details, and these same lines may have been removed from Q in an attempt, however modest, to reduce the number. And so on.

Yet there do exist a few considerations, not susceptible to this sort of invalidation, which throw a clear light on the issue. Since they do so to varying degrees, and independently of each other, I do not attempt to connect them in a single argument.

1. One passage that appears only in F begins by completing a line that has been left metrically defective in Q. It ends, however, in metrical confusion: an alexandrine appears where the new material leads back to the next line in Q:

> [Q: The two great Princes *France* and *Burgundy*,]
> F: May be preuented now. The Princes, *France & Burgundy*,

I.i.46

The anomalous line in F, we may notice, is composed of the last half-line of the 'addition' combined with an abbreviated version of what stands in Q as a complete line. This pattern strongly suggests interpolation. It is hardly, at any rate, consistent with the alternative hypothesis, namely that the new material represents an omission from Q. The passage cannot have been accidentally omitted by an actor or by the compositor, since the accident must have been accompanied by the deliberate expansion of the half-line quoted above to exactly the length of a pentameter. One is equally reluctant to believe in a deliberate cut since whoever made it must have given careful attention to expanding this half-line, while beginning the cut casually in mid-sentence, leaving a metrical gap:

> Q: Confirming them on yonger yeares,
> The two great Princes *France* and *Burgundy*,
>
> F: Conferring them on yonger strengths, while we
> Vnburthen'd crawle toward death. Our son of *Cornwal*, . . .

I.i.41–2

Aside from the metrical deficiency, no manner of hiatus is noticeable in Q: the lines supplied in F are not essential.

2. On two occasions it is fairly evident that the continuity of Q has been disturbed by the intrusion of fresh matter.

(a) (I quote the F text, enclosing the additional lines within square brackets.)

> *Foole.* Prythee Nunkle tell me, whether a madman be a
> Gentleman, or a Yeoman.
> *Lear.* A King, a King.
> [*Foole.* No, he's a Yeoman, that ha's a Gentleman to his Sonne:
> for hee's a mad Yeoman that sees his Sonne a Gentleman before
> him.
> *Lear.*] To haue a thousand with red burning spits
> Come hizzing in vpon 'em.

III.vi.10–17

It was evidently thought necessary that the Fool should supply the answer to his riddle, but it is a clumsy expedient to make him do so in the middle of Lear's bitter outburst, thereby depriving its latter part not only of sense but also of grammatical structure. So clumsy is this, indeed, that one is led to speculate whether lines 16 and 17 in F were intended for omission: a cut immediately follows (ll. 18–59). Directly after the cut, however, we find Kent attempting to pacify Lear (*O pitty: Sir, where is the patience now / That you so oft haue boasted to retaine?*, ll. 61–2). Although the occasion for this speech has disappeared along

68 with the material removed, lines 16 and 17, immediately preceding the cut, provide an adequate substitute. Hence, it appears, their retention, at the cost of some discontinuity and muddle. The passage provides particularly clear evidence of editorial interference.

(b) Lear's speech beginning at IV.vi.161 is, if we reckon two half-lines as one, five lines longer in F than in Q. The speech dwells bitterly on the hypocrisy of institutionalised justice, which enables those in authority, protected by 'robes and furred gowns', to punish their inferiors for sins of which they themselves are equally guilty, as though the office vindicated the man. In Q this train of thought leads Lear immediately to offer the blind Gloucester a piece of ironical advice: *get thee glasse eyes, and like a scuruy polititian seeme to see the things thou doest not.* In F several lines intervene which develop a related, but different, theme: the rich are safe from the law; indeed, the King himself will protect, it is implied, even the worst of them:

> F: Thorough tatter'd cloathes great [Q: smal] Vices do appeare:
> Robes, and Furr'd gownes hide all. [Place [*i.e.*, *Plate*] sinnes
> with Gold, and the strong Lance of Iustice, hurtlesse
> breakes: Arme it in ragges, a Pigmies straw do's pierce it.
> None do's offend, none, I say none, Ile able 'em; take that
> of me my Friend, who haue the power to seale th'accusers
> lips.] Get thee glasse-eyes, and like a scuruy Politician,
> seeme to see the things thou dost not.
>
> IV.vi.168–76

The new lines form a curious digression, to the purport of which we must return later. The chief clue to their extraneousness occurs, in fact, at the point of reversion to Q. Lear's advice to Gloucester takes on, in F, a different, though not perhaps unsatisfactory, meaning. It has, however, entirely lost its special aptness. In Q the idea of factitious visibility or invisibility (*through tottered raggs, smal vices do appeare, robes & furd-gownes hides all*) leads directly to the idea of factitious vision (*get thee glasse eyes*); in F no such connection is apparent, since the lines interposed stray from the point. It would be strange if the more natural succession of ideas in Q had been achieved by the omission of these lines. It is much less improbable that the new matter in F constitutes an interpolation.

3. In one case, at least, it is evident that misunderstanding has prompted the addition of a line in F. The passage reads in Q:

> *Bast.* In wisdome I sholud aske thy name,
> But since thy outside lookes so faire and warlike,

> And that thy being some say of breeding breathes,
> By right of knighthood, I disdaine and spurne . . .
>
> V.iii.141–3, 145

It is obvious that *By* is a mistake for *My*. Edmund is saying that he waives his right, by the rules of trial by combat, to know the identity of his appellant (Edgar). In the copy of Q known as BM2 a manuscript correction restores the required reading. But in F the misprint *By* is overlooked and preserved. Two consequences follow: (a) the phrase 'by right', being unidiomatic, must be modified, and (b) the verbs 'disdain' and 'spurn' must be supplied with an object. An extra line comes in aid, and, in the event, the unnecessary effort results in confusion:

> What safe, and nicely I might well delay,
> By rule of Knight-hood, I disdaine and spurne:

What must refer to the coming combat, yet that is not the object of Edmund's disdain, as the structure of the sentence seems to imply. The sense requires 'delay' as an object, or the predicate 'to do so' after 'spurn'.

More significant, however, than the muddle itself is the clear evidence that a misunderstanding has initiated it. There can be no question but that F's extra line was inspired by a failure to identify the corruption in Q.

This evidence is not, of course, wholly conclusive. We cannot argue that, if *some* of the passages unique to F display the marks of interpolation, *all* must therefore be interpolations. Nevertheless, a strong presumption is created in favour of that possibility, and, in the circumstances, the kind of evidence we have hitherto rejected as ambiguous may now reasonably be cited as corroborative. The fact, for example, that none of the fresh material in F is strictly necessary may, in the absence of other evidence, argue either addition in F or omission in Q; but when we know that some of it *has* been deliberately added we may find it more significant that the Q text does not actually require the expansions it has received.

We should except, perhaps, its defective lines which need, and frequently receive, metrical expansion. Here, however, it is very significant that none of the words or phrases supplied in F contributes materially to the sense or even modifies it, although in one or two cases what is already clear is made further explicit. The vacuousness of these stopgaps descends on occasion to fatuity. Two examples merit quoting. They are enclosed below within square brackets. The remainder of the text in each case follows Q without material change:

F: I am a very foolish fond old man,
Fourescore and vpward,
[Not an houre more, nor lesse:]
And to deale plainely,
I feare I am not in my perfect mind.

IV.vii.60–3

(The phrase added here is doubtless intended to demonstrate Lear's madness. Yet there is good dramatic cause why his madness should not appear as idiocy; nowhere else in the text is it allowed to do so. It is also worth observing that F's attempt to remedy the metre results in a greater irregularity than before. Q, without the interpolation, presents a somewhat clumsy but not impossible pentameter. F, achieving a smoother line, leaves after it an obvious loose end in the half-line *And to deale plainely*.)

F: *Edg.* What in ill thoughts againe?
Men must endure
Their going hence, euen as their comming hither,
Ripenesse is all come on.
[*Glo.* And that's true too.]   *Exeunt.*

V.ii.9–11

(Comment would be superfluous.)

Among the more material additions there is one which, it might well be argued, is indeed necessary since it fills an obvious lacuna. Q reads at this point as follows:

        . . . there is diuision,
Although as yet the face of it be couer'd
With mutuall cunning, twixt *Albany* and *Cornwall*
But true it is, from *France* there comes a power
Into this scattered kingdome, who alreadie wise in our negligēce,
Haue secret feet in some of our best Ports,

III.i.19–21, 30–3

Between *Cornwall* at the end of line 21 and *But* at the beginning of the next line there certainly occurs an awkward break both in sense and in syntax. This might well argue the accidental omission of one or more lines. Can we accept, however, that the lines omitted are those supplied by F? The version in F runs:

. . . There is diuision
(Although as yet the face of it is couer'd
With mutuall cunning) 'twixt Albany, and Cornwall:
[Who haue, as who haue not, that their great Starres
Thron'd and set high; Seruants, who seeme no lesse,
Which are to France the Spies and Speculations
Intelligent of our State. What hath bin seene,
Either in snuffes, and packings of the Dukes,
Or the hard Reine which both of them hath borne
Against the old kinde King; or something deeper,
Whereof (perchance) these are but furnishings.]
[But true it is, from *France* there comes a power . . .]

The last line I quote from Q, since it is wanting in F, as is the remainder of the speech. This omission in F, however, must certainly be accidental: a compositor's mistake, attributable, perhaps, to some difficulty in the copy.[1] It is the new lines which must claim our attention.

To the 'dear thing' that Kent 'commends' to the Gentleman in Q (an intimation of dissension between the Dukes) they add that spies, evidently 'servants' of the Dukes, have been active in conveying information to France, and that this intelligence has been directly responsible for the French landing. The news taken to France may have concerned the Dukes' quarrels, or their unkind treatment of the King, or 'something deeper'.

It is evident from the continuation of the speech in Q that in the original text, whatever may be missing from it, the main emphasis is placed upon the political divisions in the country, and the opportunity which this affords the French:

But true it is, from France there comes a power
Into this *scatter'd* Kingdom, who, already
Wise in our negligence, have secret feet
In some of our best ports . . .

If there are lines missing just prior to this, we should expect them to contain speculation of some sort, since the sentence takes a turn (apparently) from surmise to certainty with the phrase 'But true it is'. Furthermore, that Kent should in these lines speculate on the means by which the French have acquired their information is plausible enough. But that he should make fresh suggestions, as he does in the F addition, about their motives for invading (mistreatment of the King, or 'something deeper') is surprising in view of the fact that his

1   See Appendix B2, p. 235 below.

72   mind is on such matters as 'division', 'scattering' and 'negligence'. If the additional lines, however, create an odd diversion in the train of thought, they do not, perhaps, produce a logical inconsistency in the strict sense: Kent may be speculating upon several possible *motives* for the invasion while remaining certain about its *occasion*, namely, the disarray of the kingdom.[2]

But that is not all: the additional suggestions are wrong — one of them, at least, quite clearly so. The news of the King's mistreatment cannot have reached France before the invasion, as Kent is made to suggest. He speaks here on the night of the storm in the course of a scene (III.i) which immediately follows the one in which Lear has had his first and only quarrel with Regan (II.iv). Now, we must suppose that Kent's secret information respecting the French landing derives from a letter he has received from Cordelia the previous day (II.ii.170ff.), the very day, in fact, judging from other indications, upon which Lear parted from Goneril (I.iv). If this is so, Cordelia's letter cannot possibly have been written with any knowledge of the indignities offered the King, and Kent, therefore, cannot possibly now (III.i) suggest that the King of France has been moved by a report of Lear's distress.

But this is, perhaps, to take the ostensible time-scheme of the play too literally. As in other plays of Shakespeare, specifications of time in *King Lear* limit the action to an interval too short for its broader, unseen developments. One has to imagine these taking place on a second, undifferentiated, but more extensive, plane of time which obtains, as it were, in the background of events. Even so, with every allowance for a wider time-scheme, it is clear that no report is made to the French of Lear's sufferings: not, that is, until the very scene before us (III.i), in the course of which Kent asks the Gentleman to make a 'just report' to Cordelia of 'how unnatural and bemadding sorrow / The King hath cause to plain'. We learn subsequently (IV.iii) that he has written her a letter to which she has reacted with every appearance of discovering the truth for the first time.[3]

---

2   The grammatical structure of the transition back to Q (What [= whatever] . . . Either . . . Or . . . or . . . *But* . . .) is still faulty. But this may not be significant since the continuation of the speech, absent in F but doubtless present in the 'copy' for F, had no doubt been suitably modified in syntax.

3   The whole of IV.iii and the lines in III.i which look forward to it are in fact omitted from F. Thus in the text of F as it stands no

inconsistency appears. If this is significant, it can mean only that a deliberate attempt was made to alter the plot of the play. The evidence, however, is not clear. The omissions are otherwise certainly explicable, that in III.i being accidental in its immediate origin.

The plot, in any case, does not admit of being altered in the direction suggested by the additional lines. Not even the convention of double time will allow the French invasion to be prompted by news of the King's misfortunes: the two sets of events are clearly contemporaneous.

Greg, in an interesting article ('Time, Place and Politics in King Lear', *Collected Papers*, ed. J. C. Maxwell (Oxford, 1966), pp. 322–40), agrees: 'It is . . . difficult to escape the conclusion that at the time of Lear's quarrel with Goneril (*a fortiori* at that of his quarrel with Regan) the French army must have been in the act of landing, if not already landed, and this conclusion does not depend on any nice calculation from the time-data, but must be at once obvious to spectators' (p. 336). Curiously, he does not remark on the fact that the additional lines given in F to Kent in III.i contradict the conclusion, though he says that the speech is 'obscure, and probably incomplete as well as in part perhaps corrupt' (p. 335n). To assume, however, that Cordelia knows nothing of Lear's mistreatment before her arrival in England leads to difficulties later. At IV.iv.23–8 Cordelia says:

> Oh, dear father,
> It is thy business that I go about:
> Therefore great France
> My mourning and importunate
> tears hath pitied.
> No blown ambition doth our arms incite,
> But love, dear love, and our ag'd father's right.

This seems to imply clearly enough that Cordelia has persuaded France to the invasion for the sake of redressing Lear's grievances — although she has apparently only just learnt that he has any. To add to the puzzle, it appears that the King of France has no sooner arrived but he has returned to his own country to deal with an unexpected crisis, and that he has done so *before* Cordelia's receipt of Kent's letter informing her of her father's misfortune. There is a curious insistence on these details (IV.iii.1–7, 39).

Greg offers a rather involved solution to the problem which, in so far as I can understand it, I do not find altogether plausible. It seems to me, in any case, less profitable to enquire, as he does, into the possible motives of the characters concerned for their wayward sayings and doings, than to look for a possible *dramatic* motive for the anomalies.

It seems to me likely that the audience is intended at first to gain the impression, from the various references to impending civil strife, that the King of France is seizing an opportune moment to restore Cordelia to her rightful inheritance. Both Kent and Gloucester make the connection between the Dukes' quarrels and the invasion. The impression may be strengthened by the fact that Regan and Cornwall are convinced that Gloucester is an agent of the French, and that he has treacherously sent the King to Dover to help the French cause (III.vii). Though Gloucester is clearly not the spy they think him, Regan and Cornwall are putting the same interpretation on the motives of France: the invasion is the fruit of a 'confederacy', which goes to imply that it is a piece of political opportunism.

But that it is not, as the audience finally discovers in Act IV. There is no plot; and there cannot possibly be one. The French King has returned home before Lear arrives in Dover: there is only Cordelia to meet him, and no suspicion can attach to *her* motives. Then (in the lines quoted above, IV.iv.23–8) she reveals the full truth: her husband has merely yielded to her entreaties, and those have been prompted by love, not ambition. There can be only one implication: she has meant all along to rescue Lear from her sisters, whose true nature she had penetrated though he had not; she has not needed to wait for evidence of their cruelties. We are intended, it seems, to recall the threatening prophecy with which she takes

74   There seems little doubt that the plot will not at this point accommodate a suggestion of the kind we find in the additional lines, *viz.* that spies may have conveyed information to France about the mistreatment of the King; especially not when the suggestion is accompanied by a still more obvious mistake. Kent is made to say that *both* the Dukes have 'borne a hard rein' against the King. It is quite clear, however, that Albany has not done so, but on the contrary treated him with forbearance. Kent knows this very well, since he was witness to their last meeting (I.iv).

The phrase 'something deeper' (l. 28) may well fall under suspicion also. It suggests some sinister and mysterious circumstance, more shocking than the quarrels of the Dukes or the mistreatment of the King, which will later come to light. But it is never alluded to again, much less is the mystery revealed.

There is no mystery, however. The phrase appears to derive from a passage later in the play. At III.iii.8–14 Gloucester (who is also in secret communication with France) imparts to Edmund the very same news that in III.i Kent confides to the Gentleman:

> Q: . . . ther's a diuisiō betwixt the Dukes,
> And a worse matter than that, I haue receiued
> A letter this night, tis dangerous to be spoken,
> I haue lockt the letter in my closet, these iniuries
> The King now beares, will be reuenged home
> Ther's part of a power already landed . . .

Here we have again a 'worse matter' than the division between the Dukes; again it is something secret and ominous, 'dangerous to be spoken'. But the hint in l. 14 is enough for the audience, who are already fully aware of what Edmund is allowed only to guess at: the French have begun an invasion of Britain.

It looks, in other words, very much as though the mystery in Gloucester's speech has been transferred to Kent's on the same theme, and by someone not familiar enough with the exposition of the plot to notice that Gloucester's 'mystery' does not and cannot concern some further circumstance, hitherto unmentioned.[4]

---

leave of Goneril and Regan in the first scene of the play:

Time shall unfold what pleated cunning hides.
Who covers faults, at last shame them derides.
Well may you prosper!
(I.i.283–5)

4 One might further speculate that the mention of 'spies and speculations' (l. 24) was also suggested by a misunderstanding relating to Gloucester, *viz.* that he played the role of informer to the French. Gloucester is a 'servant' of Cornwall (see II.i.60–1), though,

We may notice further inconsistencies. Kent does not speak elsewhere in the   75
high-falutin' style here attributed to him:

> . . . Who haue, as who haue not, that their great Starres
> Thron'd and set high; Seruants, who seeme no lesse,
> Which are to France the Spies and Speculations
> Intelligent of our State.

This sounds more like Oswald's euphuistic vein, so scornfully parodied by Kent
himself in an earlier scene (II.ii). We may be surprised, too, that Kent, of all
personages in the play, should refer to Lear sentimentally as 'the old kind King'.
This appears to be another instance of inappropriate association with a detail
elsewhere in the text (*cf.* Lear's 'your old kind father', III.iv.20).

All things considered, it is hard to avoid the conclusion that whoever wrote
these lines was not as intimately familiar with the play as he ought to have been.
The passage, therefore, the only one of F's additions which might at first sight
appear necessary to the completeness of the text, may be more emphatically
categorised as spurious even than those we previously considered.

Other interpolations in F show similar inconsistencies and contradictions.[5]
At the same time nearly all, it may be argued, find their *raison d'être* in some real
or fancied deficiency in Q. (The principal exceptions are two pieces of doggerel
introduced for no apparent dramatic purpose at II.iv.46–55 and III.ii.79–96,
and four brief passages found at the very beginning of the play – I.i.41–6, 50–1,
65–6 and 86–7 – which seem rather to be free expansions of Q than to meet any

---

being an Earl, he might 'seem no
less (i.e. no inferior)'. There seems
no other reason why these details
should be emphasised. Gloucester,
of course, is not a spy, though
Regan and Cornwall arraign him as
such.

The phrase 'seem no less' is usually
glossed, I acknowledge, 'seem no
less (*sc.* than servants – though
they are spies)'. But this is scarcely
intelligible, unless we can
legitimately extend the implication

– 'seem no less (*sc.* than absolutely
loyal servants – though they are
spies)' –, which I very much
doubt. The context, in any case,
emphasises social, not moral,
superiority. The Dukes' 'great
stars' have 'thron'd' and 'set [them]
high' – so high, it is implied, that
their servants seem no inferior in
station.

5   See Appendix B2(b), pp. 238–48
below, nos. 7, 15, 18, 19.

76 particular need.⁶ These latter passages, however, may well be seen as the supererogatory product of the reviser's initial enthusiasm, before he realised how much arduous rewriting would be imposed upon him. As for the doggerel verses, appearing as they do in the guise of improvisations from the Fool, there are much weaker grounds, if any, for supposing that they may have formed part of the original fabric of the play.)

The more important additions in F are listed, with analysis and comment, in Appendix B2 (pp. 238–48 below), and the reader is referred there for further corroboration of the evidence already presented. One last example is worth discussing in some detail here. It is an interesting and problematical case.

In Q I.iv comes to a close with the following sequence of events: Lear leaves the stage and Goneril orders the Fool to follow him. The Fool does so with a final gibe at Goneril in five lines of doggerel. There immediately ensue these lines (without a stage direction to indicate Oswald's entrance):

> Q: *Gon.* What *Oswald*, ho. *Oswald.* Here Madam.
> *Gon.* What haue you writ this letter to my sister?
> *Osw.* Yes Madam.

Goneril orders Oswald to deliver the letter to Regan and, on his departure, turns to reprove Albany for his 'milky gentleness' towards Lear. Albany demurs mildly, and the scene concludes.

In F several lines intervene between the Fool's exit and Oswald's entrance. They are obviously essential neither to the sense nor to the development of the action at this juncture, yet equally obviously they do fulfil a function. They provide a much smoother transition to Oswald's entrance and the subject of the letter, both of which supervene abruptly in Q; and they offer further evidence of Albany's 'milky gentleness', which has so far been apparent only in his polite dismay before Lear's outbursts and in one brief exchange with Goneril:

> F: *Gon.* Do you marke that?
> *Alb.* I cannot be so partiall *Gonerill*,
> To the great loue I bear you.
> *Gon.* Pray you content . . .
>
> I.iv.333–6

6 The first of them does, it is true, emphasise the arrival on the scene of Albany and Cornwall, who receive no special introduction in Q. On the other hand, since they play a merely passive role in the ensuing scene, there seems no reason to call particular attention to their presence. (We have of course learnt their identities, and of their relationship to Goneril and Regan, at the very opening of the play.)

I give below the new lines in F, together with its revised version of Oswald's 77
entrance. Goneril's speech, it should be noted, begins with a reference to the
Fool's parting words.

> F: [*Gon.* This man hath had good Counsell,
> A hundred Knights?
> 'Tis politike, and safe to let him keepe
> At point a hundred Knights: yes, that on euerie dreame,
> Each buz, each fancie, each complaint, dislike,
> He may enguard his dotage with their powres,
> And hold our liues in mercy. *Oswald*, I say.
> *Alb.* Well, you may feare too farre.
> *Gon.* Safer than trust too farre;
> Let me still take away the harmes I feare,
> Not feare still to be taken. I know his heart,
> What he hath vtter'd I haue writ my Sister:
> If she sustaine him, and his hundred Knights
> When I haue shew'd th'vnfitnesse.]
>
> *Enter Steward*
>
> How now *Oswald*?
> What haue you writ that Letter to my Sister?
> *Stew.* I Madam.

> I.iv.345–58

It will be observed that Goneril now calls Oswald several lines before his
entrance, and that her summons to him in Q (*What* Oswald, *ho*) has, at the
equivalent point in F, become a response to his appearance (*How now* Oswald?).
But the summons in its original form has not disappeared: it has been removed
to a point still further back in the text. At this point it is extra-metrical, as will
immediately be seen in comparing the two versions of the passage:

> Q: *Duke.* I cannot bee so partiall *Gonorill* / to the great loue I
> beare you.
> *Gon.* Come sir no more, / you, more knaue then foole, after
> your master?

> F: *Alb.* I cannot be so partiall *Gonerill*
> To the great loue I beare you.
> *Gon.* Pray you content. What *Oswald*, hoa?
> You Sir, more Knaue then Foole, after your Master.

> I.iv.334–7

78   There can be no doubt that the half-line *What* Oswald, *hoa?* was interpolated here: perhaps, therefore, the rest of the preparation for Oswald's entrance should fall under suspicion. When we come, however, to examine the remainder of the added lines, we find no grounds for suspicion: rather the opposite. The style, we are bound to feel, not only may, but must, be confirmed as genuine: not many poets could bestow such variety and vitality on a relatively inconspicuous exchange of dialogue. But there is clear evidence as well of a more objective kind. In two respects the passage is quite unlike the other Folio additions and resembles instead the text of Q. First, it contains extra-metrical expletives (*yes* in l. 347, *Well* in l. 351). These, as we have seen, abound in Q. None appears elsewhere in the lines peculiar to F. Secondly the passage concludes with an interrupted sentence (l. 356: 'When I have show'd the unfitness . . . How now, Oswald?'). Interruptions, again, are strikingly frequent in Q (F showing a marked tendency to complete the broken sentences).[7]

The passage shows no other anomalies or inconsistencies. It may, perhaps, seem a little surprising that Goneril should apprehend physical danger from Lear's knights, yet the same idea later occurs to Regan (II.iv.308–10). Nor is it odd that Goneril speaks of having written to Regan immediately before asking Oswald whether *he* has written the letter: no doubt she commissioned him to do so. That she expects an attempt on Lear's part to carry his hundred knights with him to Regan may seem strange in view of Lear's claims later that she has dismissed fifty of them (II.iv.162: *She hath abated me of halfe my traine*). But we are apparently to understand that, even at this later stage, she has not yet fulfilled her threat, and that Lear is exaggerating his plight by taking the word for the deed (*cf.* II.iv.205–7 and 233–4).

The evidence, then, is somewhat ambiguous. At the beginning of the passage we find clear enough signs of interpolation (the transference of *What* Oswald, *hoa?*). The genuineness of the rest, however, cannot easily be questioned. At the same time, if it is genuine, it is very doubtful, to say the least, that it derived from an original, or from the copy of an original, manuscript. The expletives it contains are clearly actors' expletives, introduced for the sake of emphasis in speaking. Being obviously extra-metrical, they are not very likely to have been intended by the author. We seem, in other words, to be faced with an interpolation certainly, and not a retrieval of the authentic text, but an interpolation which, unlike the others we have examined, obviously bears a fairly close relation to the original.

7   See Appendix D3(a), pp. 274–5 below.

The problem does not, for reasons which will appear, admit of a wholly satisfactory solution, and the one I have to offer is necessarily less than complete. I present it in the hope merely of showing that it is, in principle at least, possible to account for the facts. Unfortunately it will be necessary, in order to give the explanation its proper place here, a little to anticipate the general argument. There is good reason to believe, as we shall find in the next chapter, that, if F cannot be said to recover the original text, it does at least often recover a more correct or complete version of the text *as transmitted in Q*. Precisely this, I assume, has happened in the present instance.

The copy for Q, I suggest, contained the additional lines substantially as we find them in F. The Q compositor must have omitted them by accident. There are difficulties, however, in the way of explaining how the accident may have occurred since the lines as they appear in F have been slightly revised. We have seen that Goneril's *What* Oswald, *hoa?* was transferred to a different context. We may notice, too, that Oswald's *Here Madam* has entirely disappeared. It is quite likely, therefore, that the evidence which would satisfactorily explain the Q compositor's 'eyeskip' has been eliminated or obscured.

It would not be impossible to supply it speculatively, if anything were to be gained by making the attempt. There is more point, perhaps, in noticing that the most suspicious lines in the addition are the first and last, those precisely which we should expect to provide the necessary clues. The first line, or rather two thirds of it (Gon. *This man hath had good Counsell*), appears to be an interpolation intended to replace 'What Oswald, ho! . . . Here, Madam'. *This man* must refer to the just-departed Fool, but if so, supplies a false antecedent to *him* in the next line, which can only refer to Lear. It is also very odd to find one of the Fool's snatches of doggerel receiving explicit comment − if it is not too controversial a suggestion that many of the Fool's interjections (rhymes, proverbs, witticisms interrupting dialogue which does not directly involve him) are extraneous to the text and were probably contributed by the actor who played the role. The last half-line of the addition (*How now*, Oswald?) also suggests interference, though much less clearly. It is immediately followed by the question *What haue you writ that Letter to my Sister?*. The anomaly here is not especially striking, and I do not wish to insist on its significance; nevertheless it is noticeable enough that after the exclamation *How now* we do not need another (*What*) to express exactly the same nuance of meaning: the questions would flow more naturally one from the other without it. Since *What* appears in Q, it is possible that *How now* Oswald? was added in F; alternatively, that a few words originally separated the two questions (a brief response from Oswald?).

80   The reader may find this explanation insufficiently circumstantial to be fully persuaded by it. He has yet, in any case, to be reassured that the 'version of Q', allegedly drawn upon for the addition in F, is more than a convenient fiction. But he will, perhaps, accept provisionally that the special difficulty this addition presents may be resolved without recourse to altogether impossible assumptions, given that the simplest assumptions (either that the additional lines in F are entirely authentic or that they are entirely spurious) do not meet the case.

By and large, as we have seen, the evidence indicates that the new material in F has been added. So clear, in fact, are the indications in a handful of cases, and so conspicuous everywhere the absence of counter-indications, that we cannot avoid a general assumption in favour of interpolation. One passage exceptionally offers contradictory evidence. But it is an exception which proves the rule. Even where, that is to say, we discover good grounds for supposing the recovery of genuine matter, we find as well (however we choose to explain the anomaly) clear signs that it does not stem from a wholly authentic source and that it has been subjected, in any case, to editorial tinkering.

It needs, perhaps, no very extended argument now to show that if the additional matter in F was introduced into the text, as it must have been, at some time after the publication of Q, then it is most unlikely that the author himself was responsible.[8] As we have seen, a good many misconceptions, misconstructions and careless mistakes attend the interpolated passages. I am unwilling to believe that Shakespeare could have been guilty of such errors, even if we suppose him to have retained, after the lapse of several years, a very indistinct notion of his original intentions. They strike me as much more probably the inevitable minor inaccuracies and miscalculations of someone paid to perform a piece of dramatic repair-work within a limited time. The evidence of style cannot be assessed altogether objectively: nevertheless it might be argued that (over and above the lines at II.iv.46–55 and III.ii.79–96 which have often in any case been condemned as spurious) the style of the additional

8   It was in fact suggested as long ago as 1910, and on the evidence precisely of the F additions, that Shakespeare himself revised the text. (R. H. Cunnington, 'The Revision of "King Lear"', *Modern Language Review*, V (1910), pp. 445–53). This article contains some shrewd analysis, and I am indebted to it for one or two details of my discussion; but its thesis is necessarily weak, founded as it is almost exclusively on the *prima facie* evidence of the additions themselves. The hypothesis of authorial revision has been recently revived (E. A. J. Honigmann, *The Stability of Shakespeare's Text* (London, 1965)), but in respect only of a limited category of verbal variants.

passages, though not poor certainly, and not even perhaps merely mediocre, is never (with the one exception we have noticed) particularly distinctive. It would not be beyond the competence of several of Shakespeare's contemporaries and immediate successors.

We must return in due course to the question of how, when and in what circumstances the text of F was prepared. There remains a problem that requires more immediate attention. It was suggested above that a more correct and complete version of the text as it appears in Q was available to the reviser, even though, as all the evidence so far goes to show, no authoritative manuscript lay at his disposal. It is easy to see that, if this were the case, we should be in a position to understand not only the recovery of genuine matter accidentally omitted from Q, but also the appearance in F of some remarkable emendations. These would prove extremely difficult to explain if we believed the reviser to be working without help of any kind. The hypothesis now, therefore, demands justification. What grounds can there be for distinguishing between 'a more correct version of Q' and some entirely independent authority? What evidence can be brought forward to show that the reviser, although no copy of the authentic text was available to him, must have received assistance from another quarter? And how may the source of assistance be identified?

CHAPTER FIVE
THE MANUSCRIPT SOURCE OF CORRECTIONS IN F

There can be no question whatever that, in addition to the printed Quarto, a manuscript of some kind was used in the preparation of the F text. The proof of this is simple.

The reader will recall that certain pages of the text of Q exist in two states of correction, and that we have designated these states Qa (uncorrected) and Qb (corrected). The corrections are confined, in the extant copies, to certain sheets of the book, and, in most cases, to one forme (inner or outer) of the sheet. We know, in fact, from a mass of evidence in contemporary printed books, that Elizabethan printing practice favoured the forme as the unit of press-correction. All four pages, that is to say, of a single quarto forme would be proof-read and corrected together before being returned to the press.[1]

One page of Q (in the inner forme of sheet C) shows *three* states of correction. This does not, however, imply a second revision of the whole forme, or even of this particular page. Since its third state shows the correction merely of a single very minor error, it is virtually certain that the slip was noticed and put right by a simple *ad hoc* operation during printing. For the rest, the twelve existing copies of Q show no inconsistencies. The pages of any given forme appear uniformly either corrected or uncorrected; in no case do we find some pages of a forme in one state and some in the other. We are bound to assume on the evidence that this was a feature of all the copies printed.

The copy of Q used in the preparation of F must have showed the same characteristics. It follows that, if a particular reading in F can be traced with certainty to the uncorrected version of the text, Qa, then we can be equally certain that the copy for the rest of that page, and for the three other pages in the same forme, must have stood in the same uncorrected state. We could not argue that a reading or readings elsewhere on those pages derived from *corrected* copy (Qb) without involving ourselves in contradiction.

Just such a contradiction, however, is entailed by supposing that the F reviser corrected a copy of Q without help from another source. This is illustrated very concisely by a comparison of two sets of variants which belong (in Q) to the outer forme of sheet E:

---

1 See Gaskell, *New Introduction*,
   p. III.

	Qa	Qb	F
II.ii.133	ausrent	miscreant	ancient
II.iv.133	fruit	tombe	Tombe

Let us assume the first of F's readings to have been derived from Qa, as must certainly have been the case in the absence of a manuscript. (It would be too much to suppose that the reviser, reading *miscreant* in Qb, converted it to *ancient*, and so happened by chance to strike upon a neat emendation of *ausrent* in Qa.) That being so, how are we to account for the second reading? It is scarcely more likely that the reviser, working, as we must now suppose, on Qa, replaced Qa's *fruit* by *Tombe*, thus chancing to fall in with the widely dissimilar reading in Qb. (Even though the context of this reading limits somewhat the available choice of emendations, such a coincidence would be remarkable.)

Similar incompatibilities are to be found elsewhere. Four of the more heavily-corrected formes in Q (besides the one already cited) produce examples:

		Qa	Qb	F
I.iv.366	[D°]	alapt	attaskt for	at task for
II.i.122		prise	poyse	prize
III.iv.10	[G°]	raging	roring	roaring
III.iv.114		come on	come on	Come, vnbutton
		bee true		heere
IV.ii.12	[Hⁱ]	curre	terrer	terror
IV.ii.29		whistle	whistling	whistle
IV.vi.230	[K°]	to saue thee	to boot, to boot	To boot, and boot
IV.vi.247		battero	bat	Ballow

It will be seen that, of each pair of F readings, one stems from Qa and one from Qb. In no case is it at all likely, and in most it is impossible, that both of the F readings can have been derived from the same state of Q, whether Qa or Qb. We are obliged, therefore, to believe that more than one version of the text was available to the reviser, a possibility that is naturally excluded if he were working from a single printed copy.

84   But did he perhaps obtain more than one copy and collate them? He might have done so, but it is in the highest degree improbable that he did. Besides the *a priori* unlikelihood of anyone with immediate practical aims undertaking so laborious and unrewarding a task (very few variants would be found in proportion to the total number of words in the text), he would have to be exceptionally fortunate to chance upon two copies of the text which exactly complemented each other, so that the uncorrected state of a forme in one corresponded with the corrected state in the other, and *vice versa*. It must be remembered that, since no attempt was made to distinguish between the corrected and the uncorrected in binding sheets up into copies, most specimens of the book would contain a random assortment.

To suppose, alternatively, that the reviser would compare *more* than two copies of the book takes us quite beyond the realms of likelihood. We are left, then, virtually certain that he must have had recourse to a manuscript.

Are we bound, however, to suppose that he consulted an independent and authoritative manuscript? And do we now, therefore, risk falling into an inconsistency? It will perhaps be worth pausing a moment to survey the position. The longer additions in F do not appear, with one probable exception, to have been derived from an authoritative source. That exception, furthermore, does not appear accurately to reproduce the original text of the play. These considerations throw serious doubt on the presumption of an independent manuscript, nevertheless are not perhaps altogether inconsistent with the incorporation of incidental *corrections* into F from an independent source. The Q text may have been corrected first from this source, and afterwards revised without reference to it. We saw earlier, however, that F is so frequently guilty of errors taken over from Q or prompted by Q's obscurities that the independent manuscript, if it existed, must have been often and wilfully neglected. The hypothesis of a careless and arbitrary collator is an inconvenient one. It makes every choice between variants a matter of perplexity. But as long as it remains not wholly incompatible with the evidence we should not, perhaps, altogether abandon it, since it does provide the simplest solution available to the problem we are now concerned with, namely the appearance in F of readings which must have derived from a source more informative than Q.

One sort of evidence would effectively exclude it. If we could be sure that on certain occasions the collator *had* consulted his manuscript copy, but had nonetheless failed to discover the true reading there, we could as surely deduce that, whatever its nature or provenance, the manuscript itself was not always reliable, and that there remained, therefore, little reason to suspect the collator of neglecting it elsewhere.

Evidence of just such a kind appears in the relationship between certain of the press-correction variants in Q and the readings corresponding to them in F. The variants in question appear on sheets E and H.

In the copy of Q1 used by the collator sheet H (inner forme) appeared in its uncorrected state. We can be confident of this since two Qa errors (one certain — *seemes* for *shewes* at IV.ii.60 – and one virtually so – *Iustices* for *Iustisers* at IV.ii.79) survive in F. If the collator were working from Qa copy we can quite plausibly assume that he overlooked these mistakes; if he had Qb copy before him, no plausible inference is possible: we should have to suppose that he was dissatisfied with the correct readings and rejected them in favour of his own misreadings of the manuscript copy, and furthermore that his misreadings coincided fortuitously with the Q compositor's, i.e. with the readings of Qa.

On sheet H at III.vii.60 the reading *layd* appears in Qa. The press-corrector probably intended to have this emended to *boyd* (for 'buoy'd'), but the corrected reading appears in Qb as *bod*. F reads *buoy'd*. Given that the collator was at this point using Qa copy, we must conclude that he consulted his manuscript for the emendation. Though *buoy'd* is accepted in all modern editions it makes no sense, either literally or figuratively, in the context. The true reading is obviously *boil'd*, as Warburton long ago suggested. The reader may judge for himself in considering the passage in its entirety, as I give it below. It should be remembered that at this period the phrase 'to buoy up', used intransitively, was capable of one interpretation only: 'to rise to, or float on, the surface of a liquid'; hence, to speak of the sea 'buoying up' would violate not only idiom but logic. Although the *OED* admits another significance, 'to rise, swell (as the sea)', it is expressly in order to accommodate the anomalous reading before us. I quote the passage from the Globe edition:

The sea, with such a storm as his bare head
In hell-black night endured, would have buoy'd up,
And quench'd the stelled fires . . .

III.vii.59–61

If *boil'd* is correct, as it surely must be, it appears that the copy for Q contained a naive mishearing or a slip of the pen: *boyd* instead of *boyld*. The Q compositor read the word first as *layd*, then miscorrected it to *bod*. The F collator, on consulting *his* manuscript, gleaned only as much as enabled him to change *layd* to *buoy'd*: clearly his source of information can have improved little if at all on the copy for Q.

86   On the evidence so far before us it is not possible to determine with certainty the state of the collator's copy in respect of sheet E (outer forme).[2] But there is no need to do so in order to find here further evidence of the inadequacy of the manuscript he consulted. Supposing him to have worked from uncorrected copy he must have found at least one 'correction' in the manuscript (*Turlygod* for *Tuelygod*, II.iii.20) which makes no sense at all. If, on the other hand, as seems much more likely, he was following Qb copy, he derived from the manuscript at least one reading (*dawning* for *euen*, II.ii.1) which is certainly wrong.[3]

It is again an obvious inference from both the sets of readings I cite below that the collator, whatever the state of his copy, must have consulted the manuscript to obtain his version of the text. Since the variants in question follow one upon the other within the space of three lines we shall consider them together.

	Qa	Qb	F
II.iv.103	come and tends seruise	commands her seruice	commands, tends, seruice
II.iv.105	The fierie Duke	Fierie Duke	Fiery? The fiery Duke

It does not, perhaps, need emphasising that in both cases F agrees partly with Qa and partly with Qb and that whichever of the two readings stood in the collator's copy his approximation to the other implies that he consulted a manuscript to achieve it. Yet once again the results are most unsatisfactory. The reading *commands, tends, seruice* does not often recommend itself to editors: it is improbably clumsy as to rhythm and rhetorically extremely weak:

> F: The deere Father
> Would with his Daughter speake, commands, tends,
> seruice,

Many editors resort to the smoother reading of Qb, even though, on the evidence of Qa and F, it is obviously a sophistication.

---

2   The evidence offered, albeit tentatively, by Greg is invalid. See introductory note to Appendix C1, p. 249 below.

3   Qa has *deuen*, showing that the word in the Q copy began with 'd'. The collator was certainly, therefore, influenced by manuscript copy, where he probably read *dawn*. That Q is right and F wrong about the time of day at this juncture is argued in Appendix A3, p. 194 below.

The second F reading cited above should carry as little conviction, though it appears in all modern editions. Its spuriousness becomes apparent when we compare the line in which it appears with its counterpart in Q:

F: Fiery? The fiery Duke, tell the hot Duke that —

Qa: The fierie Duke, tell the hot Duke that *Lear,*

Since both lines are acceptable metrically, we have to ask: Is it likely that the F version is the original and that an actor corrupted it, forgetting a word at the beginning of the line and conscientiously restoring the metre by tacking on another word at the end? Or is it more probable that Q represents the authentic text and that the F editor 'improved' it with rhetorical padding, adjusting the metre to suit? (Note the preceding line in F which does not appear in Q: *Are they inform'd of this? My breath and blood,* and the change several lines earlier at line 197 from *what fierie quality* to *Fiery? What quality?.*) It is hard to resist the conclusion that F's version of the line is the less authentic, especially when one considers that the repetition *Fiery? The fiery* combines the readings of Qa and Qb. If F is correct, we must assume an unusual concurrence of accidents in the setting of Q: the compositor must first have omitted one half of the reading (*Fierie*), then (at the direction of the press-corrector, or perhaps misunderstanding his direction) omitted the other (*the fierie*). Both mishaps will have resulted fortuitously in a perfect pentameter, though the line as it stood in the copy must have been too long by a foot:

Fierie the fierie Duke, tell the hot Duke that *Lear,*

It seems much more likely that the rhetorical repetition was suggested to the F collator (who must certainly, therefore, be viewed as performing the function of editor or reviser as well) by the discovery of one reading in his printed copy and the other in the manuscript.

I do not wish, for obvious reasons, to lay very much stress on conjectural emendations in the course of this argument. This does, however, seem an appropriate point at which to hazard one. The passage is so puzzling that, unless I am able to suggest where the errors in it lie, the reader may feel disinclined to lend much weight to the evidence it provides.

I believe that Qa preserves the most accurate text of the passage, and that the main source of the trouble is traceable to the misplacement of the phrase *tends seruise* which correctly belongs at the end of the line *below* the one in which it appears in Q. The disturbance possibly originated in the manuscript copy where

88 the phrase may well have been squeezed in at the outer margin, somewhat above its proper position, so that it appeared as a continuation of the previous line. I give the text of Qa, showing the necessary line-arrangement, incorporating the transposition I have suggested, and indicating three further emendations that are called for, two of them taken, the other adapted, from Qb:

> Qa: *Glost.* I my good Lord.
> *Lear.* The King would speake with *Cornewal*, / the deare fate
> [Qb: *father*]
> Would with the [Qb: *his*] daughter speake, / come and [i.e. *command*]
> The fierie Duke, tell the hot Duke / that *Lear* tends
> seruise . . .
>
> II.iv.101–3; 105

'Command' here takes the sense (as often) 'order to come', and 'tends' means 'awaits', while 'service' has its feudal significance of 'homage', or perhaps less strongly in view of the context, 'the paying of respects'.

The phrase *that Lear tends seruise*, since the immediately following line is complete, now occupies a short line by itself. One might argue that the break in the metre reflects an interruption in the thought: the next line starts a new train of ideas (*No but not yet may be he is not well*). But in fact the text is full of such truncated lines of two or three feet and it would place a considerable strain on critical ingenuity to have to justify each one. They might have resulted without exception, for all we know, from deliberate cuts or accidental omissions.

If this interpretation of the difficulty is correct, the alterations in Qb stand revealed as sophistications. F, we must assume, takes the process of corruption still further, with its amalgamation of the a and b versions of Q and its interposition of an extra line (l. 104), though it represents a much more intelligent attempt than the press-corrector's to make sense of the passage as a whole.

I am, however, less anxious that the reader should accept this solution to the difficulty than that he should be aware of the difficulty itself. The Q text of these lines is corrupt, and F fails to remedy the corruption. The collator's failure, moreover, occurs at a point where he has demonstrably exercised due care in consulting his manuscript. We have noticed other instances of the same incapacity. In this case, as in the others, we cannot fail to be impressed above all by his apparent inability to break free of the errors of Q: he repeats or sophisticates them without being able to correct them. How can this be accounted for?

There is in fact only one conceivable explanation: the manuscript consulted by the editor of F was not an *independent* manuscript, but one related to the manuscript copy used for Q. In fact, not to multiply hypotheses unnecessarily, we may just as reasonably suppose that it was the *same* manuscript as that used in the setting up of Q.

The supposition does not, it is true, recommend itself as immediately plausible. The interval of fifteen years separating the two editions makes it particularly difficult to accept. Nevertheless, if we can defer for the moment the question of how so intrinsically unlikely a possibility may, in fact, have materialised, let us consider how, put as a hypothesis, it explains the evidence.

It explains it perfectly. It accounts, of course, for the facts we have just been considering, the facts which led us to formulate it in the first place. It is easy to see that if the collator consulted the same manuscript as did the compositor and corrector of Q, he would be unlikely to get much beyond their mistakes wherever confusion or corruption in the manuscript itself was responsible for them. The same explanation, of course, will cover all those occasions on which F repeats or sophisticates the errors in Q, whether or not we have direct evidence that the manuscript was consulted in the process.

At the same time, the corrections in F are accounted for. The vast majority of the certain corrections are emendations of Q misreadings, to explain which we need not suppose any recourse to an independent manuscript. The same goes for the repairing of small omissions. As for the larger omission at I.iv.345–56 (the major addition in F which, as we saw in the last chapter, shows no sign of extraneous origin), the traces in it of actors' 'gag' disturbing the regularity of the metre make it far more likely that it was retrieved from the copy for Q than from any more authoritative source.

Only a very small number of corrections in F need be ascribed to the collator's unaided ingenuity. Phonetic mistakes in Q must have appeared as such in the copy, yet we do find a few of them emended. Of these, however, only two represent anything of a feat: *miracles* for *my rackles* at II.ii.172 and *a Dogg's obey'd* for *a dogge, so bade* at IV.vi.163. To these we should, perhaps, add *shoo . . . Felt* for *shoot . . . fell* at IV.vi.188–9, which shows the collator correcting what appears to be an actor's spoonerism.

The survival in F of other forms of error is also easily explained. Indeed it would be difficult to explain it on any other hypothesis. Faulty line-arrangement in Q was miscorrected, or escaped detection altogether, because the manuscript offered no help at all in this respect. We have seen (Chapter Two) that the copy for Q was very irregularly lineated. Q's mistakes in the ascription of speeches may easily, for the same reason, have been transferred to F:

90   the manuscript contained the same mistakes.

We may, on this hypothesis, require very often to question the collator's judgement or acumen, but there is no need, in fact, to suspect him of a far more ruinous failing: that of negligence. If we suppose that he was checking his printed copy against the manuscript from which the Quarto was itself produced, then there is very little evidence to convict him of careless oversights.

The wider question respecting the collator-reviser's work[4] – the question whether he effected interpolations, omissions and substitutions on his own authority – is, in a sense, independent of the question we are now considering. We discovered, in the last chapter, good reason to conclude that the reviser's more extensive additions do not proceed from an authentic source. Yet he may in theory have carried out these and other unauthorised alterations whether he disposed of an independent manuscript or merely the manuscript available to the printers of Q.

One may quite reasonably, however, postulate a connection between the nature of the reviser's proceedings and the kind of materials at his disposal. Supposing him to have had access to an authoritative manuscript, it is *a priori* highly unlikely that he would have been permitted any large measure of editorial freedom in making use of it. It is indeed unlikely, seeing that the necessary task would then amount merely to a mechanical collation of print with manuscript that anyone capable of editorial freedoms would have been sought after to undertake the work. It is otherwise if we assume that no other sources of copy were available but two: the printed edition of Q, obviously corrupt, its dubious origin known, and the manuscript associated with it, which cannot have inspired any greater confidence. One may well imagine that in such circumstances an editor of some competence would be in demand, who would, in carrying out his task, be allowed the greatest liberties consistent with preserving the spirit and substance of the original.

---

4   We cannot but assume that collator and reviser were united in one person. It would be strange if more than one were commissioned to prepare the copy for F, and, if it were so, it would be impossible to distinguish between their respective spheres of activity. Collation must often have prompted small alterations (sophistications, substitutions), which in turn may have led to changes in the surrounding context. Between the smallest changes and the most radical every degree of innovation is represented: we could not easily mark off the minor revisions from the major. This is not to exclude the possibility that the work of collation may have preceded that of revision, or that some of the more obviously redundant interpolations in F may have been contributed by different people at different times.

Thus the hypothesis of revision, which resolves some of the major difficulties in interpreting the relationship between F and Q, is assisted rather than otherwise by the further hypothesis that the reviser was able to call in aid no separate authority but only the manuscript which had already seen service in the composition of Q; besides resolving most of the remaining difficulties presented by the evidence, the second hypothesis supports the first, since it uncovers an intelligible motive for the revision we assume to have taken place.

Though there still remain to be examined in what follows numerous minor problems connected with the origin of the Folio text and its relationship to Q, the major problem concerning that relationship seems to me best resolved by the theory advanced above. Clear proof is not forthcoming, as it rarely is in textual investigations. But the circumstantial evidence, of which there is an abundance, seems consistent with only one conclusion. F is a freely edited text, based on 'copy' provided by an exemplar of Q. This copy was corrected by collation with a manuscript, the same manuscript which underlay the original edition.

We shall have to return later to consider in more detail the procedure adopted by the reviser and the conditions and circumstances which dictated it. We must turn for the moment to questions which arise immediately out of the argument so far, and which might well be raised as common-sense objections to it. Why of all things was the Quarto manuscript in requisition? And how could it possibly have been obtained?

It may seem, at first sight, intrinsically unlikely that the manuscript copy for Q would have been preserved by printer or publisher and, if it were preserved, that it could have survived for long enough: fifteen years separate the publication of Q from the appearance of F. The question cannot, of course, be conclusively decided. No evidence of any kind exists, apart from the texts themselves, to help us settle it. Remembering, however, that the evidence of the texts strongly suggests the continued existence of the manuscript, it could be argued at least that no obvious improbability is entailed in supposing its survival.

A certain amount of printer's copy of the period is still extant: not much, certainly, but enough to indicate that manuscripts were not destroyed as a matter of course after they had served their purpose.[5] Indeed, it would be surprising to learn that immediate destruction was the rule, since we must assume that the printer's copy bore on it, or carried affixed to it, the publisher's

---

5 See R. B. McKerrow, *An Introduction to Bibliography* (Oxford, 1927), pp. 217–18. Gaskell (*New Introduction*, p. 41) says that 'many examples' survive, but he has in mind the whole period of hand-press printing.

92   licence from the State authorities to print the work in question, or his 'allowance' from the Wardens of the Stationers' Company to proceed with its publication, or both.[6] (Both were obtained in the case of the *Lear* quarto.) Neither licence nor 'allowance' constituted in itself a title to possession of the copy,[7] but both provided (in theory at least) a guarantee – the one of legality, the other of the regular conduct of business – and they must to some extent have been regarded as safeguards in case of dispute or prosecution. We should expect, therefore, if only because it would be advantageous to preserve the accompanying evidence of official sanction, that the manuscript copy of any substantial publication would be returned by printer to publisher and preserved by him, at least as long as the book retained its commercial value.[8] It is, perhaps, a matter of doubt whether *King Lear* retained its commercial value for long, at least in the estimation of its publisher, Nathaniel Butter. He issued no reprint of it. The second edition of 1619 (Q2) was, as we have seen, a piratical production.

6   See Kirschbaum, *Stationers*, p. 37; Greg, *Folio*, p. 71, note F.

7   Copyright – in the strictly limited sense of a recognition by the Stationers' Company of a right to property legitimately claimed by one of its members – appears to have been established as a rule by entrance in the Stationers' Register.

8   McKerrow notes (*op. cit.*, p. 186n): 'It has been held, I know not on what grounds, that the MS. of a book when once printed from was destroyed. This seems unlikely, as it would in most cases bear the signature of the licenser, and it would therefore be important to preserve it for a time in case any question should arise as to the book having been duly passed by the authorities. The only piece of evidence bearing on the matter which is known to me is Jaggard's epistle in Vincent's *Discovery of Errors* . . . where the printer states that the original manuscript of the work [printed by Jaggard] against which Vincent was writing was extant, and it could therefore be proved that the errors in the printed book were not due to the printer's carelessness.' I have discovered another piece of evidence in the records of the Court of the Stationers' Company (ed. W. A. Jackson (London, 1957)). The entry of 5 March 1631 (pp. 236–8) relates, amid a welter of incidental circumstances, that a consortium of three printers were engaged in reprinting an abridgement of the *Book of Martyrs*, to which abridgement they may possibly have acquired a right granted under Royal patent some sixteen or more years previously, when it was reported that they were including in their reprint copious 'additions' from the complete text, to which they had no right whatever. The Clerk of the Court records (I modernise the spelling): 'the Master of this Company being informed of the abusive printing of the said Book with large additions by the forenamed Young, Flesher and Haviland about a month ago went in person to the printing house of the said Flesher. And there finding the said new Abridgement in the Press, called for the Copy, some part whereof being delivered unto him, he found that it was almost all a new written Copy and such as

Nevertheless we need not assume that Butter was at pains to guard his copy without object for as long as fifteen years. We shall later find very good reason for believing that the Folio text was prepared not for the publishers but for use in the theatre, and at a somewhat earlier date than we should suppose if it had originated as printer's copy. This being so, the Q manuscript would have been obtained by the players at a date a little earlier still — within ten years, we may not unreasonably assume, of the original publication.

It is rare at this period to find an interval of fifteen years or longer between the first and second editions of a play, if we leave out of account collected editions and special cases.[9] Obviously the more popular plays, those with the longest commercial life, would be precisely the ones most likely to be reprinted very soon after their first appearance. Nevertheless, several instances are recorded of an interval of ten years, more or less, between a first and second issue.[10] It is apparent that certain plays, less immediately popular, still held the public interest, or were capable of reviving it, after a space of ten years or so. It seems therefore *prima facie* unlikely that publishers would relinquish their assets in dramatic copy, or lose interest in them, before the lapse of a comparable length of time.

Given that we are now considering the plausibility of certain assumptions rather than seeking to establish their truth, there seems no reason to dismiss the possibility that Butter may have kept the manuscript 'copy' of *Lear* for such a period of time. And there is, equally, nothing to prevent us supposing that the King's Men obtained it from him temporarily, for a consideration. We might, indeed, assume that the transaction involved a permanent transfer of the copy, *de facto* if not *de jure*. Butter's copyright was, in fact, officially transferred (i.e. by

had never formerly been printed with the said Abridgement.' The implication is clear (though just possibly it may not have been intended) that the part of the copy not 'new written' was the manuscript of the original abridgement, preserved from the date of its first printing in 1615. But more direct evidence has come to light since McKerrow wrote. No fewer than five manuscripts are now known which not only show signs of use as printer's copy but bear the signatures of official licensers: Hooker's *The Laws of Ecclesiastical Polity* (Bk.V), Taylor's *The Causes of the Diseases of the Kingdom*, Harington's *An Apologie*,

Herbert's *The Temple,* and (of somewhat later date) Milton's *Paradise Lost* (Bk. I). See Kirschbaum, *Stationers*, pp. 37 and 391–2.

9 Chapman's *Byron* provides an example: it does not appear to have been reprinted between 1608 and 1625.

10 Three examples might be cited from among plays associated with the King's Men, *viz. Mucedorus* (Q1: 1598; Q2: 1606); *Thomas Lord Cromwell* (Q1: 1602; Q2: 1613); *The Faithful Shepherdess* (Q1: n.d., but c.1610 according to *STC*; Q2: 1629).

94 entrance in the Stationers' Register) to another publisher upon his retirement from business in 1639. Flesher, however, the new owner, who seems to have acquired the rest of Butter's stock at the same time, took no steps to reissue the play. It was not republished in quarto form until 1655, when Jane Bell, who it appears had no claim to *Lear* at all, but had probably acquired the copyright of the earlier *True Chronicle History of King Leir,* issued a reprint of Q2.[11] Since Q2 (Pavier's 1619 reprint) was itself produced under irregular auspices, we are left with the publication of the Folio in 1623 and its reprint in 1632 as the only occasions before the Restoration on which the play was reissued in the way of lawful business. It is true that Butter's copyright was never made over to the publishers of the Folio, who entered in the Stationers' Register only those plays in the collection that were 'not formerly entred to other men'. And it may well be, as is usually suggested, that Butter received a fee for consenting to the use of his property. But it is just possible, if the players had acquired and retained his 'copy', that his consent was never sought. The players could not, of course, purchase a copyright: since copyright was conferred by the Stationers' Company exclusively on its own members, they were not empowered to do so. But they could presumably, by buying the 'copy' of a play and thus gaining possession of the licences which authorised the printing of it, reduce the copyright of its publisher to a dead letter. They might then make future dispositions as they saw fit, supplying another publisher with the necessary authority for reissuing the play, or reselling the copy to him.[12]

11 An advertisement appearing in the two quartos published by Jane Bell in 1655 indicates that she had acquired the copies of a publisher, Oulton, to whom the rights in *Leir* had been transferred in 1640. If Flesher ever disposed of his interest in *Lear*, no record of the transaction exists.

12 There would be nothing at all unusual, or (apparently) irregular, in the publication of a book by someone other than the stationer who, by virtue of an entry in the Register, ostensibly held the copyright. There are very many known instances of the proceeding. A simple reassignment of copy by bill of sale did not, it appears, require the sanction of entrance in the Stationers' Book, so that what appears to be piracy is, more often than not, the result of a perfectly valid, though unrecorded, transfer of rights (see Kirschbaum, *Stationers*, pp. 74 and 334–6). The players in securing control of a copyright thus 'off the record' would be, to all intents and purposes, converting the publisher's original entrance in the Register into a 'blocking entry' – preventing other publishers from making use of the copy without limiting their own right to dispose of it later as they pleased. They could, of course, neither in these nor in any other circumstances appeal to the Stationers' Company for protection against piracy, but they would have other means of dealing with attempts upon their property: the records show that the Lord Chamberlain was not unwilling to intervene on their

Such speculations are tempting since they reduce by one at least the number   95
of copyrights supposedly waived by arrangement in favour of the publishers of
the Folio, who cannot have sought, or felt entirely satisfied with, the mere
permission to reprint.[13]

behalf. He did so, for example, in 1619, apparently on the occasion of Pavier's reprints (see Greg, *Folio*, p. 15 and p. 24, note D). (For discussions, too complicated to be summarised here, of the 'blocking entries' known to have been put to use – not always successfully – on behalf of the King's Men, see Kirschbaum, *Stationers*, pp. 185ff., and Greg, *Publishing*, pp. 112ff.)

13 If we accept what is usually maintained, that the copyrights in three of the previously published plays were 'derelict', there remain eleven plays the rights in which were owned by seven publishers outside the Folio syndicate, *viz.* Law (*Richard II, Richard III, 1 Henry IV*), Pavier (*2 Henry VI, 3 Henry VI, Henry V*), Johnson (*The Merry Wives of Windsor*), Walkley (*Othello*), Hayes (*The Merchant of Venice*), Walley (*Troilus and Cressida*) and Butter (*Lear*). It is remarkable that none of these plays was reprinted again in quarto until six years after the publication of the Folio, and that no subsequent reprint, with one or two questionable exceptions, was issued by any of the publishers mentioned. Neither Pavier's nor Walley's copies were ever republished, nor, as we have seen, was Butter's *Lear*, although it was pirated in 1655. In 1628 Walkley transferred *Othello* to Hawkins, and in 1630 Johnson *The Merry Wives of Windsor* to Meighen. These plays were reprinted in 1630 by their new owners, both reprints drawing on the *Folio* text, to which neither publisher was strictly entitled. By this date, however, the Folio was presumably out of print, since in

the following year, 1631, Smethwick himself, a member of the syndicate, republished two of his copies (*The Taming of the Shrew* and *Love's Labour's Lost*) in Folio texts. In 1632 the Second Folio appeared, and we find Meighen and Hawkins as members of the new syndicate. By the end of 1629 (when his will was proved) Matthew Law had died, leaving a part of his estate to a daughter 'Alice Norton'. In that year John Norton (her husband?) issued a reprint of *Richard III* 'printed by John Norton and are to be sold by Mathew Law, dwelling in Pauls Churchyeard, etc.' – which may or may not indicate an initiative of Law's, since it was in fact Norton who in subsequent years republished at intervals all three of Law's Shakespearean copies. Only Hayes, of all the copyright owners at the time of the original collection, himself reprinted his copy – or so it seems on the face of it, although the circumstances might be regarded as somewhat suspicious. Hayes's name last appears in the Stationers' Register in 1630 and in the records of the Court of Assistants in 1632. Though he had never been, it is true, a very active member of the Company, the absence of any later references to him is fairly good *prima facie* evidence that about this time he must have died, retired or sold his business. It is surprising, therefore, that Q3 of *The Merchant of Venice* bears the date 1637 – a full five years after his last recorded appearance in publishing history. Whatever may be the precise significance of the pattern of events outlined above, it seems to show that the publishers of the

96   However, it is not necessary to go so far in order to explain how the players may have acquired the manuscript copy of *Lear* belonging to Butter. The transaction might well have been of the simplest: a fee in exchange for a loan.

Why they should have acquired it is a more important question which must now claim our attention. There can only, of course, be one explanation of their being under any such necessity, one which is borne out, as we have seen, by the evidence of the printed texts. No authoritative manuscript existed: the prompt-book must have been lost. The printed Quarto, by itself, would have presented a daunting editorial challenge to the most accomplished mender of plays. To obtain, therefore, the 'copy' from which it had been produced must have seemed, if a desperate recourse, at least better than none.

There can be little purpose, perhaps, in pursuing this largely speculative enquiry further into the circumstances of the case. The prompt-book may have been lost in a hundred different ways, and one might find a hundred equally plausible reasons why no authorial manuscript survived from which to copy a new one. But the date of the loss, which we can fix approximately, is interesting. The revision of the play cannot have occurred very long before Shakespeare's death, and in any case not before his retirement from the theatre in 1613 or thereabouts, or we should certainly expect to find evidence that he had carried out the task himself. The evidence, however, as we have seen, points to the intervention of another hand. It seems fair to assume, therefore, that the prompt-book disappeared not much earlier than 1613 and (since there is internal evidence, which we shall examine later, to suggest a date for one or two of the additional passages) perhaps not later than five or six years from that date.

Much scorn has been heaped upon Sir Sidney Lee for asserting that the King's Men lost many of their manuscripts, among them some of Shakespeare's plays, in the Globe fire.[14] Yet the fire, which took place in 1613, would fit very satisfactorily into the sequence of events which, as we have inferred, led to the preparation of the F text of *Lear*. It took place very late in Shakespeare's career, at

First Folio made some attempt to control the copyrights not in their immediate possession, not merely to seek *ad hoc* their owners' permission to reprint; or else (if it is significant that the Stationers' Register records no transactions supplementary to the entrance of the unpublished plays) that the players themselves were active to this end.

14 Sir Sidney Lee, *A Life of William Shakespeare* (London, 1915), p. 560.

precisely the time when, as scholars now agree, he had ceased to produce new
plays and had retired to Stratford, or was about soon to do so. Had important
manuscripts of his work been irretrievably lost or destroyed at this time he
would not, one imagines, feel prepared promptly and willingly to make good
the damage. We need not place implicit faith in any such hypothesis: no direct
evidence is forthcoming to support it. Yet the circumstantial evidence has, I
feel, been too glibly dismissed and Sir Sidney Lee taken too cavalierly to task for
an assertion which is far from arbitrary, though doubtless he might have spoken
with more reserve and taken more care to substantiate his statements. The facts,
in any case, are interesting enough to bear a further review.

We might assume, even without supporting evidence, that the stock-in-
trade of an Elizabethan theatrical company (costumes, properties, playbooks
and so forth) would be held in safe-keeping at their headquarters, the theatre
itself. There is, however, very clear corroborative evidence. On Shrove Tuesday
1617 riotous apprentices invaded the Cockpit theatre, under lease at the time to
the Queen Anne's Men. Having entered the house, we learn from John Chamberlain, they 'defaced yt, cutting the players apparell all in pieces, and all other
theyre furniture, and burnt theyre play books, and did what other mischeife
they could'.[15] A few years later, in 1621, the Fortune playhouse, the headquarters of the Palsgrave's Company, was destroyed by fire. 'It was quite burnt
downe in two howres', writes the same John Chamberlain, '& all their apparell
and play-bookes lost, whereby those poore companions are quite undone'.[16]

It is not far-fetched, therefore, to suppose that prompt-books were in store at
the Globe playhouse when it, too, was consumed by fire in 1613. Numerous
contemporary accounts of the fire testify that it very rapidly destroyed the
building – 'in a very short space', 'in less than two hours', 'within less than an
hour' – and that the destruction was complete – 'the whole building was quite
consumed', 'to the very grounds', 'nothing but the piles / Left'.[17] A set of verses
describing the incident emphasises that the fire attacked the tiring-house

15 *The Letters of John Chamberlain*, ed.
N. E. McClure (Philadelphia,
1939); letter of 8 March 1616/17.
See G. E. Bentley, *The Jacobean
and Caroline Stage* (Oxford,
1941–68), I. 161–2, for an
account of the incident.

16 Letter of 9 December 1621. *Cf.*
Bentley, *op. cit.*, I. 141;
Chambers, *Stage*, II. 442.

17 The accounts are cited complete in
Chambers, *Stage*, II. 419–23.

98   (where, we must presume, the players' property, including their manuscripts, would have been lodged) directly after it commenced:

> This fearfull fire beganne aboue,
> A wonder strange and true,
> And to the stage-howse did remoue,
> As round as taylors clewe;
> And burnt downe both beame and snagg,
> And did not spare the silken flagg.
> Oh sorrow, &c.[18]

It must be evident from these details that the players would have some ado to save themselves together with such of their belongings as lay immediately to hand, without having much leisure to bestow on the removal of manuscripts from their archives. It is, in any case, arguable that, had they any time to spare, they would have devoted it instead to saving their costumes. 'Apparel' represented to them a far more valuable capital asset than prompt-books since it was constantly in service and expensive to replace, whereas their collection of manuscripts must have contained, among many old plays long since dropped from the repertory, a comparatively small number worth (from a business point of view) the rescuing.

It is true that Chamberlain's description of the accident makes no mention of losses to the players, as do his accounts of the later occurrences at the Cockpit and the Fortune. He says, merely, that no one was hurt. This is perhaps significant, though not necessarily so. No weight, in any case, can be attached to the statement in one of Sir Henry Wotton's letters that 'nothing did perish but wood and straw, and a few forsaken cloaks', a statement sometimes advanced as proof that the movable property of the King's players suffered no damage. Wotton is referring, as did Chamberlain, to the fact that the occupants of the building escaped unharmed. That he was not at all interested in the fate of the players and their property is clear from his summary description of the theatre itself as 'wood and straw': the same indifference is indeed obvious in every line of his elegant and ironical commentary on the incident, which makes of the disaster an amusing anecdote, and expresses throughout a well-bred disdain of things theatrical.[19]

---

18 'A Sonnett upon the pittiful burneing of the Globe playhouse in London', preserved in manuscript; possibly by William Parrat. See Chambers, *Stage*, II. 420–2.

19 The relevant portion of Wotton's letter is cited by Chambers, *Stage*, II. 419–20.

It seems to me quite likely that the King's Men did suffer considerable loss of property, including playbooks, as a result of the fire: the presumptive evidence is, in my view, much stronger than is usually allowed. No doubt, however, the consequences of such a disaster were much less serious for them than they were to be later for the companies at the Cockpit and Fortune, since the King's Men possessed another theatre in the Blackfriars where a considerable portion of their assets survived.

It is not necessary to suppose that one of these consequences was the destruction of the manuscripts (prompt-book and actors' parts) relating to *King Lear*: though the date of the fire fits conveniently into the textual history of the play, it must be admitted that a single small collection of documents may be lost in innumerable ways. If, however, it is likely, as Sir Sidney Lee maintained, that several Shakespearean manuscripts besides that of *Lear* disappeared, and if it could be shown (as Lee made no attempt to do) that they must have disappeared at about the same period, towards the close of Shakespeare's career, then naturally the hypothesis of their common destruction in the fire of 1613 would acquire much greater plausibility. We should not, I think, dismiss Lee's theory out of hand. A far more thorough and unprejudiced examination of certain Shakespearean texts will be necessary before the requisite evidence, either for or against such a theory, can come to light: but while the relationship between the Quarto and Folio versions of these plays remains a source of perplexity, the question must, in my view, remain open.

In the case of *Lear*, the textual evidence clearly indicates that the authoritative copy of the play, the prompt-book, had disappeared and that an earlier manuscript, a theatrical report which had been used in the setting up of Q, was procured to help in the editing and revision of the text presented in Q. We have seen that, in drawing such inferences from the texts themselves, we are not committing ourselves to implausibilities. We have seen, too, that, though no further evidence is forthcoming to explain precisely how and why the series of events we have postulated took place, possible explanations are not far to seek.

We must now return to the evidence at our disposal. At least one feature of it remains anomalous and requires special attention.

CHAPTER SIX
THE MANUSCRIPT 'COPY' FOR F

We have so far examined, and found unwarranted, one of the two principal assumptions supporting the 'orthodox' theory, namely that the text of F derives in part from an independent manuscript. With the other – that the Folio text was set up from a corrected copy of the Quarto – we have so far found no occasion to disagree. Yet critics in the past have demurred to it, and not wholly without reason.[1]

They rest their case on a series of small errors in F which, set beside the spectacular corruptions in Q, do not appear very striking or significant, but which, since they are errors of a kind the accepted hypothesis does not lead one to expect, cannot well be overlooked. We have encountered these errors before, without, however, fully examining them. They have all the appearance of manuscript misreadings. If they are such – and they seem not to be susceptible to any other explanation – they lend support to the argument that F was set up not from printed copy but from a manuscript.[2]

A list follows of the more obvious instances. The reader will note, in consulting the relevant portions of the text, that in each case: (a) the Q reading does not require correction, or, if it does, does not receive any, so that editorial emendation is not in question; (b) the F reading is inferior, wrong or merely a deteriorated version of its counterpart in Q, so that editorial interference of any kind may reasonably be ruled out; (c) the error in F cannot plausibly be explained as a casual misprint; and (d) its written outline, in secretary hand, would bear a close similarity to the written outline of the reading in Q (or some alternative spelling of that reading).

1	I.iv.267	great	grac'd[3] (from *grate?*)
2	II.i.54	lancht	latch'd (from *lācht*)
3	II.i.78	spurres	spirits

---

1 Notably Madeleine Doran. She went further, it is true, to postulate that F and Q derived independently of each other from the original, a theory which is no longer tenable. But her argument maintaining that F was not set from printed copy deserves consideration.

2 Or, at least, that a manuscript intervened in the transmission of the text from Q to F.

3 Usually accepted into the editions, though both rhetoric and metre plainly require a more unemphatic word in this position. The main stress must fall on the following word, 'palace'.

4	II.i.79	Strong	strange (*strong* read as *strang*, a variant spelling of *strange*)
5	II.i.81	why	wher (superscript 'y' read as 'r')
6	II.i.89	strange newes	strangenesse (from *strange nes*?)
7	III.iv.83	iustly	Iustice (from *iustlie*)
8	III.vi.73	tike	tight (*tike* read as *tite*)
9	III.vi.73	trūdletaile	Troudle taile (from *trondle taile*, an alternative spelling)
10	IV.i.71	stands[4]	slaues
11	IV.ii.17	armes	names
12	IV.iv.3	femiter	Fenitar
13	IV.iv.4	hor-docks	Hardokes
14	IV.iv.18	distresse	desires (from *distres*)
15	IV.vi.17	walke	walk'd
16	IV.vi.71	enridged	enraged
17	IV.vi.83	coyning	crying[5]

Some of these errors *may* represent errors of judgement on the part of the F reviser, if we can suppose that in consulting the Q manuscript he sometimes misguidedly preferred his own misreadings of it to what he found in the printed copy.[6] But many (such as *strangenesse, Iustice, tight, desires*) make hopeless nonsense, and these we certainly could not ascribe to the reviser's interference. We have, besides, in *Troudle taile, Fenitar* and *Hardokes* corruptions which are most unlikely to have been perpetrated by the F compositor if he were following printed copy.

4 A perfectly acceptable reading, indeed a necessary one in the context, although it has not hitherto, as far as I know, found any favour with editors: *'stands* is a recognised aphetic form of *withstands*, the sense of which is precisely the one required.

5 This list does not comprise all the readings cited by Miss Doran (*Text*, pp. 91ff.), who includes several trivial errors which may be misprints, as well as one or two which might well be taken as genuine editorial changes. Also excluded from the list are three errors which might be misreadings from printed copy (II.iii.10, Q: *else all*, F: *elfe all*; II.iv.174, Q: *tēder hested*, F: *tender-hefted*; III.iv.53, Q: *foord*, F: *Sword*) and three which might have resulted from the compositor's failure to decipher manuscript corrections on printed copy (IV.vi.247, Qb: *bat*, F: *Ballow* — for *Batton*; III.vii.10, Q: *festuant*, F: *festiuate* — for *festinate* or *festinant*; II.ii.84, Q: *Reneag*, F: *Reuenge* — possibly the misreading of a spelling correction, *viz. Renegue*).

6 *Crying* for *coyning* at IV.vi.83 is, I feel, the most likely instance, since the letter 'o' in the handwriting of the Q manuscript was easily confused with 'r'. The passage in question is allusive, and the reviser may have missed its drift.

102   Should we look for an explanation, perhaps, to the character of the printed copy? It may be that these errors originated in the uncorrected state of certain pages in the specimen of QI used by the reviser, pages which in all the specimens known to us display the Qb version of the text. The notion seems at first to have much to recommend it. The errors, all except one (IV.ii.17: *names*), occur on formes which appear in one state only in the extant copies. Since these formes show no variants in as many as twelve exemplars, it is reasonable to assume that we know them in their corrected state — the earlier, uncorrected, state is generally, and for obvious reasons, the rarer. The errors tend to occur, furthermore, in groups (for example, those in II.i and IV.iv), much as do the press-corrected errors of which we have evidence. The nature of the mistakes, the nonsense spellings and obviously unacceptable misreadings, puts them well within the capacity of the Q compositor.

But there are serious objections to this otherwise attractive hypothesis. We might not be too surprised if a thirteenth copy of the Quarto were one day discovered which brought to light two or three further variant formes. From a statistical point of view, however, it is very highly unlikely that a copy would appear which displayed new variations in as many as five formes: and it is just such a copy we should have to postulate as responsible for the errors we are considering. It would show the following formes in an uncorrected state: D inner (readings numbered 1–6 in the list above), G inner (7–9), H outer (10), I outer (12, 15 and 16), I inner (13, 14 and 17).[7]

Still, if it is *a priori* improbable that a copy showing so much additional variation could ever have come into existence, it is perhaps open to us to suppose that some at least of the F errors may represent uncorrected readings in Q. Alternatively, we may argue that, though all the errors may indeed be misreadings from manuscript copy, this may only indicate that certain parts of the corrected Quarto were recopied by hand, perhaps because they were especially heavily marked, leaving it no less probable that the bulk of F was printed directly from QI.

The first possibility there seems to be little point in investigating: if one or more of the apparent misreadings are in fact relics of uncorrected Q (and there is no means of establishing whether that is so, and, if so, which) we are still left with the problem of the remainder. But the second hypothesis deserves consideration.

It will be worth recalling, first, that the additional passages in F, which must

---

7   The error numbered 12 (*names*) is excluded since it occurs on a forme (H inner) of which we possess both   the uncorrected and corrected states, showing an invariant Q reading (*armes*).

presumably have been printed from manuscript copy, contain very few errors, and only one misreading of the kind we have been discussing – indeed a rather less obvious one which might, on the most cautious criteria, be discounted as a possible printer's slip (*Place* for *Plate*, IV.vi.169). We may infer, from the appearance of a single misreading in about a hundred lines, that the copy for the additional passages was easily legible. Avoiding the multiplication of hypotheses, let us assume that it was the very scribe responsible for this copy who was required to transcribe further portions of the text from the corrected specimen of Q. These portions gave rise, on the evidence, to a further score or so of misreadings (for to those listed must, in reason, be added a handful from among many doubtful instances, not all of which can be attributed to purely mechanical error). Assuming a low incidence of such errors (one in every hundred lines or so) we should have to infer from the discovery of more than twenty in the non-additional passages a very extensive use of manuscript copy.

The evidence, however, is not quite susceptible to so straightforward an interpretation. Most obviously because the errors listed as nos. 2–6 do not square with the hypothesis of a low incidence of error. Here indeed is a positive cluster of mistakes, to which might be added several more from the same neighbourhood not much less certainly identifiable as misreadings. We shall see later (Chapter Nine) that evidence of another kind exposes this phenomenon as highly anomalous, and that it is of very limited significance here. Elsewhere the appearance of misreadings in the same line or in successive lines (nos. 8 and 9, 12 and 13) is not, I think, suspicious. The best manuscripts may include brief passages of comparative illegibility. But for that very reason (i.e. because both errors in each pair were probably determined by the same cause) they should not, perhaps, be admitted into our quasi-statistical computation as independent items.

Counting each of these pairs of errors, therefore, as one error, and excluding errors 2–6, we find the list reduced to a minimum of ten misreadings. Let us suppose that we might elsewhere find up to half as many again of the more trivial kind, represented by *Plate / Place*, which has been excluded from the list. (Examined singly not one of these errors is indubitably a misreading, yet some of them must be.) We are now encouraged to infer that between 1000 and 1500 lines of the text at least must have been set from manuscript copy.

This argument receives some support from the fact that more than half the errors listed (*viz.* nos. 7, 10–17) derive from passages in Q which received very little correction or relineation before their incorporation in F, so that, had these passages alone been recopied by hand, one would be hard put to it to explain why.

104   The portion or portions of manuscript copy we are postulating must, of course, have been transcribed from a marked-up copy of the Quarto: we have found no reason to discard the hypothesis that the F text throughout was founded on a revision of the earlier edition.[8] If, however, a substantial proportion of the text was transcribed by hand, and if, as it seems, there was no practical advantage in so transcribing many of the particular passages which offer the clearest evidence of transcription, then it is difficult to resist the conclusion that the whole text must have been copied fair in the interests, if nothing else, of neatness and consistency. Can we suppose, then, that the printers of F received as copy not the original 'corrected' specimen of Q but a manuscript transcript of it?

How such a supposition might accord with the conclusion we have just derived from the number of the misreadings, namely that something less than half only of the text was actually set up from manuscript, will later become clear (Chapter Eight). Meanwhile two more general considerations make it virtually certain that the copy delivered to the printer was a manuscript transcript.[9]

First, we know that the Folio compositors used cast-off copy. A printed book would, of course, normally be very easy to cast off: but a much altered print, strewn with numerous additions and deletions, one especially in which the arrangement of lines had been drastically revised, would make any summary and time-saving method of computation very hazardous (and no printer willingly resorts to an actual count of words). Yet it is not apparent in the result that the copy used presented any difficulty. Though there is some evidence of crowding on the last two pages of quire rr and rather more of space-wasting on the first of quire ss, it is clear that no serious misjudgement occurred. It would not, I think, be unreasonable to maintain that the casting-off operation could not have

8   We have ruled out the possibility that an independent manuscript, or even incomplete portions of an independent manuscript, may have been used in preparing the copy for F. There is, as we have seen, no clear evidence anywhere in the text for its origin in an independent source, and we cannot use the mere *lack* of evidence for or against independent derivation in certain portions of the text as a pretext for reviving the hypothesis. It remains possible that derivation directly from the manuscript copy for Q (without the mediation of the print) is in question here. The

evidence, however, of common Q/F errors such as misreadings, mislineations, mispunctuation and a few common misprints testifies throughout to the dependence of F on printed Q: such coincidences are not likely to have arisen in the course of independent transmission from the same source, the manuscript copy for Q. It is theoretically conceivable, since passages of F may be found free from any sign of this dependence, that the copy for these passages was transcribed directly from the Q manuscript, or that the manuscript copy for Q was itself

been conducted so successfully, or indeed willingly undertaken at all, had not the printers been supplied with reasonably 'clean' copy.

Secondly, there is further evidence in the text itself to indicate that F must have derived from Q through the mediation of a manuscript. We have already noticed the fact that a large number of the disagreements in reading between F and Q are wholly unimportant, in the sense that the variants in F make no difference to grammar or meaning. Plurals are changed to singulars, and singulars to plurals, when either would be acceptable; one form of the relative is substituted for another; synonymous prepositions are interchanged. There is no discernible purpose in the large majority of these trivial alterations.

It is impossible to imagine that the reviser marked so large a number of trifling changes in his printed copy: no one, surely, with so laborious a task in hand, would waste time and energy altering *which* to *that, betwixt* to *between*, and the like, on so large a number of occasions. A few of the changes might be attributed to the F compositors. Reprints of the time normally show a scattering of just such indifferent variants, the result of inattention or memorial failure. But the compositors cannot possibly be held responsible for extensive interference of the kind we have to account for. All the evidence goes to show that, then as now, in the matter at least of substantive readings, compositors were accustomed to set about a strictly accurate reproduction of copy. Frequent, unimportant changes of wording are more to be expected from a scribe. If the text he were given to copy offered, as in the present instance, a somewhat provisional appearance, if, that is to say, it were covered with corrections, revisions and interpolations, he might be especially inclined to treat its details with some freedom. The likelihood is increased if we suppose that the copyist was connected with the theatre, or that, being engaged by the players, he was

re-used in part in the printing of F, but I do not know what would constitute sure evidence in favour of so complicated a hypothesis. One has only, in any case, to try and envisage the reasons for a proceeding of such oddness and inconsistency to decide that there is no probability of its having ever occurred.

9 That a manuscript *intervened* between Q1 and F was suggested originally by Philip Williams ('Two Problems in the Folio Text of *King Lear*', *Shakespeare Quarterly*, IV (1953), pp. 451–60.

Williams's argument is based on assumptions and evidence I cannot accept, for reasons which will not become apparent until later in this study; but he was, I believe, correct in concluding that F must derive from a manuscript transcribed for some reason from an 'altered' copy of Q1. He surmises that the transcript was commissioned to serve as printer's copy, and that the altered Q1 was the current prompt-book consisting in 'a conflation of "good" pages from Q1 supplemented by inserted manuscript leaves to replace corrupt passages of Q1' (p. 460).

acquainted with the circumstances of the case and with the need for a thoroughly rehabilitated text.

There would, of course, be no need to conjecture the employment of a scribe if we could suppose that the reviser himself transcribed the text he had prepared. Small changes of the kind we are considering would have come very easily from his pen, since he had affected so many more radical ones. But, on this supposition, the persistence of error becomes difficult to explain. The reviser would surely have become clearly aware of his frequent minor oversights if he had been obliged to copy them: and he would surely then have made the attempt to repair them. Transcription, therefore, by a person or persons other than the reviser appears the likeliest hypothesis, if we are to explain the apparently pointless alteration of so many of the unimportant readings in Q.

One final consideration remains to direct us to the assumption of manuscript copy. It is generally agreed that the F text reflects many of the characteristics of a prompt-book. The proponents of the theory now most widely accepted hold, in fact, that F represents a conflation of Q with the version of the prompt-book current in the theatre at the date of printing, or just before. We have found reason to believe, however, that no such conflation took place, that in fact no text of the play existed before the preparation of F other than that to be found in Q and its related manuscript. If F, therefore, does indeed show signs of derivation from a prompt-book, only one inference is possible: it derives *directly* from a prompt-book. The version of the text which it presents may, in other words, have been prepared in the first place not for the printers but for use in the theatre. Indeed if we infer, as we have done from other evidence, that the original exemplar of the text had been lost or destroyed, we may be led by another line of argument to the same conclusion. The loss of the original prompt-book would very probably have caused the players to commission a new one, certainly so if they wished to revive the play. And we should expect the undertaking to have followed a course not markedly different from that which explains the genesis of F: a revision of the sole surviving text, that of Q, ridding it so far as possible of corruptions and obscurities and adapting it to new conditions.

It scarcely needs adding that, if a prompt-book were delivered as copy to the printers of F, it would certainly have taken the form of a manuscript. It would be absurd to suppose that a copy of Q, much obscured by corrections and revisions, could serve the practical purposes of a theatrical book-keeper. We have still, however, to review the arguments for supposing that a prompt-book should come into question.

Two kinds of evidence witness the theatrical origin of the F text: firstly, certain features of its lay-out and of its apparatus of stage-directions; secondly, certain alterations in the text itself.

A small clue is supplied by the division of F into acts. Q is not so divided. Few early texts are. But the division is a regular feature of surviving contemporary prompt-books.[10] It must, of course, have been necessary to subdivide the text of a prompt-book wherever pauses in the performance were required. It seems that, although such breaks were not customary in the early public theatres, they became a regular feature of performances in the private theatres, whence they were adopted into the public theatres from about 1607 onwards.[11]

Much more informative are the stage directions in F. These are exactly of the kind we should expect to find in a theatrical manuscript. They are, first of all, regularly and correctly marked and in all important respects complete. The errors in Q (e.g. *Edmund* for *Edgar* at IV.vi. 1) are corrected, its ambiguities (e.g. *Duke* for both Albany and Cornwall) removed, and its gaps supplied. Only one anomaly remains. Edmund is indifferently *Edmund* and *Bastard* in stage direc-tions; his speech prefix, on the other hand, is always *Bast.*, except in two short passages in the first two scenes where it appears as *Edm.* This is a muddle, but hardly a serious one in that it would be unlikely to unsettle a book-keeper familiar with the play.

Several exits are missing, two thirds of them relating to supernumeraries: attendants, soldiers and the like. I have counted seven involving major charac-ters. But it is not at all uncharacteristic of prompt-books to be lacking in a few necessary exit directions.[12] Actors can be relied upon to make their way off-stage at the correct times: it is their entrances over which a stage-manager or book-keeper needs to keep watch. It is significant that not a single entrance is missing from F.[13]

10 Of those, certainly, which may be dated c. 1605 or after. See W. W. Greg, *Dramatic Documents from the Elizabethan Playhouses* (Oxford, 1931), I. 210.

11 See Andrew Gurr, *The Shakespearean Stage* (Cambridge, 1970), p. 97, citing W. T. Jewkes, *Act Division in Elizabethan and Jacobean Plays* (New York, 1958), pp. 100–1.

12 See Chambers, *Wm. Sh.*, I. 120.

13 Greg says one entrance is wanting (*Folio*, p. 385). I assume he refers to the re-entrance at I.iv.53 of the Knight who has been sent to summon Oswald. But Greg himself observes (*Folio*, pp. 361, 464) that exits followed by immediate re-entrances often go unmarked in texts of the period.

108   The nature of the stage directions in F is also suggestive of theatrical usage. Q tends, as we might expect, to describe the details of a particular production: F confines itself, in a more businesslike way, to indications of what is basically required. For example:

> Q: *Sound a Sennet, Enter one bearing a Coronet,*
>   *then Lear, then the Dukes of Albany, and Cornwell,*
>   *next Gonorill, Regan, Cordelia, with followers.*

> F: *Sennet. Enter King Lear, Cornwall, Albany, Gonerill,*
>   *Regan, Cordelia, and attendants.*

I.i.35

> Q: *Shee takes a sword and runs at him behind.*

> F: *Killes him.*

III.vii.80

Except for a final *He dies* at V.iii.311, and for the direction last quoted (the absence of which immediately after Regan's speech might have left it doubtful whether it were she or Cornwall responsible for the killing), F contains no instructions as to action.[14] It is, however, far more explicit than Q about sound effects, a matter of some importance to the book-keeper, who, as he was responsible for their management backstage, would need precise indications of what was required and when. F abounds in flourishes, tuckets, horns, etc., which are mostly missing from Q, as is also the direction for music, *Exeunt with a dead March*, at V.iii.326. The storm is carefully noted at II.iv.286, two lines before Cornwall first mentions it. The direction *Storme still* is repeated six times to remind the book-keeper that the appropriate effects are to continue through III.i, III.ii and III.iv.

One would expect to find equal care devoted in F to properties, but this is not quite the case. On three occasions, it is true, F draws attention to necessary properties which go unremarked in Q (II.i.39: *Torches*; II.ii.144: *Stocks*; III.iv.115: *a Torch*). On three further occasions, however, F omits to mention properties noted in Q (II.ii.47: *with his rapier drawne*; III.iii.1: *lights*; V.iii.222: *a bloudie knife*). One might argue, perhaps, that of these the first two are not

---

14   The following directions in Q are omitted from F: *sleepes* (II.ii.181); *draw and fight* (III.vii.78); *He*   *kneeles* (IV.vi.34); *He fals* (IV.vi.41); *they fight* (IV.vi.249); *He dies* (IV.vi.256).

strictly called for. But the omission of the 'bloody knife' is odd: it is referred to explicitly two lines further on in the scene, and one must suppose that the book-keeper would require a reminder of the point at which it was, in the hands of the 'Gentleman', to appear on the stage.

Much more positive evidence is supplied by the placing of entrances. In the text of Q characters enter, for the most part, immediately before they first speak or are spoken to. Modern editors also assume that the point at which a character begins to participate in the action normally marks his entrance. This accurately enough reflects what would occur in a production of the play on a modern stage. But in an Elizabethan playbook the placing of certain entrances had to be differently judged. The Elizabethan outdoor stage was, by our standards, extraordinarily large.[15] Actors who were required, for whatever reason, to cross the whole expanse of the stage before speaking, would need the space of two or three lines of dialogue in which to do so. Their entrances would have, accordingly, to be marked two or three lines early in the prompt-book. Such anticipations are a noticeable feature of extant theatrical manuscripts.[16] We find the following instances in F:

15 According to the builder's contract, which has survived, the Fortune theatre (built in 1600) was to be supplied with a platform forty-three feet in length, extending in breadth 'to the middle of the yard' (i.e. $27\frac{1}{2}$ feet).

16 These should be distinguished from the marginal notes occasionally to be found still further in advance of moments of entry, which evidently served to warn the book-keeper that an actor or actors were to be got ready at the tiring-house door (see Greg, *Folio*, p. 139). About anticipatory entrance-directions as such there have been differences of opinion. Greg is surely right to dismiss the suggestion that they were signals to the book-keeper to summon the actors required: 'if an actor was not on the spot to make his entrance, two or three lines would afford no sufficient time in which to fetch him' (*EPS*, p. 38). But his own theory is not more convincing ('It appears to have been the prompter who needed warning of action

ahead'), and he seems not to be convinced by it himself ('Actually there would seem to be no need for such anticipation, since the direction if boldly written, as it usually was, could easily be picked out by the eye' – *EPS*, p. 38). One must, I think, concur with Chambers: 'It is [the author's] tendency to place an entry just before the first speech of the character concerned. The cautious book-keeper sometimes shifts it to an earlier point, so as to allow time for the character to cross the stage' (*Wm. Sh.*, I. 120).

Of course, not *all* entries were marked early in prompt-books, but only those which required the actor to travel across the length (or breadth) of the platform in full view of the audience. It is too readily assumed, I think, by writers on the Elizabethan theatre that the *upstage* area would be avoided as far as possible in production. They, no doubt unconsciously, identify this area with the back of a modern stage, and associate it, accordingly, with

110	I.ii.146	Edgar	4 lines early
	II.iv.87	Lear and Gloucester	2
	II.iv.185	Oswald	3
	II.iv.191	Goneril	2
	III.ii.36	Kent	2
	III.iv.115	Gloucester	17
	IV.i.10	Gloucester and Old Man	3
	IV.vi.81	Lear	2
	IV.vii.21	Lear (in a chair carried by servants)	4
	V.iii.102	Herald	5
	V.iii.230	Kent	3
	V.iii.231	Goneril and Regan (their dead bodies carried on)	7

We may note that actors carried in (IV.vii.21, V.iii.231) require slightly longer than the normal two or three lines. Edgar's entrance (I.ii.146) is protracted because Edmund pretends for a while not to notice him, Gloucester's (III.iv.115) because he is supposed to be wandering about in the storm: five lines elapse before the Fool catches sight of him, and a further twelve before he is addressed by Kent. The Herald's five lines' allowance (V.iii.102) seems to be the result of an error: his entrance is actually marked before the speech in which Albany summons him.

It is noteworthy that sound effects are also carefully marked in F in advance of references to them in the text, e.g. *Storme and tempest* (II.iv.286 – two lines or so

acoustical difficulties and obstructed lines of sight. But the rear of the Elizabethan stage stood as much within the auditorium as its forward edge: the line of the so-called 'tiring-house wall' corresponds in relation to the placing of the audience with the line of the proscenium arch in a modern theatre. There would thus be no difficulty about upstage action, and one must assume that there was plenty of it. Hence plenty of opportunity, too, for rapid entrances and exits requiring no more time than is necessary on a modern stage.

That time was, however, occasionally needed, and allowed for, is indicated not only by anticipatory entrances in

prompt-books. A multitude of examples shows that new scenes frequently began with the actors advancing downstage from the tiring-house door. Two or three lines of unimportant, or even irrelevant, dialogue are provided to 'cover' the protracted entrance before the main business of the scene begins. Likewise, mid-scene entrances or exits may be accompanied by comments from the characters already on stage, or remaining there, comments which imply that the character arriving or leaving is in view but out of earshot. Greetings and valedictions, again, may be prolonged to allow plenty of time for actors to approach or withdraw.

before *'twill be a Storme*) and *Drum afarre off* (IV.vi.289 – two lines before *Farre off* 111
methinkes I heare the beaten Drumme).

An equally revealing clue appears in the language of certain directions. It is
well known that in Elizabethan theatrical parlance the stage was 'out' or
'without' and the tiring-house 'in' or 'within', though a spectator would most
naturally take the opposite view. In Q Goneril's and Regan's bodies are brought
in (V.iii.238), in F they are brought *out* (231), as are the stocks at II.ii.144. This
single small detail is almost enough by itself to illustrate the different sources of
the two texts.

There is ample evidence, then, in stage directions to attest the prompt-book
origin of F. The text itself, however, provides further confirmation, if confirmation is needed.

It is clear that, in spite of numerous brief additions of new material scattered
through the play, a more serious effort was applied to shortening the text than to
lengthening it. Additions to Q total about one hundred lines; the omissions
amount to three hundred. This abridgement is, in part, clearly connected with
the elimination of minor speaking-roles. At the end of III.vii, for example, an
exchange has been cut between two servants who do not otherwise contribute to
the scene. The whole of IV.iii has been omitted: it employs a 'Gentleman' who
cannot be played either by the actor who as 'Messenger' brings IV.ii to a close or
by the one who as 'Gentleman' ('Doctor' in Q) begins IV.iv. In IV.vii F's
'Gentleman', represents two characters in Q ('Doctor' and 'Gentleman'), and
speaks the lines of both. At the point in Q where the two characters separate, the
Doctor leaving the stage, the Gentleman remaining behind for a few further
lines of dialogue with Kent, F brings the scene to a close, omitting the final
exchange. A further economy is effected in IV.vi when three Gentlemen,
emissaries from Cordelia, are reduced to one. This evidence makes it plain that
the text of F was adapted to the needs of a smaller company of players than had
been necessary for the performance of the Q version, and that its abridgement
was, partly at least, determined by the demands of theatrical expediency.

There is reason to believe, furthermore, that one or two at least of the major
additions and omissions in F formed no part of the original revision but were
incorporated into the text by the book-keeper in the theatre. The relevant
evidence will be examined in the next chapter. Meanwhile we may notice that at
least one of the more extensive interpolations – the Fool's 'prophecy' at the end
of III.ii – is most unlikely to have recommended itself to a reviser of any literary
pretensions. It has little poetic merit and absolutely no dramatic relevance. It
was obviously introduced to afford the company's clown an opportunity to
impress with a piece of lively and doubtless topical satire, and can only have

112 originated during a production in the theatre.

When we consider these clear indications of theatrical editing in connection with the evidence of stage directions, we can scarcely avoid the inference that the F text reproduces a manuscript used in the theatre, in other words a prompt-book. This inference, as we have already observed, is entirely consistent with the conclusion we drew earlier that the copy submitted to the printers was written by hand.

It must follow that the initial editing and revision of the Q text was performed in the first place not for the printers but for the players, its object being the provision not of printer's copy but of a prompt-book for the King's company. If this prompt-book was used, and further revised, in the theatre, it is possible that it came into being some considerable time before being handed to the printers. I have, in fact, already suggested that it may have been produced within ten years or so of the publication of Q. It is now time to offer grounds for proposing so early a date.

There follows in the next chapter a review of the various stages by which, as seems most probable, the F text reached its penultimate shape as copy for the printers. The evidence relevant to dating will be best considered in the course of this historical account.

The text of F, we have seen, gives no sign of derivation from a source more authoritative than Q. It shows, on the other hand, the clearest marks of editing and revision. We are bound to assume that, at the time of its preparation, no authentic copy of the play existed. We can only indeed infer, in the circumstances, that the text of F would never have come into existence were it not for the loss or destruction of the original manuscript: the prompt-book, the actors' parts and the author's rough draft, if there ever were one. (If we are to believe that Shakespeare's colleagues 'scarce received from him a blot in his papers' — and, as long as we do not take the phrase *au pied de la lettre*, there is no reason to be sceptical,[1] he may well have submitted his original drafts to the theatre for use as they stood.) The manuscripts may have perished in the Globe fire of 1613. There is no evidence that they did so. But since they must have disappeared at approximately this period, the supposition seems not too implausible.

We must further assume that the new prompt-book was commissioned for a revival of the play. Records of performances at this period are unfortunately even scantier than they usually are. We know of only two productions of *Lear* before the Restoration: the one mentioned on the title-page of Q, which took place at Whitehall on 26 December 1606, and one by strolling players in the provinces in 1610, for which apparently 'printed books' (i.e. copies of Q) supplied the text. As we noticed, however, F gives every indication of having been adapted for use in the theatre, and there seems no reason to suppose that the work was done gratuitously. If there was a revival, it may be that the second edition of the play (the Pavier Quarto of 1619) gives us a clue to its date. A publisher of the time would be most unlikely to reissue a play after many years, even one by Shakespeare, unless it had been recently re-introduced into the theatre and were fairly fresh in the public mind. It is sometimes not implausibly maintained that Pavier was venturing upon a collected edition of Shakespeare's works. Complete sets of the 1619 Quartos have indeed survived bound together in single

---

1   The boast of Heminges and Condell (if they it was who wrote the Prefatory Address in the Folio where the phrase appears) was not trumped up to impress the credulous reader. That it represented a genuine belief among the players is attested by the famous passage in Jonson's *Discoveries*: 'I remember, the Players have often mentioned it as an honour to Shakespeare, that in his writing, (whatsoever he penn'd) hee never blotted out line. My answer hath beene, Would he had blotted a thousand.'

114 volumes. Nevertheless it is clear from bibliographical evidence that the reprint of *Lear* was intended primarily for separate sale.[2] Pavier, therefore, must have anticipated a market for it independently of the other plays in the collection.

We shall return in due course to this matter of a date, but the reader may like to be reminded of a circumstance touched on earlier which sets one outside limit for it, as the publication of the Folio sets the other. The person responsible for editing and revising the Q text was not Shakespeare. The number of errors remaining in F is enough to arouse suspicion. Far more significant, however, is their nature. We cannot plausibly suppose an author so forgetful of his original intentions that he would fall into obtuse mistakes and misconceptions of the kind we have noticed. Still less can we suppose that Shakespeare would have baulked at the many difficulties and obscurities we find glossed over or hesitantly tinkered with. When baffled by a garbled passage he would surely, like any other writer, have rewritten it entirely rather than rest satisfied with an unsuccessful attempt to recover it. The reviser's work, in short, is too conscientiously aimed at restoration and repair, and is too ineffectual in achieving that aim, to be mistaken for that of the author himself. If Shakespeare did not himself undertake the task of revision, then we may plausibly assume that he was not available to do so. The date, therefore, at which it was accomplished is unlikely to have preceded his retirement from the theatre in 1613.[3]

At a time, then, in all probability after that date, a copy of Q, together with the manuscript 'copy' which, as we have seen, must have been obtained from the publisher, was handed to another dramatist with a commission to convert it into a usable text. We must assume that the work was entrusted to an experienced writer, since for all his errors of misunderstanding and carelessness he carried it out in the main intelligently and skilfully. How did he proceed?

It is more than likely that he began by collating his specimen of Q with the manuscript 'copy', and that, having once accomplished the collation, he did not again revert to the manuscript. This is suggested both by general considerations and by particular evidence. It would be impractical to attempt to revise his text

2   The compositor went to some trouble in setting the final pages of the play to save space (e.g. by manipulating the lineation) so that he could complete the text on the *recto* side of the last leaf. This effort to leave the verso blank can only indicate that the book was designed to be sold separately as a pamphlet (i.e. unbound). Greg is of the opinion that Pavier's plan to publish the plays as a collection was abandoned before the edition of *Lear* went to press; furthermore that the plays were ultimately sold both singly and in sets (*Folio*, pp. 16–17).

3   It is Chambers's surmise on the available evidence that after 1613 Shakespeare wrote no more (*Wm. Sh.*, I. 87).

at the same time that he was comparing it *literatim* with another: it would obviously be more sensible first to render the printed copy as accurate as possible before proceeding to examine what further corrections and changes might be necessary. Once the exacting task of collation had been performed, it would be tedious and difficult, in the course of his second revision, to refer to the manuscript again. It was not, we may safely assume, divided into acts and scenes. Locating a particular reading, supposing the reviser determined on a fresh consultation, would prove a laborious business which might not in the end provide any enlightenment.

It is, in any case, only on the supposition of two successive processes (collation followed by revision) that certain details in the F text can be explained. It is remarkable, first, that, although F abounds in substitutions (readings which bear perhaps a lexical relation but no orthographical resemblance to their counterparts in Q), they very rarely correspond with *misreadings* in Q. I have found no more than two or three instances (e.g. *reward* at III.vi.5 for *deserue*, which should have been corrected to *deserne*, i.e. *discern*). Apparently the reviser, when faced with obvious misreadings, corrected them, or attempted to correct them, and then left them alone, although he was very frequently willing to replace words in Q which needed no correction. An obvious explanation lies in the possibility that he went through the text twice with different purposes in view, once simply to correct his printed copy against the manuscript, a second time to revise it more thoroughly and freely on his own initiative. On his second review he would naturally tend to preserve the readings he had already spent time emending.

A further clue is provided by the sophistication in F of Q errors which must have been overlooked during the work of collation. We have already examined a striking instance; at V.iii.145 an uncorrected Q misprint (*By* for *My*) prompted the reviser to a radical misinterpretation of the sense, which he had to justify by the addition of a line. We can only assume that he did not have the manuscript beside him when he committed this extravagance, and that he did not because he had already checked his copy against it, as well as he was able, for mistakes of precisely the kind which here led him astray.

It seems, then, reasonable to assume a double recension of the Q text. The first stage of collation with the manuscript would result in a number of corrections and in the recovery of matter accidentally or mistakenly omitted from Q. But we should expect a few errors to go unnoticed. And we should expect here and there to find the F reviser as much misled by the handwriting of the manuscript as had been the Q compositor: to find him, that is to say, confirming the compositor's misreadings or compounding them. Wherever, on

116 the evidence of Q, we have reason to infer more radical corruption in the manuscript copy, it is not surprising to discover the reviser hazarding emendations (if he attempts any at all) which are self-evidently speculative and wrong.

The second stage of revision would produce substitutions, expansions and cuts. There is evidence, which we shall be examining below, to show that some major additions and cuts were effected at a later stage, but smaller adjustments of the text would certainly have been taken care of by the reviser himself. He would now deal more summarily with corruptions in Q (e.g. at I.iv.307, *cadent Teares* for *accent teares*, which can hardly represent the correction of a misreading). He would also at this point, no doubt on the presumption that he was dealing with a much-debased text, allow his own taste and judgement much freer play. The F text shows, on comparison with Q, a great deal of regularisation of grammar, syntax and idiom. Not all of it is necessary or even correct, but it betokens the reviser's fastidiousness in such matters. He valued a smooth style, and was liberal with small 'improvements' of wording and arrangement. Where he replaced a (satisfactory) reading of Q with his own choice of word, it was sometimes to substitute the current for the uncommon,[4] sometimes for a gain in emphasis,[5] but often, apparently, simply because he preferred one word to another.[6] He had, too, a strong sense of logic, and many of his corrections and expansions were clearly dictated (not always advisedly) by his suspicions of irrationality in the original text.[7] It is a curious fact that he was inclined at the

4   e.g. *sticke* for *rash* (III.vii.58); *sterne* for *dearne* (III.vii.63); *stop* for *stople* (V.iii.155).

5   e.g. *falls* for *stoops* (I.i.151); *condemne* for *dislike* (I.iv.365); *Coward* for *caytife* (II.i.64). The stronger word, needless to say, is not always the more effective.

6   *Strike* for *smite* (III.ii.7) is an example which may stand for a considerable number.

7   In changing *smal* to *great* at IV.vi.168 the reviser misunderstood the point in a rather literal-minded way. The same might be said of his alteration of *vertues* at V.iii.170 to *vices*, though most editors preserve the change. ('Virtue', however, might here mean, as elsewhere in Shakespeare, 'accomplishment, power'.) In the first scene of the play the reviser evidently thought it unreasonable that Lear, in banishing Kent, should allow him four days for preparation, and five for travel: in F the proportions are reversed (I.i.176 and 178). A similar fastidiousness apparently causes the change from *British* to *English* at IV.vi.256 – Lear was not King of Scotland. Here and there the reviser was offended by rhetorical exaggerations, rephrasing them in more temperate terms (e.g. *houres* at II.ii.65 becomes *yeares*; *a 100* at II.iv.72 becomes *twenty*). A similar intellectual discomfort seems to prompt one or two of the additions. The Fool's riddle 'whether a mad man be a gentleman or a yeoman' is tidily supplied with an answer (III.vi.13–15), even though the answer disrupts Lear's reply as given in Q,

beginning of his work to adventitious elaborations and embellishments, but 117
that he soon abandoned this policy, confining himself to more purposeful
changes.[8]

Metre was one of his chief concerns: he completed or recast scores of faulty
lines in Q, or lines which he regarded as faulty. He must, too, as he revised, have
marked new line-divisions for the copyist wherever necessary. This part of his
work left in its turn a residue of error. It is clear that on a few occasions the
reviser omitted to correct a wrong line-division in Q, or inadvertently marked a
new division in the wrong place; that he was not always careful in completing
defective lines; and that he sometimes discovered a defective line where none
was.

It is hardly surprising that his task of marking up a badly mislined copy
resulted in several errors of this kind. Nor is it extraordinary that, apart from his
many unsuccessful attempts to resolve textual difficulties, he failed sometimes
even to notice them (or, if he did notice them, to tackle them). It is a fair
assumption that he was paid to perform his task in a given time, and that he
would approach it conscientiously enough, no doubt, but scarcely in any spirit
of scholarly meticulousness. The work would involve much reading back and
forth, since every problem would have to be assessed in its context, and it is not
remarkable that in the process a few oversights occurred. We might also suppose

---

making nonsense of it. An
amusing instance of this orderliness
occurs at II.iv.142–7. Regan's
immediately preceding speech
appears to convey the opposite of
what she intends, i.e. a defence of
Goneril:

Q: *Reg.* I pray sir take patience, I
haue hope
You lesse know how to value her
desert,
Then she to slacke her dutie.

The reviser adds a gloss:

F: *Lear.* Say? How is that?
Reg. I cannot thinke my Sister in
the least
Would faile her Obligation. If Sir
perchance
She haue restrained the Riots of
your Followres,
'Tis on such ground, and to such
wholesome end,
As cleeres her from all blame.

8 The additions at I.i.50–1,
I.i.65–6, I.i.86–7 and I.i.90–1 do
not fill any gap in narrative logic
or continuity of sense. The same
might be said of I.i.41–6,
although this passage does fulfil
the function of introducing Albany
and Cornwall by name at their first
appearance on the scene. I.i.41–6
and I.i.86–7 may also have been
partly intended to restore broken
metre, but if so the trouble
expended on them was lavish in
comparison with the simple filling
up of gaps which characterises the
reviser's later procedure. Most
subsequent additions fulfil a
strictly practical purpose, either
that of regularising metre or that
of clarifying sense or action. The
exceptions are (a) one or two
passages which appear to be
recoveries of the Q text, (b) one or
two passages which appear to have
been added in the theatre (see
Appendix B2).

118 that in a copy receiving copious corrections details temporarily held over for later attention would tend soon to be obscured and lost sight of. It must be acknowledged, however, that the reviser cannot have reviewed his work thoroughly once he had finished it or the accumulation of small oversights would certainly have come to his notice.[9]

A third stage in the production of the F text was reached, as we have seen, when a scribe was commissioned to copy the refurbished text of Q. This manuscript transcription was to serve the King's Men as a prompt-book. The copyist would have regularised the spelling of names and the form of speech-prefixes. It was possibly he, too, rather than the reviser, who filled in missing stage directions, omitted some he regarded as superfluous, and recast others to suit the expectations of a book-keeper.

A great many small and unimportant changes of wording must be attributed to him. He may also have tampered with line-division, and it is probable that on one or two occasions he made clumsy attempts to remedy the reviser's oversights.[10] The copy he produced, however, was evidently a very clean one. The text of F shows the usual scattering of compositor's slips, but comparatively few misreadings, few significant errors of spelling or punctuation and, one or two interesting lapses aside which we are about to notice, no other sign of confused or garbled copy.

9 The reader should, perhaps, be reminded, in case a suspicion of special pleading has entered his mind, that the reviser, on the argument presented here, was employed on a taxing and complicated piece of work with very little in the way of extraneous help at his elbow. We might, with perfect consistency, allow him many more errors of carelessness than is in fact necessary, while yet demurring at the frequent oversights we are required to ascribe to the collator of the traditional theory, who is alleged to have engaged in a far simpler undertaking.

10 For example, at IV.vii.36–8. The reviser evidently failed to notice that the preceding cut had left a short line in the middle of Cordelia's speech or he would undoubtedly have expanded the line to the required length. It was very likely the copyist who, reluctant to transcribe an obviously short line, made matters worse by redistributing the two following lines in order to disguise the gap. Had he faithfully reproduced the short line as left by the reviser it is unlikely that the F compositor would have interfered. Similar errors occur elsewhere, e.g. at IV.vi.109–34. Here the reviser must have begun by marking line-divisions, perhaps up to the fourth line of the speech (though to this line he added a word, *dye*, which makes its scansion problematical). After that, realising his mistake, he gave up, but forgot to erase his markings, thus misleading the copyist, who persisted in the effort to versify: he divided five further lines, only one of which forms an acceptable pentameter. The speech at

The misreadings apart, two errors only suggest that the copy was at all
difficult to decipher. They are interesting in that they demonstrate a further
stage in the history of the text: revision in the theatre. At I.iv.154 the F printers
misinterpreted the direction for a cut. The break in continuity at this point
makes it obvious that the deletion should have started three lines earlier (at line
151). At III.i.22 the compositor inserted a passage into the text which had
clearly been written in the margin of his copy, or on a separate slip pasted into it.
After setting the additional matter (III.i.22–9) he returned to the text at the
wrong point, omitting several lines (ll. 30–42) which, again, a hiatus in the
sense makes apparent should not have been dropped.[11] Both errors must have
originated in the printing house: the copyist who prepared the prompt-book
cannot have been to blame. No prompt-book in use could have shown the
discontinuities of sense which appear: such glaring anomalies would certainly
have been corrected as soon as noticed. So that it must have been alterations
marked *in* the prompt-book which caused the trouble.

In inferring that the prompt-book itself was modified by the introduction of
cuts and interpolations (one, at least, of each) we are assuming, of course, that
the text was further revised after reaching the theatre. In fact many of the longer
cuts, and some of the additions, may have been prompted at this later stage by
the exigencies and interests of production – very probably, at any rate, those
cuts which made possible a reduction in the personnel required for the play; and
almost certainly those additions which, self-evidently irrelevant as they are,
seem to have been introduced for a purely theatrical purpose, i.e. II.iv.46–55
and III.ii.79–96.

IV.vi.161–77 demonstrates the
opposite error. It begins with three
lines of prose, but the rest of it is
clearly verse, and intended by the
reviser as such (he revised line 166
to make it scan, and added the
passage, 169–74, which,
beginning and ending with
half-lines, fits perfectly into the
metrical scheme). But the copyist
again continued as he began – in
prose. One or two sophistications
in F seem beneath the reviser's
intelligence. It is possible that
they represent the copyist's
attempts to emend errors left
uncorrected at the collation stage
(because the manuscript offered no
help) and then overlooked at the

stage of revision. An example is
the extraordinary reading *Questrists*
at III.vii.17.

11 It is quite likely that a slip
containing the additional lines was
pasted by its lateral edge to the
left margin of the manuscript and
positioned immediately beneath
line 21 so that, when folded down,
the flap obscured the rest of the
speech. A prompt-book belonging
to the King's Company survives in
which this method of interpolation
has been employed (see *Second
Maiden's Tragedy*, ed. Sir W. W.
Greg (Malone Society Reprints,
London, 1910)).

These two passages are alien, and significantly inferior, in style to the rest of the play and may well have been contributed by the actor who spoke them. The other additions, whether supplied before or during production, argue a professional pen. It would be reasonable to suppose that the reviser, even after he had submitted his finished work, would be ready to furnish additional matter as required, and that, if the new material needed were integral to the play, he would be approached before anyone else as the man most familiar with its details. There is, in other words, no point in multiplying hypotheses: we should probably assume, unless there were clear evidence to the contrary, that all the interpolated matter, regardless of the likely circumstances of its interpolation, was contributed by the same hand.

Among the additions are two which offer indications of the approximate date at which they were written, hence of the approximate date by which the text had been revised and the play revived in the theatre. These indications are, no doubt, slight, but in the absence of any other evidence they are by no means too slight to be worth examining. One clue occurs in the course of the Fool's 'prophecy' (III.ii.79–96), a passage which appears to have been interpolated in the theatre; the other is supplied by the addition to Lear's speech on authority (IV.vi.169–74), which probably formed part of the original revision.[12]

The Fool's 'prophecy', as Warburton first observed, falls into two sections: lines 81–4, which evidently apply to the contemporary present, and lines 85–90, which refer to a Utopian future. Warburton was doubtless right in supposing that of the two concluding couplets one, though it must surely be the first (ll. 91–2) and not the second as he surmised, rightly belongs at the end of the first section (after line 84).[13] If his interpretation of the first section (that it alludes to current circumstances) is correct, as it is generally understood to be, then the lines are full of interest. The allusions seem by no means too vague to be traceable to topical matters.

---

12 The lines, though manifestly written as verse, appear in F as prose. It might in other circumstances be argued that, being added in the theatre, they were placed in the margin of the prompt-book and there laid out so unclearly that the compositor mistook them for prose. But the fact is that the *whole speech*, of which these lines form part, is printed as prose. The error appears to be the copyist's (see p. 118, n.10); if so, the additional lines must have appeared in the text handed him by the reviser.

13 I cite Warburton's comment from Duthie's New Cambridge edition (p. 203): 'The judicious reader will observe . . . that this is not *one* but *two* prophecies. The first, a satyrical description of the *present manners as future*: And the second, a satyrical description of *future manners, which the corruption of the present would prevent from ever happening.*' Duthie observes that lines 91–2 'are set as a single line in F, which suggests a marginal

Despite which, I do not know, I confess, what may be made of the priests or   121
the brewers in the first couplet. The second, however, contains an apparently
unambiguous reference to a well-known circumstance of James I's reign:

> When Nobles are their Taylors Tutors,
> No Heretiques burn'd, but wenches Sutors;

Edward Wightman and Bartholomew Legate, the last heretics to be burned in
England, went to the stake in 1612. Naturally, some years would go by before it
began to be realised that they were the last. It was not, in fact, until 1618 that a
royal reprieve confirmed the final abandonment of a barbarous practice. The
Church historian Frere observes: '. . . it is a sign of the gradual growth of
toleration in matters of religious belief that, when next such treatment came
into question, public opinion had so far grown as to prevent any further
repetition of it, and in 1618 the King reprieved a Portuguese ex-monk who, on
a charge of blasphemy, had been handed over to the sherriffs to be burnt'.[14]

It seems reasonable to infer, then, that the observation implicit in *No
Heretiques burn'd* would make little sense before 1612, or for some time after, and
that it would not altogether pass for apt or accurate until the latter part of 1618
(the crucial reprieve having been granted in the spring).[15]

insertion'. I agree. The single-line
setting is not an attempt to save
space: the passage appears at the
head of the first column of page
rr3, a page which elsewhere shows
no sign whatever of crowding or
compression. The book-keeper, in
writing out the interpolated speech
(perhaps on a separate slip), must
have accidentally omitted this
couplet and inserted it later in the
margin without showing its
division into two lines. The
compositor then committed a
double error in setting the two
lines as one and inserting them at
the wrong point.

14   W. H. Frere, *The English Church in
the Reigns of Elizabeth and James I
(A History of the English Church*,
vol. V) (London, 1904), p. 371.

15   The pun on *burn'd* customarily
noted by editors (to burn = to
infect with venereal disease, this

sense applying of course to the
'wenches' suitors') raises the
possibility that a similar
double-entendre is intended by the
word *Taylors* in the preceding line.
The clearest candidate, however,
for the object of any such improper
allusion in the 1610s would be the
King himself, who affected to
tutor his favourites. In 1607 or
1608 he had given daily
instruction in Latin to Robert
Carr, and from 1614 onwards
Carr's successor, George Villiers,
received much the same
schoolmasterly attentions (see
G. P. V. Akrigg, *Jacobean Pageant*
(London, 1962), pp. 206–7).
Perhaps the word *Nobles* is a
cautious euphemism for *Princes*. A
hint so dark, however, could not
be caught with any pretence to
confidence. I leave a more obvious
solution, if there is one, to scholars
better versed in the *minutiae* of
Jacobean history.

122   The interpolated passage IV.vi.169–74 has already been briefly discussed (see above, pp. 68 ff.). Seen in context, it is curiously beside the point, dealing as it does with the judicial immunity of the rich, and the power of the King to confer that immunity, in the middle of a speech the theme of which is the *hypocrisy* of judicial authority. The idea that the rich enjoy a special protection is of course suggested by the phrase *robes and furd-gownes hides all*. But the point of that phrase is that the trappings of *judges* (not the rich at large, who are not particularly to be associated with 'robes and furred gowns') cover the same human frailties that those judges presume to condemn. It implies not a complaint against unjust privilege but a protest, more fundamental and more bitter, against the very recognition of judicial authority. The attack on privilege is thus introduced not only irrelevantly, but anti-climactically.

The inappropriateness of the interpolation in a speech which, as it stands in Q, requires no expansion not only reveals it as an interpolation but strongly suggests that it was introduced for a purpose. It does not contribute to the advancement of the action; it obscures, by its irrelevance, the idea developed in the rest of the speech; and it is almost startlingly inconsistent with the character of Lear, who is required to utter it. One finds it difficult, therefore, to avoid the conclusion that the point of the passage lies outside the play, that is, in topical reference of some kind. The reviser, one may imagine, saw the tenor of Lear's speech as bearing in general on some subject of contemporary concern and seized on the opportunity for including a more particular and telling reference to it even if it proved not altogether *à propos* in the context.

The additional lines run (they are not aligned as verse in F):

> Place {i.e. *Plate*} sinnes with Gold, and the strong Lance of Iustice, hurtlesse breakes: Arme it in ragges, a Pigmies straw do's pierce it. None do's offend, none, I say none, Ile able 'em; take that of me my Friend, who haue the power to seale th'accusers lips.

The underlying ideas, it will readily be seen, are: (a) that the rich are proof against the law, whereas (b) the poor have no defence against it; that the King (c) can uphold any criminal (with the implication: even the worst) and (d) has the power, if necessary, to prevent his prosecution.

The pointers are few, yet, if they have a bearing on contemporary events, it would be difficult to mistake it. The two last suggestions, especially, totally irrelevant as they are to Lear's situation, and at odds (coming from him) with what we know of his character, are entirely in keeping with what was believed in the 1610s of James I. The whole passage, in fact, exactly reflects the interpretation placed by contemporaries upon the King's very ill-judged handling of the most notorious scandal of his reign, namely the Overbury affair.

Sir Thomas Overbury was alleged to have been murdered during his imprisonment in the Tower at the instigation of the Countess of Somerset, with the help of various agents and accomplices. The Earl, her husband and James's reigning favourite, was accused of complicity in the crime. According to the practice of the time, the alleged agents and accessories in the plot — four of them (a fifth case was postponed) — were examined and tried first, before the chief conspirators. All but one were people of modest birth and means. They were all summarily disposed of, the 'gentleman' executed, the others hanged. There then ensued the trial of the Countess, who pleaded guilty, followed by that of the Earl, who refused to admit any part in the crime, but was nevertheless condemned. Both were sentenced to death, and sent to the Tower, ostensibly to await execution. A mere seven weeks later, the Countess received the King's pardon. Sentence on the Earl was never carried out, though he, stubbornly maintaining his innocence, had to wait longer for the royal absolution. Within six years of the trials the couple were given their freedom.

Neither the guilt of the protagonists in the affair nor even indeed the fact of murder was ever, it seems, satisfactorily proved. Yet there was no doubt at the time in the public mind about either. The contrast that appeared between the ruthless treatment of petty criminals and the leniency shown towards murderers of exalted station did not pass unnoticed. That the King had promised the latter clemency if they pleaded guilty was doubtless not generally known, although the Countess was publicly assured as sentence was passed on her that her peers would recommend mercy. The King's prompt redemption, however, of his promise in the case of the Countess appalled contemporary opinion.[16] This was indeed 'abling' the offender. As for the Earl, it was an almost equal outrage that within weeks of his commitment to the Tower the King refused to have him expelled from the Order of the Garter. 'Yt is much spoken of', says John Chamberlain, 'how forraign princes of that order (to let our own passe) can digest to be coupled in societie with a man lawfully and publikely convicted of so fowle a fact . . .'.[17]

16 '. . . yt seemes the common people take not this [the pardon] for goode payment, for on Saterday last the Quene with the Countesse of Darbie, the Lady Ruthen and the Lord Carew comming privatly in coach to see somwhat here in towne, there grew a whispering that yt was the Lady Somerset and her mother, wherupon people flocked together and followed the coach in great numbers rayling and reviling, and abusing the footmen, and putting them all in feare . . .' (John Chamberlain, letter of 20 July 1616, *Letters*, II. 17).

17 *Ibid.*

124   But there were more sinister aspects to the affair which produced far more serious repercussions in public opinion. Long before the Countess came to trial it was being bruited abroad that not all the powerful offenders had been brought to book, and that further crimes were involved. Even the King's name was mentioned. Suspicions against him seem to have persisted: he later found it necessary, it is reported, to swear on his knees before his Council that he had neither knowledge of, nor complicity in, Overbury's murder. The rumours emanated from one principal source: Coke, the Lord Chief Justice, who directed all the early examinations and prosecutions and was nothing if not zealous in the discharge of his duties. At what seems to have been a critical point in his enquiries, the King intervened. The fifth trial in the series, that of Sir Thomas Monson, he commanded to be postponed. The accused, however, was arraigned in due form and Coke took the opportunity, before breaking off the proceedings, to proclaim at length and in open court that further disclosures were impending of a highly sensational kind. The consequences were extraordinary. Monson's trial was deferred yet again, and then forgotten about. He was soon pardoned and released. Coke was never permitted to make his revelations. He was not appointed, as he might have expected, to conduct the trials of the Earl and Countess. His career from that moment went into a decline which, within the year, had reached a nadir of total disgrace.

Though the King's part in these events may well be fully explained and justified, it impressed critical contemporaries very unfavourably. Appearances strongly suggested that he had succeeded in 'sealing the accuser's lips'. Contemporary reaction, as it is illustrated in the memorialists, letter-writers and 'gossips' of the day, is clearly summed up by a modern historian: 'Those who thought poorly of the Crown's case concluded that there must have been some undisclosed facts implicating the King to account for the hesitations of the prosecution and the leniency with which the prisoners were treated afterwards. Moralists who thought the Earl guilty were shocked that the King condoned such wickedness in high places.'[18]

That the King was willing to sanction the crimes of the mighty and, worse still, that he was ready, when he could, to prevent them from coming to light – these were the lessons which, together with the more obvious moral that there existed one law for the rich and another for the poor, were inevitably drawn from an affair which received full publicity and excited intense public interest for the

18   William McElwee, *The Wisest Fool in Christendom: The Reign of King James I and VI* (London, 1958), p. 232.

best part of a year. No other series of events or set of circumstances in the course of James's reign could have given rise to reflections of such a kind in such connection with each other.

It seems, then, not at all improbable that we have to do, in the additional passage at IV.vi.169–74, with covert but (to a contemporary audience) direct and telling allusions to the Overbury affair.[19] If so, we may date the interpolation fairly exactly.

Overbury died, or was murdered, in 1613 ; but the alleged crime was not investigated until two years later. The Somersets were tried and sentenced in May 1616, and in July of the same year the Countess received her pardon. The allusions in the play, if such they are, could not have originated at an earlier date. One need not, on the other hand, assume that they belong to the immediate aftermath of the affair. The series of trials created so much of a sensation that they must have lived longer than is usual in the public memory. They would probably not have ceased to excite interest before the lapse of a year or two.

Of the two passages we have examined one suggests a date close to 1618, the other a date soon after 1616. It is not, of course, essential to suppose that both passages were added to the play at the same time. Indeed, as we have seen, the addition to Lear's speech probably formed part of the reviser's text, whereas the Fool's 'prophecy' must have been added later in the theatre. If the arguments put forward above have any weight, we might conclude, without attempting too

19   Scholars occasionally declare themselves sceptical about the 'hits' at political figures so often alleged to be intended in Elizabethan and Jacobean plays. So strict and punitive a censorship prevailed, it can be argued, that no writer of the time would dare to comment except flatteringly upon the actions and motives of the great. Certainly it can be shown, on the evidence of existing theatrical manuscripts, that the censors could be extremely fussy, suspecting libels where none could conceivably have been intended or sustained. It is as much a fact, on the other hand, that dramatists did comment critically on contemporary affairs and even assail public figures, and that the censors were not always alive to the significance of what they read.

Two celebrated cases vouch for the fact. Neither *The Isle of Dogs* (1597) nor *A Game at Chess* (1624) was banned until it had reached the stage. The then Master of the Revels (responsible for theatrical censorship) must be presumed to have read the first; it is known that his successor of a later day read the second. It is doubtful, in any case, whether the revised version of *Lear* would have been submitted to the Censor. We find Sir Henry Herbert, who performed the functions of Master of the Revels from 1623 onwards, insisting in 1633 that copies of old plays be re-submitted to him before revival. His remarks clearly imply that the practice, if it was ever customary, had, before that date, fallen into disuse.

126 much precision, that the play was revived at some time within the period 1616–20.[20]

This dating squares extremely well with plausible inferences from other facts. Since Shakespeare was not himself responsible for the revision, it must have been commissioned after his retirement (c. 1613) and very possibly after his death in 1616. Furthermore, it is most likely that a revival closely preceded the second edition of the Q text, which appeared in 1619. It might not be too arbitrary, therefore, to limit the date for revision and revival more narrowly to the years 1616–18. No proof is possible in these matters, but that seems a not unlikely guess.[21]

About the identity of the reviser it is scarcely prudent even to guess. Nevertheless, there are certain considerations which restrict speculation. We should expect the leading theatrical company of the day, anxious to rehabilitate a play by their leading playwright, to entrust the task to a writer of some competence. It is obvious, in any case, that the work was, in all important

20 It is interesting to find a contemporary commenting at the beginning of this period on the apparently growing practice of refurbishing old plays for revival. His remarks relate to the plays performed at Court during the Christmas season of 1614–15. 'They have playes at court every night . . . being for the most part such poore stuffe that in stead of delight they send the auditorie away with discontent. Indeed our Poets braines and invention are growne very drie insomuch that of five newe playes there is not one pleases, and therfore they are driven to furbish over theyre old, which stand them in best stead, and bring them most profit.' (John Chamberlain, letter of 5 January 1615: *Letters*, I. 567). The King's Men contributed eight plays to this season.

21 I have developed the argument about dating at some length since I find it interesting that a number of clues, faint and uncertain though they may be, concur in their indications. I should, perhaps, stress that this question is entirely adventitious to the main argument. The material hypothesis, inferred from quite other evidence, is that at some date between 1608 and 1623 the prompt-book of *King Lear* must have been lost and a revision of Q commissioned. Two objections might be levelled against this hypothesis on purely chronological grounds: (a) that a date close to 1608 would lead one to expect that Shakespeare himself had performed the revision which, *ex hypothesi*, he did not; (b) that a date close to 1623 would make it difficult to believe in the survival of the 'copy' for Q which, *ex hypothesi*, did survive and was made use of in the revision. Both objections might be avoided by narrowing somewhat the postulated time-span, and there letting the matter rest. The reader will thus appreciate that, if there are, as I speculatively propose, indications of a positive kind to fix the date more precisely, they serve merely to confirm suppositions about chronology which are not, by themselves, exceptionable.

respects, efficiently performed. More probably than not the man approached 127 was one who had himself contributed to the company's repertoire. His credentials are likely to have consisted in some previous or current professional connection with the company.

At the period in question the obvious candidates are Jonson, Fletcher and Massinger. The first two exclude themselves on grounds of style: neither could have written the additions to *Lear* without producing a much stronger effect of inconsistency than is in fact apparent. Massinger, on the other hand, is known now, and may well have been known then, as a passable neo-Shakespearean. He had already acquired some standing, collaborating with Fletcher and others in plays some at least of which were written for the King's Men. There is good evidence for believing that he was also engaged, at precisely this period, in revising and 'reforming' old plays, no doubt to supplement his income.[22] I do not propose his name with any great confidence. But it is not at least inconceivable that it was he who undertook the revision of *King Lear*.[23]

22 See T. A. Dunn, *Philip Massinger* (London, 1957), pp. 15–16, for evidence relating to Massinger's earliest years as a playwright, a 'period of collaboration and hackwork' from about 1613 onwards into the early 1620s; and pp. 24–7 and 267 for a summary of what is known, or may be inferred, about his work as a reviser of plays. (See also Bentley, *Profession*, pp. 239–40, for evidence not cited by Dunn.)

23 Besides the interesting evidence that Massinger was at the appropriate date employed in the revision of plays, other considerations, though rather less objective ones, might be adduced in support of my suggestion. Dunn's analysis of Massinger's style reveals much that is remarkably consistent with what has been observed here of the reviser's work. Massinger's plays abound in Shakespearean echoes, 'verbal or phrasal recalls and parallels in thought and image. They are so common as to be one of the Massingerian stigmata and lead us to the inevitable conclusion that Massinger must have been a very close student indeed of Shakespeare's work . . .' (*op. cit.*, p. 203). In respect of its fluency and dignity, at least, Massinger's style is not very clearly distinguishable from Shakespeare's less impassioned vein. But its faults are, perhaps, more characteristic, and more interesting in the present context. Dunn comments at length on Massinger's involuted syntax, his fondness especially for periodic sentences and for every kind of parenthetic construction (*ibid.*, pp. 214ff). The examples he gives of this mannerism parallel very closely, in their stiltedness and tortuosity, the addition in the F text of *Lear* at III.i.22–9 (see above p. 75). Massinger displays too, as Dunn notes, 'a logical and methodical turn, a necessity to get everything cut-and-dried, a vein of pedantry' (*ibid.*, p. 232) – precisely the characteristics noticed here in the reviser's alterations. The reviser's predilection for a smooth-running style might also be Massinger's, about whose fastidiousness it is observed: 'every sentence says what

128   The textual history of F does not quite conclude with its modification in the theatre. There is no indication that further revision was carried out in the printing house or at the behest of the editors of the Folio. (Indeed the state of the Folio texts in general does not suggest that the 'copy' received was subjected to any very careful scrutiny.) But further changes and corruptions inevitably took place at the hands of the printers: changes to the 'accidentals' of the text (spelling, punctuation, capitalisation) and corruptions in its readings, traceable to the compositor's occasional difficulty in deciphering the copy or to accidents in the setting of type.

The most important and interesting changes, however, were brought about by the reconstitution, or partial reconstitution, of the copy in the printing house. Not that the variants which resulted from this proceeding are either very numerous or very significant — indeed most of them are quite valueless. But they have set a puzzle for textual critics which has never been satisfactorily solved. We cannot hope, therefore, fully to explain the characteristics of the F text without pursuing its progress somewhat further, that is, into the printers' workshop. In doing so we shall at last be taking up the question, first broached in Chapter One, of the apparent affinities between F and Q2.

it means to say and says it with a regard for verbal usage and grammatical and syntactical orthodoxy' (ibid., p. 217). I do not wish to labour what must remain, from the nature of the evidence, a weak argument. One final point may be worth mentioning. If we assume, as has been argued here, that the additional passage at IV.vi.169–74 alludes to the Overbury affair, it is not inconsistent with what we know of Massinger to suppose that he may have felt strongly enough on the subject to contrive, somewhat clumsily, a reference to it. We do not know enough, certainly, to speak of his political loyalties at this time, yet he was connected indirectly through his father (a retainer of the Herbert family) with one of the leading contemporary figures at James's court, the Earl of Pembroke, whose party were the bitter enemies of the Somerset faction. It would not, in the circumstances, be surprising to find him amongst those who voiced indignation at the corruptions of justice which spared Somerset's life.

CHAPTER EIGHT
THE RELATIONSHIP BETWEEN F AND Q2

We saw in Chapter One that Q2, although it appears to be merely a reprint of Q1, displays a large number of variants. Some of these may be attributed to error in the printing house, but the majority are obviously the result of a calculated attempt to improve the text.

Not only the readings received attention. Q2 is much neater typographically than its predecessor. It shows a more generous use of space, hence a clearer lay-out (except on the last few pages: here the compositor was forced to compress his copy so that he finished the text on the last leaf of the quire). Capitals and italics are somewhat more liberally and more rationally employed than in Q1. Punctuation is very much improved: errors are corrected and a greater diversity of stops replaces Q1's ubiquitous commas. Many misprints are emended, as are most spelling mistakes, and a rather more up-to-date system of spelling is adopted generally.[1] This evidence of care in polishing the surface of the text lends some weight to the theory that the collection of Quartos of which Q2 forms part represents a first, abortive attempt to issue the plays of Shakespeare in a comprehensive collected edition.[2]

Also consistent with the theory are the unmistakable signs of editing in Q2. Attempts have been made here and there to correct line-arrangement, speech-prefixes or stage-directions which in Q1 are obviously faulty. Readings are emended, if not always happily; on occasions a word is added or deleted to perfect the sense. Details are freely altered, though not as frequently as in F: we find an occasional substitution of 'he' for 'a', or 'if' for 'and', but for the most part these 'indifferent' changes consist in the contraction of certain locutions (e.g. *where's* for *where is*) and the expansion of contractions. There are, besides, a variety of more important changes which we shall later examine in detail.[3]

---

1 The following spellings, for example, and all those analogous to them, are consistently altered: *maister* to *master*; *graund* to *grand*; *cary* to *carry*; *drawen* to *drawne*; *hould* to *hold*; *nise* to *nice*; *cursse* to *curse*.

2 Greg (*Folio*, p. 13) suggests that Pavier may have intended to gauge the probable success of such a venture with a preliminary batch of ten plays.

3 D. F. Mackenzie found it difficult to decide whether a series of very similar changes in Q2 of *The Merchant of Venice* (another of the Pavier Quartos) was due to compositorial negligence or to deliberate revision of the copy, though he inclined to the former supposition ('Compositor B's role in *The Merchant of Venice* Q2 (1619)', *Studies in Bibliography*, XII (1959), pp. 75–90. Many of the changes in both Q2 *Merchant* and

130   Apart from these calculated alterations we find, as is only to be expected, a series
of fresh errors, chiefly misprints and omissions.

It is generally accepted that Q2 was printed from a copy of Q1 in which sheets
D, G and H stood in the uncorrected state. The evidence is indeed very clear on
this point. The uncorrected readings on these sheets nearly all recur unchanged
in Q2.

It is sometimes suggested, furthermore, that Q2 may reflect the variant state
of yet another Q1 sheet, or rather forme, I outer, which in the extant copies of
Q1 shows no variation. On the last page of this forme (I4^v) Q1 ascribes two
successive speeches to Lear (IV.vi.198–201 and 202–4). The repetition of the
prefix makes it clear that they are intended as separate speeches. F prints both
speeches (somewhat revised) as one, but it is quite likely that the anomaly in Q1
signifies the accidental omission of a line or lines of which the F reviser had no
knowledge. Q1's separate speeches reappear in Q2 with the interesting addition
of a further speech placed between them (*Gent.* Good Sir). The question arises
whether this brief addition in Q2 represents (a) a corrected version of the text, of
which Q1 shows the uncorrected counterpart, or (b) an uncorrected version
(since the additional speech, set at the latter end of a line of print, may have been
accidentally eliminated while corrections to the Q1 page were in progress), or (c)
merely an editorial interpolation (since it would have appeared as obvious to the
editor of Q2 as it does to us that something was probably missing from Q1).

The balance of probabilities favours the third alternative. If Q2 does reproduce a variant state (corrected or uncorrected) of outer I, we should certainly
expect to find corroborative evidence elsewhere in that portion of Q2 which
derives from the same Q1 forme. None, however, is discoverable. None,
certainly, of further *corrections*. A pair of Q2 errors, *beake* for *beach* and *aboue* for *a
boui* (from page I2^v in Q1), might be construed as further relics of *uncorrected* Q1.
But it is very slight evidence, and is, besides, more readily susceptible of a
different explanation (see below, pp. 153ff.).

It is a curious fact that a remarkably high proportion of Q2 variants reappear
in F. This has encouraged certain critics to believe that Q2 must have played a

Q2 *Lear* could no doubt be
attributed to the compositor's
carelessness in reading or
memorising copy. But I am
reluctant to believe that changes
involving an appreciation of
meaning (substitu.ions,
sophistications, corrections) would
often occur to a compositor, unless
the evidence in his copy of error,
or apparent error, both leapt to the
eye and suggested some obvious
remedy. Mackenzie acknowledges,
somewhat against the drift of his
argument, that changes to stage
directions and speech-prefixes in
The Merchant of Venice 'have all the
characteristics of planned rather
than impromptu editing' (p. 76).

part in the transmission of the text, whether because the F compositor consulted it occasionally, or because his copy was composed partly of Q2 pages imperfectly corrected.[4]

That F is in some way related to Q2 seems indisputable. Nevertheless the views advanced so far do not adequately explain the relationship – partly because they are based on a rather uncritical appraisal of the evidence, but partly too because they assume highly unlikely practical procedures as the means by which one text was brought into relation with the other.

Let us start with the evidence. The first step must be to discount a great deal of it as merely speciously relevant. Q2 and F were produced by the same printer, William Jaggard, within the space of four years. We should expect near-contemporaneous products of the same printing house to show a considerable similarity in their surface features. It is therefore not particularly significant that the punctuation in F, which carries the improvements initiated in Q2 several stages further, frequently agrees with Q2 against Q1. Such coincidences are easily explained if we assume that the F compositors re-punctuated the Q1 text on the same principles as their colleagues of Q2, but in general more assiduously. The same goes for spelling. The style adopted in F is very close to, though not identical with, the one favoured in Q2. Both are comparatively remote from the old-fashioned style of Q1. Agreements between F and Q2 against Q1 are accordingly to be counted by the score.

F and Q2, again, are both edited texts, and, in one or two minor respects, edited along identical lines. Obvious misprints are emended in both, small functional words supplied or deleted as required by sense or metre, common colloquial locutions expanded or contracted according to taste. In both texts such minor changes are frequent, especially so in F. It is unsurprising, therefore, that on several occasions their revisions coincide, particularly when we take it into account that F, with its far greater number of small alterations, more often than not *disagrees* with the changes in Q2.

Much of the apparent similarity between the texts must, therefore, be disregarded, not of course because we can be sure that it is purely coincidental but because it could be plausibly explained as the product of coincidental purposes and procedures. It is unreliable as evidence.

There remains, however, a small residue of identical readings, agreements between F and Q2 against Q1, which it would be much more difficult to explain away as in the nature of things predictable. They consist of (a) common

4 Doran, *Text*, pp. 109ff. (Q2 consulted); A. S. Cairncross, 'The Quartos and the Folio Text of *King Lear*', *Review of English Studies*, VI (1955), pp. 252–8 (Q2 copy).

132 anomalies of spelling, (b) common omissions apparently unprompted by the context, (c) common interpolations apparently unnecessary to sense or metre and (d) common substitutions where the original requires no emendation. I list them below according to category, alongside their parallels in Q1:

		Q1	Q2	F
(a)	I.iv.4	raz'd (C3^v)	raizd (B4^v)	raiz'd
	II.iii.4	vnusuall (E3)	vnusall (D4^v)	vnusall[5]
(b)	II.ii.158	Come my good Lord away? (E2^v)	Come my Lord, away. (D4^v)	Come my Lord, away.
	V.iii.250	the Captaine (L3)	om. (L3)	om.[6]
(c)	I.iv.33	canst doe? (C3^v)	canst thou do? (B4^v)	canst thou do?
	I.iv.151	Doo'st know (C4^v)	Dost thou know (C2)	Do'st thou know
	IV.vii.59	Pray doe not mocke, (K2^v)	Pray do not mocke me: (K2)	Pray do not mocke me:
(d)	I.iv.111	on's (C4^v)	ones (C1^v)	ones[7]
	IV.vi.236	durst (K1)	darst (I4)	Dar'st
	V.iii.155	stople (L2)	stop (L2)	stop

5 These are not merely variant spellings but genuine anomalies. *Race* and *rase* occur in F as alternatives for *raze*, but no other instance appears of *raize*. *Vsuall* and *vnusuall* do not vary.

6 I exclude the common F/Q2 omission of IV.vi.276a: *and for you her owne for* Venter. The phrase makes no sense in Q1 and it is not at all unlikely that the editors of Q2 and F would omit it independently for that reason. (It is, incidentally, omitted from the Globe and subsequent modern editions.) In both Q2 and F the omission has prompted a doctoring of the syntax in the immediately preceding portion of the sentence and F's method here is, significantly, quite different from that of Q2:

Q1: your wife (so I would say) your affectionate seruant

Q2: Your wife (so I would say) & your affectionate seruant,

F: *Your (Wife, so I would say) affectionate Seruant.*

7 An agreement in error. The context reveals that Q1 is perfectly correct and that *on's* stands for *of his*: *Why for taking on's part, that's out of fauour* . . . For *on's = of his* see, three lines further down, I.iv.114: *why this fellow hath banisht two on's daughters*. For the common practice of following a verbal noun with pleonastic *of* see Abbott § 178, and, for a further example in *Lear*, II.i.40–1 (Q: *Here stood he . . . warbling of wicked charms*).

A few further cases must be regarded as somewhat more doubtful evidence: 133

(a)	I.i.166	Physicion (B3)	Physition (A4)	Physition
	I.i.270	farewell (B4ᵛ)	farwell (B1ᵛ)	farwell
	III.iv.2	tyrannie (G1)	tirrany (F3)	tirrany
	V.iii.159	arraine (L2)	araign (L2)	araigne

(These spellings must be considered unusual in F though they are not un-exampled in the F texts of other plays. All other apparently anomalous spellings shared between Q2 and F, one or two of which have been cited in the past as significant evidence, are in fact quite normal in the Folio. Examples are *prize* (for *price*), *pezant, rellish.*)

The following appear more doubtful still:

(d)	I.ii.148	sith (C2ᵛ)	sigh (B3ᵛ)	sighe
	V.iii.292	So thinke I	So I thinke	I so I thinke
		to (L4)	too (L4)	

(Of the first of these two substitutions it might be said that both editors predictably prefer the more modern form of the word. Though both forms are, in fact, of ancient descent, and though the form *sithe* was still current in the seventeenth century, it was arguably at this time dropping out of everyday usage. The second substitution is more complex. It will be seen that F prefers in part the word-order of Q2 (*I thinke*) to that of Q1, but that this alteration in F is associated with a re-formation of the whole sentence of which there is no hint in Q2. It might plausibly be argued that the reading in F is just as likely to have originated in Q1, since if *So thinke I to* were changed to *I so thinke I* the next obvious step, on grounds of euphony, would be a further alteration to *I so I thinke*.)

In addition to this list a single common emendation might be advanced as possibly significant, though one may think it somewhat too obviously sug-gested by the original error to count as conclusive. At IV.i.10 Q1a (H2) reads *poorlie, leed.* Q2 (H1) alters this to *poorely led* and is followed to the letter by F, though in F the subsequent comma becomes, more correctly, a mark of interrogation.

Eleven sets of variants constitute the significant evidence. A further seven may be put forward with less confidence, the last three very tentatively. There is no abundance of facts, but they are quite sufficient to prove that F is in some way associated with Q2.

134   Let us consider the possibilities in turn. We may summarily rule out the hypothesis that Q2 was in some way derived from F, or from the copy supplied to the printers of F: the evidence of every line shows unequivocally that its editor knew nothing of F. The possibility that F was derived solely from Q2, or rather that a copy of Q2 was used by the reviser as the sole basis of his text, must also be dismissed: agreements between F and Q1 against Q2 are very frequent. Let us continue to suppose, however, that the manuscript copy for Q1 was available to the reviser, but that he used it in marking up a copy of *Q2*. There still remain unexplained the clearest traces of *printed* Q1 in F. Anomalous spellings, for example, not found in Q2: *weild* at I.i.56 (Q2: *wield*), *hizzing* at III.vi.17 (Q1: *hiszing*; Q2: *hissing*); the survival of a press-corrector's sophistication in F at I.iv.366 (*at task for*), whereas Q2 at this point reprints Qa (*alapt*); and, most significant of all, the mislineation of V.iii.46–7, lines which are correctly divided in Q2.[8]

Are we, then, to assume that the copy for F derived partly from Q1 and partly from Q2? There seems no alternative,[9] yet there are difficulties involved in the supposition. It remains, at all events, no more than a guess unless we can find acceptable answers to the questions it immediately raises: why should two copies of the text be used, and how, when, and by whom were they combined?

Somewhat improbably it is the evidence of punctuation which provides a clue. Indeed, a close comparison of the punctuation in the three texts virtually, as will emerge, resolves the problem. Let us start by examining the punctuation of Q2.

8   This page of Q2, being derived from Q1b (K4ᵛ), contains the phrase *and appointed guard* missing from Q1a and from F, consequently enough material for two complete lines. But the point is that, in contrast to Q2, Qa and Qb misalign the passage, Qa printing its one and a half lines, and Qb its two lines, as one. F, whether it derives directly from Qa at this point, or indirectly from Qb (which would imply that the words *and appointed guard* were deliberately re-omitted — see Appendix B2a, p. 237 below), repeats the error of lineation, printing one and a half lines as one.

9   I do not take seriously Miss Doran's suggestion that the F compositors 'consulted' Q2 occasionally. Apart from the implausibility inherent in the notion of seventeenth-century compositors looking up doubtful readings in a second version of their copy (with never a scene-division, much less a line-numbering to help them locate the object of their search), no compositor, then or now, would go to this trouble in order to copy a spelling mistake. Agreement between F and Q2 in spelling and other errors (e.g. omissions) is also enough to rule out any possibility that Q2 was 'consulted' by the reviser, whether systematically or sporadically.

We have noticed that it is more elaborate and more correct than that of Q1. Indeed, the number of errors retained (where the text is comprehensible) is small.[10] On sheets A to H (inclusive) of Q2 the punctuation remains fairly light, and diverges relatively little from that of Q1: commas are redistributed, several are added and some dropped; question-marks are supplied where necessary; and a few semi-colons introduced to separate sentences and to mark the heavier pauses, though by no means according to any consistent principle. Sheets I and K, on the other hand, present a different picture. Not only is a much larger number of stops added to those in Q1 (which may be partly an effect of the scantier punctuation in the earlier text at the end of the play) but a qualitative difference is strikingly apparent. Colons and full-stops appear in quantity for the first time. Whereas on the earlier sheets they are heavily out-numbered by semi-colons, being absent altogether from long stretches of the text – it should be remembered that these remarks apply to *additional* stops in Q2 – the proportion is now reversed. The effect is, of course, of a far more thoroughly punctuated text.

So marked is the contrast between the two sections of the book that we can only assume it was brought about by a change of compositor.[11]

10 i.e. errors of positioning (due allowance made for the differences between seventeenth-century practice and our own). It is hazardous to pronounce on errors in the choice of stop in an early printed text.

11 The second compositor was first noticed by Madeleine Doran (*Text*, pp. 132–4). Her discovery has been confirmed by a detailed analysis of punctuation, spelling and other features of the text in J. F. Andrews, 'The Pavier Quartos of 1619 – Evidence for Two Compositors' (Vanderbilt, 1971, an unpublished dissertation, most of which is devoted to a study of the *Lear* quarto). Andrews's analysis is somewhat vitiated by an unexplained reluctance on his part to examine the data page by page. Instead he compares statistical totals for two blocks of the text, confining himself to testing Miss Doran's hypothesis that one compositor set all of sheets A–H, and another all of sheets I–K. He overlooks in consequence the real possibility that one compositor may have set isolated pages (or perhaps half-formes) in the block attributed to the other. Had any such interventions occurred, of course, the data signalling them would be entirely obscured in the comprehensive totals calculated for the block. It seems possible, in fact, that pages H1^v and H2 were set not by the first compositor but the second. These pages show the differentiating pattern of punctuation; they show, too, the spelling *Gloster* and the appearance of proper names in roman instead of italic type which are among the marks of the second compositor's work. There can be no doubt, however, that in the main Andrews's conclusions are correct, and that they supersede, as Andrews claims they do, the findings of W. S. Kable (see 'Compositor B, the Pavier Quartos, and Copy Spellings', *Studies in*

136   Just as the punctuation of Q1 is largely carried over into Q2, where it is elaborated and extended, so is the punctuation of Q2 largely assimilated into F. At first sight the two later texts seem to stand in the same relation as the two earlier: the punctuation of F is heavier than that of Q2, and more correct, but it does not differ significantly in the positioning, at least, of the stops.

It was settled earlier that frequent agreement between F and Q2 in the matter of pointing is hardly remarkable in that they were printed at the same shop within a few years of each other: a general similarity (in comparison with Q1, a much earlier and less well-produced text) is bound to be apparent. But it may be otherwise if we are to investigate the extent to which F *exactly repeats* the stops discovered to be added or altered in Q2 when we compare Q2 with Q1. Coincidence, of course, in supplying obvious deficiencies – question-marks omitted by Q1, or full-stops at the end of speeches – would not be significant. But we should expect the choice of stops marking pauses in mid-paragraph, whether verse or prose, to show independent patterns in F and Q2 if they were printed independently of each other. It is quite clear that no hard-and-fast rules were applied at the time to the use of these stops, and that their selection was left more or less to taste. Hence, an agreement between F and Q2 in the choice, let us say, of a semi-colon to replace a Q1 comma (in preference to a colon, a full-stop or no change at all) could scarcely be regarded as predictable. Any large number of such agreements over a given portion of text must in fact constitute very good evidence for that portion of the influence of Q2 on F.

In conducting a comparison on this basis we must, of course, ignore all the stops added by F over and above those added in Q2. F is more elaborately punctuated throughout, and the extra stops tell us nothing to the purpose. We must equally ignore agreements between F and Q2 when both agree with Q1. Our attention must be focused on the stops in Q2 which show disagreement with Q1, and the extent to which these additions or alterations reappear unchanged in F.

Details of the comparison are presented in Appendix D1, p. 257 below. The

Bibliography, XXI (1968), pp. 131–61), who maintained that a single compositor was responsible for this, as for the other, Pavier quartos. Kable has been as effectively challenged by P. W. M. Blayney (' "Compositor B" and the Pavier Quartos: Problems of Identification and their Implications', *The Library*, 5th series, XXVII (1972), pp. 179–206), who agrees with Andrews in detecting the hands of two compositors. Though Blayney originally suggested a somewhat different division of compositorial stints, he has recently conceded the greater detail and accuracy of Andrews's analysis ('The Compositors of the Pavier Quartos', *The Library*, 5th series, XXXI (1976), pp. 143–5).

reader, if he will turn to examine it, will see almost at a glance that it shows an alternating pattern. In certain sections of the text the punctuation peculiar to Q2 is carried over into F with little or no change; in the remainder the correspondence is much less close, indeed might have resulted simply from chance. The parts of the text which most faithfully reproduce the pointing of Q2 coincide exactly with pages of F set by compositor E before quire ss, and with the five pages of quire ss at the end of the play. Pages set by compositor B before quire ss all show a punctuation approximating much less closely to that of Q2.[12]

Whatever may be the conclusions to be drawn from this pattern as a whole, it appears clear from the first that compositor E must have been using a specimen of Q2 as his copy. The resemblance in punctuation on his pages of F to that of Q2 is much too close to be put down to chance. No other assumption will do: it would be absurd to suppose that the pointing of Q2 was transferred meticulously to a copy of Q1, or to a manuscript, before being reproduced (and further expanded) in the text of F. Naturally, it follows that, in setting quire ss, *both* compositors were using Q2 copy.

There is further evidence to bear out this conclusion. Q1 uses brackets four times; Q2 repeats these and adds a further six, all of which are repeated in F on the pages we are concerned with. Brackets, since their use in place of commas was largely dictated by whim, and since they occur so rarely in this text, are an especially good index of connection. We find, too, that certain errors and anomalies in the Q2 punctuation are transferred to F – again, on these pages only. Finally, of the fourteen readings shared between F and Q2 which we have isolated as most likely to be significant, all occur on these same pages,[13] with the exception of one which will require special comment later.

The evidence, therefore, dictates – which is not putting it too strongly – that the pages of the F text set by compositor E, and also those on quire ss set by compositor B, were derived from Q2 copy. Naturally the specimen employed would have to be corrected by reference to a master copy, so that a number of F/Q1 coincidences in readings on these pages is easily enough explained.

What of the pages before quire ss set by compositor B? It cannot, of course, be concluded that he was *not* using Q2 copy simply because he incorporates into his

---

12 The Folio text of *Lear*, set by the compositors customarily identified as 'B' and 'E', occupies ten pages of quire qq, the whole (twelve pages) of quire rr, and five pages of quire ss. Chapter 9, pp. 141–57 below, presents the relevant details in full.

13 See Appendix D4, p. 276 below. The fourteen readings include the anomalous spellings cited as 'somewhat more doubtful evidence'. The remaining, 'still more doubtful', F/Q2 agreements prove to be coincidental.

138   text many fewer of Q2's peculiarities. He may have given himself a much freer hand than E in composing from printed copy: if he were a more experienced compositor, as Hinman maintains,[14] this would be very likely. The fact, however, that he demonstrates for a time his independence of Q2 (on pages before quire ss) but thereafter adheres to it as closely as compositor E (on pages of quire ss) suggests strongly that he did not set from the same copy throughout. At the end of quire rr he must have changed to Q2 from some other version of the text. The evidence, in fact, shows this particularly clearly. The change occurs at a point late in the text, beyond that at which the second Q2 compositor replaced the first: his more lavish punctuation supplies copious data which enable a very pronounced transformation to appear in the record of B's agreements with him.

B's pages before quire ss show no connection at all with Q2 — no shared readings, no common anomalies or errors of punctuation. Some apparent exceptions (on page qq6^v) we shall consider later. The signs are, rather, of derivation from Q1: frequent agreement in erroneous punctuation, or in punctuation manifestly inferior to that of Q2; and coincidence, too, in a few irregular readings which could not have been imported into Q2 as 'corrections' to replace their obviously correct equivalents there.[15]

That B's copy, however, was not a specimen of Q1 itself but a manuscript derived from Q1 is evidenced by the frequent manuscript misreadings discoverable on his pages. These are, of course, the misreadings we considered in an earlier chapter. A few appear anomalously on pages set by compositor E — another irregularity we must examine in due course — but it is noticeably compositor B who is responsible for the vast majority.[16]

It is tempting to find corroboration in data of another kind for the assumption that B was setting from manuscript copy; but it must be admitted that the remaining evidence is ambiguous. B's pages show certain well-defined characteristics absent from E's, e.g. a tendency to substitute full stops for Q1 dashes and marks of exclamation, and a disposition to continue in roman type when setting names. (E's text shows one instance only of a name in roman, 'Gloster' on page ss2^v, but in this it reproduces Q2.) It might be argued that such divergences from copy would be unlikely if B were setting from print. One or two instances, however, occur on the pages (of quire ss) which he did set from print – enough to prove that his eccentricities were habitual. One small part of

---

14   See *Printing*, I. 214ff., for a review of the evidence indicating that compositor E was an apprentice in Jaggard's shop.

15   Details will be found in Appendices D2 and D4, pp. 268 and 276 below.

16   See Appendix D4, p. 276 below.

this evidence is perhaps more significant. The spelling *Gloucester*, not found in Q1, appears seven times in the F text (as against thirty-six occurrences of *Gloster* or *Glouster*). On all seven occasions it appears in B's pages prior to quire ss. Furthermore, on six out of the seven it occurs in a *stage direction*. Since it is most unlikely to have been a habit of B's to reserve a particular spelling for stage directions only, it is possible that we have here a direct reflection of manuscript copy. Stage directions here and there in the prompt-book may well (as in extant manuscripts) have been recopied in the margin, or across the page, by a book-keeper – one, in this case, who used the spelling *Gloucester*. If so, it is very likely that the rest of the manuscript showed *Gloster*, the spelling of Q1. To this spelling B twice reverts in stage directions and four times in the body of the text,[17] though his own favoured spelling (fourteen instances) is *Glouster*.[18]

We have arrived so far at the hypothesis that underlying compositor B's pages on quires qq and rr is a manuscript version of the text derived from Q1, and that the rest of the copy was set from a copy of Q2, suitably altered. It needs, perhaps, no lengthy argument eliminating unlikely alternatives to enable us to conclude that the specimen of Q2 was altered by reference to the manuscript employed by B, and that this preparation of the copy was effected in the printing house. We must otherwise suppose that a composite version of the text was delivered to the printers, part of it based on Q1, and part on Q2. No such copy, however, could have originated with the reviser. He would have no conceivable reason for adopting now one edition now another as the basis of his revision. Nor could he quite fortuitously have hit upon a method of alternating between the two so as exactly to anticipate the printers' requirement of a copy divided in certain proportions and at certain points. Nor indeed could he, or anyone else, have provided an appropriately divided copy *ad hoc* during the printing, since a complete copy would be required for casting off before it could be settled how appropriately to divide it. We have reason, of course, to think, in any case, that the reviser had completed his work, that, in other words, the reconstituted prompt-book of the play was in existence, before the publication of Q2.

How then, however, do we explain the peculiar circumstances of the case? Why was a copy of Q2 brought into play, and the extensive labour undertaken of collating a large part of it with a manuscript which might have done duty throughout? I can think of only one explanation which appears reasonable. The

17 One of these contracted spellings
    may be explained as necessitated
    by a full line of print.

18 In *Richard II* and *Richard III*, too,
    Glouster is B's favoured spelling.
    Not so in the Henry VI plays,
    where for reasons not readily
    determinable we find him
    preferring *Gloster*.

140 prompt-book was supplied to the printers on loan, and perhaps for a limited time. Being a 'clean' copy of the play it would serve admirably for casting-off. But it must surely have been bound, however sketchily, inside a cover, so as to prevent the mislaying of loose sheets, and for the same reason its dismemberment in the printing house would surely have been prohibited. If such, or something like it, were the case, a second copy would have to be prepared, since the two compositors were required to work simultaneously on different portions of the text. A copy of Q2, the latest edition, and one produced in the same shop, would naturally come to hand for the purpose.

What, however, of the difficulties of setting from heavily corrected copy, which must have proved seriously if not impossibly inconvenient? It seems, as we shall see, that the problem was not entirely overcome though it was, as far as possible, circumvented. Punctuation was left to the compositor, who, as the evidence shows, merely elaborated for the most part upon what he found in Q2: the copy, therefore, would be free of alterations to the stops. Minor corrections and additions could be accommodated in the margins, as on proofs. The worst problems would be presented by the extensive relineation of verse passages and by substantial or frequent interpolations. Matters were so arranged, however, that those portions of the text which would entail especially heavy correction of the printed copy were left, wherever possible, to compositor B who held the manuscript. The procedure adopted can be traced in some detail, as the following chapter will attempt to show.

CHAPTER NINE
THE DISTRIBUTION OF F 'COPY'

The copy for F was divided between compositors B and E as shown in the table below, which lists the Folio pages in order of setting.[1] Pages are paired in formes. Where two compositors worked on the same forme they set their pages simultaneously; where one compositor set both pages we must understand that he proceeded from one page directly to its companion on the same forme before taking up work on the succeeding forme.

Quire						
Quire qq	(MS)	B	3^v	4	E	(Q2)
	(Q2)	E	3	4^v	E	(Q2)
	(Q2)	E	2^v	5	B	(MS)
	(MS)	B	2	5^v	E	(Q2)
	(*Hamlet*)	B	1^v	6	E	(Q2)
	(*Hamlet*)	B	1	6^v	E	(Q2)
Quire rr	(MS)	B	3^v	4	B	(MS)
	(Q2)	E	3	4^v	B	(MS)
	(MS)	B	2^v	5	B	(MS)
	(Q2)	E	2	5^v	B	(MS)
	(Q2)	E	1va	6	B	(MS)
	(MS)	B	1vb			
	(Q2)	E	1	6^v	B	(MS)
Quire ss	(*Othello*)	E	3^v	4	E	(*Othello*)
	(Q2)	E	2^v	5	E	(*Othello*)
	(Q2)	B	3	4^v	E	(*Othello*)
	(Q2)	E	2	5^v	E	(*Othello*)
	(Q2)	E	1^v	6	E	(*Othello*)
	(Q2)	B	1	6^v	B	(*Othello*)

It is rather surprising to find that qq4–6^v must have been allotted, at the start, entirely to E, and Q2 copy prepared for these pages. (As Hinman shows, it was customary for a compositor, once he had begun on the middle page of a quire, to proceed *seriatim*, backwards or forwards as appropriate, through the remaining pages of the quire. It seems fair to assume that E was originally intended to set *all* the pages in the second half of quire qq.) The fact is that Q2 copy would have been far more suitable for the part of the text covered by qq2–3^v, since it would

1   I rely here on Hinman's findings
(*Printing*, II. 270–9 and 286–97).

142 have required far less correction. But there is possibly a good explanation for this apparently perverse proceeding. The extent of the revision required, and the location of the most troublesome pages, may not have been foreseen (as it could not have been without a fairly careful comparison of manuscript and print). Hence it may have seemed an open question at first whether the first or second half of the quire were more suitable for Q2 copy. Other things being equal, the second half would offer advantages, since by starting with qq4 the corrector[2] could proceed through the text continuously and in the logical order of pages, preparing a large quantity of Q2 copy to cover not only the second half of quire qq but the first half of quire rr as well.

We must assume, however, for reasons which will become apparent, that the corrector had not proceeded very far beyond qq6^v in his preparation of Q2 copy before work on the setting of quire qq began. This is not implausible. The corrector would, of course, have received advance notice of requirements for quire qq as soon as the text for this quire had been 'cast off', but this may not have been attempted until work on the preceding quire pp had begun.[3] The time available to him would thus be limited, if he were not to cause an inconvenient delay in the proceedings.

We shall return to this point. Meanwhile the puzzling irregularities in the distribution of copy for quire qq require explanation. Why, if Q2 copy had been prepared for the second half of the quire, was it not brought into play exactly as planned? The evidence is entirely circumstantial, but there is perhaps just sufficient to suggest a reasonable answer. We must start, however, with the

2 I assume that copy-editing of the kind discussed would fall within the province of the press-corrector, or one of the press-correctors, in the Jaggards' printing house.

3 See Hinman, *Printing*, II. 505ff., for casting-off procedures used in the preparation of the Folio. It was not customary to cast off copy for the second half of a quire, unless special circumstances required it. An examination of the second half of quire pp shows that copy for it *was* cast off, though it is only the last page which reveals (by the unnecessary splitting of verse-lines into two at the foot of its second column) unmistakable signs of juggling with the copy. An unleaded stage-direction on the preceding page is a further possible sign of adjustment. Earlier pages in this half of the quire look perfectly normal, though, of course, this may simply mean either that the relevant portions of text were accurately cast off, or that the adjustments necessary were relegated to later pages of the quire. Since the text of *Hamlet* occupying these pages of quire pp extends on to the initial pages of quire qq, the casting off of pp4–6^v (or the latter part thereof) indicates that an estimate was required of the extent of the overspill. This could only be because the text of *Lear*, starting on qq, was itself to be cast off well in advance of the commencement of type-setting on the new quire.

somewhat arbitrary assumption that, after setting qq3^v, compositor B was temporarily unavailable. If that were so, further Q2 copy would be required for E to set qq3, and this could have been prepared while he worked on qq4^v, the page which in fact he did set first.[4] At the same time it must have become obvious that it would be far easier for B than for E to set page qq5, a page consisting entirely of Q prose relineated as verse. While E was occupied with qq3 the manuscript was still available, so that the opportunity would arise of preparing additional Q2 copy to cover qq2^v, the page now allotted in exchange to E. It is not, I think, unreasonable to speculate on such *ad hoc* arrangements. Forethought and planning must have been necessary in the preparation of Q2 copy, yet it does not seem, on the evidence, to have been carried through on any consistent principles.

Compositor E must have encountered fresh difficulties on the second half of page qq5^v and throughout most of qq6, pages which, like qq5, contain a large amount of relineation. We may wonder why he was not again relieved by compositor B, who held the manuscript. Perhaps, as far as qq5^v is concerned, it was because the more experienced compositor, B, was required to set the beginning of the play (on qq2). Hinman has suggested, very plausibly, that particular care was devoted to initial pages of individual plays.[5] It is as likely, however, that the provision of further printed copy for qq2 would have caused unnecessary delay. B was using the manuscript copy on qq5, and, until he had finished with it, nothing could be done to extend the supply of Q2 copy for E.

If the corrector had still a quantity of Q2 copy to prepare for the next quire, rr, he would require the release of the manuscript as soon as possible, and he must have claimed it while E was setting qq6 and 6^v: it would be difficult otherwise to explain why, when for once the simultaneous use of both copies was not necessitated (the companion pages being taken up with *Hamlet*), the better of the two was not brought into use.

Compositor E was therefore left to cope as best he could with the special problems of qq5^v and qq6. Not unsuccessfully, as the results show: we shall later see, however, that, for part of qq6 at least, he seems to have sought special assistance.

---

4 Hinman, *Printing*, II. 272.

5 That B was required to set the first page of *Lear* suggests, Hinman says, 'that Compositor E was not encouraged — not at any rate at the beginning of his career as a Folio compositor — to set first pages . . . The initial page of a play, a kind of title page, might well be regarded by the Folio printers as more important than other pages. And sometimes, at least, it was certainly so regarded' (*Printing*, I. 224).

144   The arrangements for quire rr present a more rational appearance: experience, perhaps, suggested a more sensible *modus operandi*. Q2 copy was prepared for those pages of the first half of the quire which did not demand heavy correction, compositor B being expected to do the rest. Relineation would not be a serious problem in this part of the text. Pages rr1ᵛ and rr2ᵛ, however, contain additional matter in F which would have needed copying into the margins of Q2: these pages were partly or wholly set aside for B.⁶ There is, it is true, no obvious reason why he was required to set page rr3ᵛ as well: it would not have demanded unduly elaborate revision of the printed copy. One can only assume that the corrector had been working through the copy in the normal sequence of pages (starting with the portion corresponding to page rr1), and that, given the limited time at his disposal, he was not ready with page rr3ᵛ when composition began.⁷

   He had plenty of time, however, to prepare Q2 copy for quire ss, since after the completion of quire rr a break occurred in the printing of *Lear*.⁸ During this interruption compositor B set the whole of *Timon of Athens*, while compositor E disposed of ss3ᵛ–4, the first two pages of *Othello*, for which the copy was evidently ready prepared. Whatever the reasons for the irregular apportionment of the compositors' stints on subsequent formes of quire ss, it had obviously no connection with the availability of copy, since only one was required and Q2 was available throughout.

   Why, though, was Q2 copy employed for the last pages of the text on quire

6 It is very likely that B set not only column b of page rr1ᵛ, but a part of column a as well. An addition to the text (II.iv.142–7) occurs at the bottom of this column. Somewhat earlier (at II.iv.132 and II.iv.137) occur agreements between F and Q1 against Q2 in anomalous punctuation (see Appendix D2, p. 269 below). The last occurrence of a damaged type identifying compositor E is still further up the column (II.iv.126 – line 40 in Hinman's facsimile). I should guess that E's copy had been prepared as far as the stage direction at II.iv.128.

7 There is nothing in the lay-out of qq6 and 6ᵛ to suggest that compositor E was working to cast-off copy, i.e. by adjusting spacing or lineation to accommodate a predetermined quantity of text. Yet the latter pages of qq must have been cast off to assist the corrector in preparing copy for quire rr. If, however, the operation were delayed, as is most likely, until the composition of qq6 was due to begin (at which point the corrector would be ready, with the manuscript at his disposal, to embark on further editing of Q2), then, since pages qq6 and 6ᵛ consist almost entirely of verse, a very accurate computation could be effected, which would place no great strain on compositor E in observing the limits it imposed upon him.

8 Hinman, *Printing*, II. 281–2.

ss, and the labour undertaken of preparing it, when a superior copy, the manuscript, was usable without extra effort? We cannot know for certain, but it may well be that the notion of 'superior' copy in Jaggard's shop attached to *printed* copy, however much corrected and at whatever expense of time to the corrector – no doubt on the principle that it was easier to handle and easier to read, and therefore much reduced the labour of composition. In the case of *Lear* the relatively good punctuation of Q2 (if the manuscript were not, as theatrical manuscripts frequently were not, very conscientiously punctuated) would prove an added attraction. But there were perhaps other, or additional, reasons for not calling the manuscript into play more often than was absolutely necessary. The King's Men would expect the return of their prompt-book, and would, it goes without saying, hope to receive it back in good condition. Manuscripts in the printing house are much subject to wear and accident, even when they are not deliberately dismembered, or defaced by printer's markings. Philip Gaskell well describes the distinguishing tokens of printer's copy from the hand-press period as 'set-off from fresh-made proofs, inky thumb-marks, and a general air of dog-eared grubbiness'.[9] It must undoubtedly have been to protect the manuscript prompt-book from too much damage of this kind that throughout the setting of the play it was kept out of the hands of compositor E and entrusted only to the relatively experienced B. Perhaps, for the same reason, compositor B himself would use it only when circumstances compelled.

The explanation may, however, be a still simpler one; the players may have required the return of their prompt-book before the setting of the play could be completed.

Such appear to have been the considerations governing the constitution and distribution of the copy for F. It remains to examine some anomalous features of the evidence, of which the most striking is the appearance in a part of the F text set by B of readings apparently derived from Q2.

There are five of these F/Q2 agreements on page rr6^v, column b:

	Q1	Q2	F
IV.vi.236	durst	darst	Dar'st
243	swaggar'd	zwaggar'd	zwaggerd
244	so	zo	zo
247	ile	chill	chill
250	sir	zir	Zir

9 Gaskell, *New Introduction*, p. 41.

146 (I do not list *Pezant*, IV.vi.235, shown by Q2 and F against Q1's *pesant*, since the former is a common spelling elsewhere in F. I exclude also the common omission of IV.vi.276a, *and for you her owne for* Venter, which may well have been deleted independently in the two editions on grounds of incomprehensibility.)

The list is impressive until one recalls that Q2's dialect spellings are not entirely novel: Q1 employs similar forms (*chill, chud,* etc.) elsewhere in the same context. The editor of Q2 uses them more consistently, and the F reviser is more scrupulous still. In Q2, it is true, *s*'s are for the first time converted to *z*'s, but there is no reason, given the context, why the same idea should not have occurred independently to the reviser of F. Edgar's assumed brogue is obviously intended as West Country, or rather as what familiarly passed for such on the Elizabethan stage.[10]

There remains the agreement in *Dar'st* against Q1's *durst*. The latter is not technically an error. Though the form *durst* served for the past and past conditional tense of *dare*, it could also be used, analogously with 'should', 'could', etc., for the indefinite present. It is so used in Q: *Wherefore bould pesant durst thou support a publisht traytor*[?] Consequently F and Q2 appear to agree in an unnecessary alteration.

But if it is, strictly speaking, unnecessary, one might argue that it was almost inevitably suggested by the context. The conditional *durst* gives a very weak sense in these surroundings, approximating closely to that of a merely auxiliary 'shouldst' or 'wouldst'. It may have been felt as doubly inappropriate since the rhetorical question with 'dare', as a form of challenge or threat, required in Shakespeare's day, as it does in our own, the use of the indicative: 'How dare you? How dar'st thou?'[11] Numerous examples of this usage might be cited from

---

10 *Cf.* in *The London Prodigall* (1605), a King's Men play, the *chil*'s and *zyrrha*'s of Oliver, described in the list of *dramatis personae* as 'a Cornish Clothier', though we are informed in the course of the play that he comes from Devonshire. See Kökeritz, pp. 35ff., for comment on the use of southern or southwestern dialect as the standard speech of rustic characters in Elizabethan drama.

11 It required equally, of course, the use of 'how' rather than 'why' or (as here) 'wherefore'. But the appearance of 'wherefore' may be explained by the construction of the sentence. 'How' in this idiomatic usage is elliptical (= 'how comes it that?'). Perhaps for this reason it resists separation from the verb. We should reject: 'How, bold peasant, dar'st thou support . . . ?' Hence, I suggest, the substitution of the synonymous 'wherefore' (= 'for what cause?')

the Shakespearean texts. None is to be found of the conditional in an equivalent context.[12] In the circumstances it is less significant that Q2 and F coincide in their alteration of the reading. The intention of both editors was very probably to rectify a lapse of style.

There is, after all, nothing on page rr6ᵛb to connect it indisputably with Q2. It is, on the contrary, dissociated from Q2 not only by the general pattern of stops[13] but by a serious error in the punctuation at IV.vi.264–5 which is clearly traceable to Q1.[14] This page contains also the reading *ice* for *ile* (IV.vi.246) which, *pace* the editors, is far more likely to represent a misreading of the manuscript (if it is not merely a compositorial slip) than the arbitrary importation of a Northernism (*ice* for 'I s'll') into a passage the reviser himself recognised as stage Somersetshire (*cf.* his change of the next *ile* following to *chill*).

The pages set by B present no further problems. It is otherwise with the pages set by E which raise difficulties as baffling as any we have so far encountered. Though the issues involved may not be of cardinal importance to the establishment of the text, they are not irrelevant to the clarification of its history.

Two problems arise. We shall first confront the more important, at the same time the less tractable, of the two. It concerns the following readings on page qq6 set by compositor E:

	Q1, 2	F
II.i.47	reuengiue	reuenging
48	their	the
54	lancht (Q2: launcht)	latch'd
78	spurres	spirits
79	Strong	strange
81	why	wher
89	strange newes	strangenesse

These readings we have met before, but the reader may like to be reminded of

---

12   The conditional *durst* occurs once in a rhetorical question, but a question of altogether different tone and implication referring to the past:

Durst thou a (= have) lookt vpon him being awake?
And hast thou kill'd him sleeping?
A Midsummer Night's Dream, III.ii. 69–70).

13   See Appendix D1, p. 265 below.

14   See Appendix D2, p. 272 below.

148   their significance in a somewhat different context. They have the following
characteristics in common: (a) They are, with the possible exception of the first,
obviously inferior to their counterparts in Q2, hence are unlikely to have been
imported into the Q2 copy as misread 'corrections' from the manuscript, much
less to have stood in the manuscript in the first place as emendations of the
reviser. In the case of the last two, *wher* and *strangenesse*, which make nonsense,
one may fairly confidently exclude the possibility that they were deliberately
substituted by anybody for the obviously satisfactory *why* and *strange newes* in the
printed text. (b) They do not, with the possible exception of *the* and *wher*, look in
the least like the products of compositorial carelessness in reading printed copy.
(c) They wear, on the contrary, every appearance of compositorial misreadings
from manuscript, above all the last, which can only have resulted from some
aberrant spelling of *newes* in the copy, or from a carelessly formed manuscript
outline of the word.

  We are faced, therefore, with an extremely puzzling question: From what
source did E derive these errors, given that his punctuation on this page is
emphatic evidence of Q2 copy?[15] It is theoretically possible that, for a time, he
used the manuscript copy normally appropriated by compositor B but temporarily available while B was setting the last pages of *Hamlet*. To this, however, he
must have added Q2 punctuation, or somehow contrived to follow two copies
simultaneously, one for readings and lineation (the manuscript), and the other
(Q2) for guidance in pointing. To the inherent improbability of this proceeding
we must add the unlikelihood that compositor E would have made such frequent
mistakes in reading from a manuscript which, as the evidence shows, was
unusually legible. We may recall, furthermore, the reasons we have found – less
than completely cogent though they may be – for believing that the manuscript
copy must in any case have lain at this time with the corrector.

  It is perhaps more likely that compositor E, finding himself with a page of
copy overcrowded with markings (every line of it will have contained directions
for relineation, apart from the score or so of incidental corrections), and
knowing the manuscript copy to be unavailable, caused the corrected print to be
recopied before setting it. Alternatively, a page or so of manuscript copy
covering the passage in question here may have been prepared in advance by the
corrector, who would foresee E's difficulties at this point in dealing with
heavily-marked print. The corrector would, of course, copy from the prompt-
book, but might well introduce the more helpful punctuation of Q2 into his
transcript.

---

15   See Appendix D1, p. 260–1 below.

This hypothesis derives some support from a curious compositorial error 149
which had to be corrected during the printing.[16] The first two lines of the page
we are discussing (qq6) read:

> But that I told him the reuenging Gods,
> 'Gainst Paricides did all the thunder bend,
>
> II.i.47–8

When compositor E, however, came to set the catchword at the bottom of the
preceding page (qq5ᵛ) he selected, not *But*, as he should have done, but *Gainst*.
By itself this would not be very strange: the phenomenon known as 'eye-skip' is
not uncommon. The oddity lies in the fact that, if E's copy were Q2, his eye
must have skipped not a complete line of verse but a length of prose irregularly
disposed as follows:

> . . . Lordship, but that
> I tolde him the reuengiue Gods, gainst . . .

Even if we assume that the Q2 copy must have borne marks to indicate
line-endings, it is unlikely that such an error would occur. Nor does it seem
probable that, as he reached the end of qq5ᵛ, E may have collected in his stick a
line more than was necessary (the line commencing *But*), discovered the error
during imposition or earlier, and then disposed of the line, but – most strangely
– without removing the catchword (*Gainst*) which he had set below it. It is
somewhat easier to assume that, in looking for the catchword, he jumped a line
in his copy, the text of which therefore must have displayed this line as,
precisely, one line. And if the assumption is correct, the copy can only have been
manuscript. Though the misreadings we have noticed occur only on qq6a, this
manuscript may well have covered the relineated text in the column before
(qq5ᵛb) and in the one after (qq6b) as well.

A similar set of apparent misreadings from manuscript occurs at II.ii.83–5 on
page qq6ᵛ, also set by E:

	Q1, 2	F
II.ii.83	Bring	Being
	stir	fire
84	Reneag	Reuenge
85	gale	gall

---

16 See Hinman, *Printing*, I. 306–7.

150 Of these, however, *fire*, though it is sometimes cited as a possible misreading, is clearly not such at all but a true correction; while *Reuenge*, certainly a misreading, may be attributed to the scribe who copied the prompt-book: it is quite possible that he misinterpreted the spelling *Renegue*, substituted in the manuscript for *Reneag* on the Q1 copy. *Being* and *gall*, too, are undoubtedly wrong, but the errors are trivial enough to constitute compositorial slips. If, at all events, *Being, Reuenge* and *gall* are true misreadings, I am quite unable to account for the supply of manuscript copy to compositor E at this point. The relevant speech in Q2 is correctly aligned, as is most of the surrounding context, and the amount of correction called for as small as it is anywhere in the text.

No obviously anomalous readings occur on the pages subsequently set by compositor E. Since he was not required, after page qq6, to set heavily corrected copy, it would indeed be strange if we found traces later of any unusual expedient of the kind apparently resorted to in preparing the copy for that page.

The remaining anomalies are less conspicuous, though no less paradoxical in their apparent implications. They are possibly all to be explained as originating in the prompt-book 'master-copy'. All occur on pages of quire ss set by E.

The strangest is the erroneous reading *heere* (Q1, Q2: *heare*) at V.iii.13 (page ss1^v). We may be fairly certain that E was not himself responsible for a misprint here, since he made a deliberate attempt to justify the reading by means of additional punctuation:

> Q2:   . . . so weell liue,
> And pray, and tell old tales, and laugh
> At gilded Butterflies, and heare poore Rogues
> Talke of Courte newes, and weel talke with them too,

> F: So wee'l liue,
> And pray, and sing, and tell old tales, and laugh
> At gilded Butterflies: and heere (poore Rogues)
> Talke of Court newes, and wee'l talke with them too,

It is possible that the press-corrector, having misread the master-copy, perversely imposed his error on E's Q2 copy at the expense of the correct reading. But it is more likely that he correctly read, and conscientiously transferred, a mistake which stood in the master-copy in the first place as a slip of the copyist's pen.

Three further details of the text set by E appear to show improbable coincidences between F and Q1 in irregularities which are absent from Q2. All three are perhaps similarly explicable as features of the prompt-book introduced into the Q2 copy by a rather too scrupulous press-corrector.

1. *Gone.* appears in F as a speech-prefix for Goneril at V.i.29 (page ss1ᵛ) instead of the otherwise invariable *Gon.* This corresponds with an equally exceptional (though not, in this case, unique) form of the prefix in Q1: *Gono.* (Q2 shows at this point, as always, *Gon.*). Since this is Goneril's first speech in the F text for some considerable space, the copyist, finding the unusual *Gono.* in the printed copy, may have been unconsciously deflected from his own standard abbreviation. Again, we should have to suppose that the press-corrector transferred this very minor aberration to Q2.

2. At V.iii.46–7 (page ss2) the texts read as follows:

> Q1a: To saue the old and miserable King to some retention,

> Q1b: To send the old and miserable King to some retention, and appointed guard,

> Q2: To send the olde and miserable King
> To some retention, and appointed guard,

> F: To send the old and miserable King to some retention,

There is reason to think that the reviser's text derived from Q1b at this point, and that he must deliberately have re-deleted the phrase *and appointed guard*, leaving the line as it stands in Q1a (see Appendix B2a, p. 233 below). We may doubtless suppose, odd as it may seem, that the press-corrector, finding this in the prompt-book, obediently mangled the complete (and correctly lineated) version of Q2 so as to bring it into agreement with the master-copy.

3. The name 'Edmund' is spelt thus in Q1 on all but one occasion. The unique occurrence of *Edmond* (V.iii.167) is repeated in F (page ss2ᵛ), although Q2 shows *Edmund*, and although the latter spelling is almost invariably preferred by compositor E.[17] Here again we should perhaps assume that the unusual spelling

---

17 The spelling *Edmond* occurs once elsewhere in E's text, in the second last line of page qq3. The speech in which it occurs is continued on the following page, set by compositor B. Since the spelling *Edmond* recurs twice on this page within the next seven lines, three times again further down, and a further five times elsewhere in B's text, and since it was in none of these instances inherited from Q1, it seems more than likely to exhibit an idiosyncrasy of compositor B's. I am very much inclined to suppose, therefore, that the last few lines of qq3 were set by B. Page qq3ᵛ looks somewhat crowded. If the amount of copy allotted to the page exceeded its capacity, B may well have decided to remove some lines from the top of the page back to qq3 (still to be set by E) rather than allow lines at the bottom of the page to intrude into qq4 (already set, or being set, by E).

152 in Q1 – isolated, as it happens, from previous and subsequent appearances of the name – influenced the copyist, although his own preferred spelling was very probably 'Edmund'. It will seem much less likely, perhaps, in this case that the press-corrector transferred the anomaly to Q2, yet he must have had instructions to alter the spelling of personal names where necessary: F invariably has *Gonerill* for Q2 *Gonorill*, and it would be surprising if such consistency were achieved without help from the copy.[18]

The reader will find these explanations less than cogent if he feels, as I am myself very much inclined to do, that the reappearance in F of Q1's irregularities, however slight, must be evidence of a more direct relationship between the two texts. Yet a glance at Appendix D4 (p. 276 below) will show that the evidence of Q2 punctuation on these pages of F is very clear, and that it is supported, in the case of page ss2ᵛ at least, by the evidence of Q2 readings.

An alternative, if somewhat radical, solution to the problem might be offered by the hypothesis that the pages of quire ss were set not from Q2 but from an earlier, lost, edition of the play (Qx) of which Q2 was an exact, or almost exact, reprint. This would account for the influence on these F pages of Q2 punctuation and Q2 readings. At the same time it would allow for the possibility that a few small irregularities, inherited from Q1, remained uncorrected in the earlier edition and were therefore, where it served as copy, carried over into F.

Entities are not to be multiplied beyond necessity, and it may be that a few problematical details in the Folio text do not create a necessity pressing enough to justify postulating an unknown edition. Yet these details, as we have seen, are certainly difficult to explain on other grounds. Certain features of Q2 itself, moreover, offer just enough reinforcement to the hypothesis to make it worth entertaining.

---

18 A fourth oddity on one of E's pages earlier in the play is less remarkable than it might at first seem. Once again F appears to repeat an anomaly in Q1 in despite of the Q2 copy which is perfectly regular. The three texts read as follows:

Q1: *Lear*. Now by *Appollo*,
     Kent. Now by *Appollo* King
          thou swearest thy God in vaine.

Q2: *Lear*. Now by *Apollo* –
     Kent. Now by *Apollo*, King
          thou swear'st thy Gods in vaine.

F: *Kear*. Now by *Apollo*,
    Lent. Now by *Apollo*, King
         Thou swear.st thy Gods in vaine.
         (I.i.162–3; page qq2ᵛ).

It is evident from the effect of spoonerism produced by F's speech-prefixes that compositor E must initially have confused the two lines, setting the second in place of the first, without succeeding subsequently in disentangling the confusion. The comma after *Apollo*, like the 'K' of *Kear*, must be a relic of the original mistake.

The fact is that the text of Q2 contains a number of extraordinary errors which $\quad$
are not, on the supposition of its derivation directly from Q1, very easily
attributable either to the compositor or to the editor who prepared the 'copy'.
They seem, in other words, to require some more complex explanation.

As we have seen, editorial changes are frequent in Q2. Most are trivial.
Where they do affect the meaning, their purpose is obviously corrective, and
this remains true even of one or two of the bolder alterations which result merely
in new errors (e.g. *lessen* for *list* at I.iv.284, *vnreuerent* for *reuerent* at II.ii.133,
instead of *liest* and *reverend* respectively). On a few occasions, however, a
radically new reading appears in Q2 where no correction could conceivably have
been required. Below is a complete list of these apparently pointless departures
from the text of Q1:

	Q1	Q2
I.ii.159	dissolutions of ancient *amities*	*armies*
III.i.47	as *feare* not but you shall	*doubt*
III.ii.50	this dreadful / *Powther* ore our heades	*Thundring*
III.iv.136	in the *furie* of his heart	*fruite*
IV.vi.17	walke vpon the *beach*	*beake*
IV.vi.19	her cock *a boui*	*aboue*
IV.vi.100	*euery thing* I saide	*all*
IV.vi.119	for I *lacke* souldiers	*want*
V.iii.152	to *answere* an vnknowne opposite	*offer*
V.iii.320	and the *goard* state sustaine	*good*

Of these apparently motiveless substitutions three (*doubt*, *all* and *want*) may
be easily enough explained away as the kind of synonymous variant to be found
here and there in many reprints. Compositors sometimes 'improved' unconsciously on their copy in this way. But no such explanation will suffice for the
other seven readings.

It is clear not only that they cannot be unconscious substitutions but also that
they cannot be misreadings of printed copy. Nor is it at all likely, since the
original readings in Q1 are perfectly intelligible and satisfactory, that they
represent editorial alterations. Indeed all but one (*Thundring*) make nonsense to
a greater or lesser degree in their respective contexts.

It is theoretically possible, though again most unlikely, that six of the seven
originate in the uncorrected state of Q1 pages: C2ᵛ (*armies*), F4ᵛ (*Thundring*), I2ᵛ
(*beake, aboue*), L2 (*offer*), L4 (*good*). Unlikely first because potentially supportive
evidence relating to these pages (or other pages in the same formes) is almost
entirely wanting; and secondly because we should not expect to find quite so

154 many instances of uncorrected sheets in the single copy of Q1 which furnished the text of Q2. There is a third consideration. The remaining reading (*fruite*) derives from a Q1 page (G2ᵛ) which we know already stood in its uncorrected state in the copy for Q2 (Q2 reproduces all the readings of uncorrected outer G, most of them without change). It is entirely unlikely, in other words, that *fruite* derives directly from Q1. We need accordingly a different explanation for this error, and if any suggests itself, it is in all probability the one we need for the others.

Two of these errors, *aboue* for *a buoi* and *good* for *goard*, might easily be misreadings from manuscript copy. Others (e.g. *beake* for *beach*, *fruite* for *furie*) are much less plausible as such. Given that Q2 was printed from edited copy, we cannot rule out the possibility that a corrected Q1 was transcribed in manuscript for use by the compositor. But if so, proof-reading was quite exceptionally thorough. Aside from the misreadings taken over from Q1, and the fresh errors at present under discussion (all of them fairly radical), Q2 is conspicuously free from the mistakes we almost invariably discover in a text set from manuscript copy, i.e. minim confusion, substitutions of 's' for 'f', 'l' for 't', and the like.

On the assumption that Q2 derives not from Q1 but from an intermediate Qx, a mistake such as *fruite* for *furie* is easy to explain. Supposing a compositorial slip in Qx which produced *fruie* (a simple transposition of letters), the next unthinking step into the sophistication *fruite* would very easily occur. It is well known that any series of reprints at this period is likely to show examples of such progressive deterioration, sometimes in a protracted sequence of error compounding error.

What, however, of the six other unexplained readings? Possibly *armies*, *beake* and *good* resulted from another type of misprint in Qx: the dropped letter. We may see the sequence of original–misprint–sophistication in each case as *amities–amiies–armies*, *beach–beac–beake*, *goard–goad–good*. (It is interesting that the latter sequence is prolonged into the next quarto edition: Q2's *and the good state sustaine* gives rise in Q3, a reprint of Q2, to *and the good sustaine*.) We need no different explanation for the reading *aboue*, except that in this case we should have to assume the omission in Qx of a space rather than a letter: *a boui–aboui–aboue*.

The error *Thundring* cannot, of course, belong to this class: it was clearly not derived from *Powther* by the mediation of a misprint. In fact it wears the appearance of a substitution, accidental or deliberate, although it is not easily explicable as such. It cannot have been introduced unthinkingly as a synonym of *Powther*, which it is not. It cannot have been intended to improve the sense, since *Powther* makes perfectly good sense. 'Powther', furthermore, is a common word and its spelling was familiar to contemporaries, though the form 'pother' is more familiar to us. I can only suggest, on an assumption as before of progressive error, that in Qx the variant spelling *Powder* was introduced, which, though equally current in the seventeenth century, may have betrayed the editor or compositor into a simple misunderstanding, hence into a mistaken decision to emend.

The last of these errors, *offer* for *answere*, is still more puzzling. The sentence as it appears in Q1 makes, once again, perfect sense, whereas the Q2 version makes none: *Thou art not bound to offer an vnknowne opposite.*[19] Were we once again to suppose that a misprint may have intervened between *answere* and *offer*, it would be difficult to imagine what it might have been. Since some unusual error must have been involved, conjecture would be useless.

It might be argued that in this case, and in most or all of the other cases we have been considering, the sophistication which appears in the Q2 text may be the work of a proof-corrector, while the mediating misprint may belong not to a prior edition but simply to an uncorrected state of the Q2 text. Certainly there is evidence that Q2 was corrected as it proceeded through the press. Two or three variants were discovered by the Cambridge editors, who collated four copies of the book. These variants show the correction of very trivial slips, but it is quite possible that more serious errors were committed elsewhere and patched up by a press-reader without reference to the copy.[20]

A more serious objection may perhaps be founded on the evidence of punctuation in Q2 and F. It is clear that if certain pages of F were printed not from Q2 itself but from an immediate ancestor, Qx, then Qx must necessarily have shown almost precisely the same punctuation as Q2, since we find that punctuation reproduced in F with remarkable fidelity. In Qx, by the same token, must have appeared the evidence we discovered in Q2 of more than one compositor – a change of style in punctuation two-thirds of the way through the text. Even if we claim to detect the influence of Qx only at the very close of the play (quire ss), at which point the more elaborate punctuation of the second Q2 compositor is already in evidence, we still cannot suppose that the whole of Qx was punctuated in this style. The more primitive style of the first compositor must also have

19 Though it is conceivable that the Q2 editor or compositor had confusedly in mind an accepted intransitive sense of the verb *offer*, 'to make an attack' (see Onions, *Glossary*).

20 Extant copies of Q2 still await collation. It is less likely that corrector's sophistications were introduced into the text at an earlier stage of proof-reading (before press-work began). If a point were made at all of pulling and correcting proofs, they would almost certainly be checked against the copy. See Gaskell, *New Introduction*, pp. 110ff.

156 passed from Qx to Q2: were Qx to have initiated a fuller and more correct pattern of punctuation throughout, we should scarcely expect to find it simplified in a large part of the later edition. Since the change of style in punctuation corresponds with a change in the spelling of certain words and names (see p. 135, n.11, above), the spellings must have originated in Qx as well.[21]

We are forced into the position, in other words, of according to Q2 a somewhat anomalous status. It might be a normal reprint, by the standards of the time, in so far as it corrects certain errors in its predecessor and sophisticates others. But the hypothesis obliges us to attribute to it as well the decidedly unusual characteristic of reproducing the spellings and punctuation of its copy almost without change.

I am not sure that such a hypothesis is tenable. It may be that further evidence can be found to decide the issue, or that the evidence I have offered may be otherwise and more convincingly interpreted. I have stated the case as I see it principally to show that, if the relationship between Q2 and F proves to be, for all practical purposes, perfectly clear, some little doubt still remains, of theoretical rather than practical importance, whether by 'Q2' we mean unequivocally the edition we know, or whether we may, at times, be referring in fact to an earlier edition very closely resembling it.

It remains only to repeat that the readings of Q2 are entirely without authority. Their appearance in the text of F is due only to the use by Jaggard's compositors of a quantity of Q2 copy in which, here and there, a mistake or variant reading was left uncorrected. The arguments advanced earlier to demonstrate the dependence of F on Q1 remain, of course, substantially unaffected.[22]

21 On the evidence appearing in F of agreements with Q2 readings on supposedly Qx pages, we are bound to assume, too, that some, if not all, of the editorial changes in Q2 first appeared in Qx.

22 Something must be added, however, to show that the evidence discussed above (of the use of Q2 copy in the printing house) does not seriously weaken the conclusions derived from the treatment in F of Q press-variants.

   Two arguments were put forward: (a) showing that F was certainly influenced by manuscript copy, (b) demonstrating that this manuscript can only have been the one employed in the preparation of Q. In support of (a) pairs of

readings from F were cited, each pair corresponding to Qa/Qb variants occurring on the same sheet of Q, and each showing one reading dependent on Qa and the other on Qb: an impossibility if only one copy of Q were used by the reviser (p. 83 above); (b) was substantiated by reference to certain readings in F which show that, though the editor must have consulted his manuscript to arrive at them, they do not improve very much on the faulty readings of Q (pp. 85ff. above).

   We are now able to see that the evidence relating to (a) would have no weight if it could be argued about each pair of incompatible readings that one came from the reviser's copy of Q1 and that the other made its way into the text through Q2; similarly, that the evidence relating to (b) would be valueless if the F readings in question were transmitted fortuitously through Q2 and therefore could not be offered as proof that the editor had looked up his manuscript copy. There is no need, however, as will be seen, to revise these arguments.

Q2 copy was used in that part of the text which covers the following press-corrected formes and pages in Q: nearly all of D outer; nearly all of E outer; page G1; and page K4. In Q2 E and K appear corrected, D and G uncorrected.

Of the pairs of readings quoted in support of (a) those derived from sheets G, H and K do not fall in that part of the text which was transmitted through Q2 copy, except for *roaring* on sheet G which is a 'corrected' reading and cannot, therefore in any case have derived from Q2. Of the pairs derived from sheets D and E, one of the pair in each case (*prize*, uncorrected, sheet D and *Tombe*, corrected, sheet E) *may* have been introduced into F from Q2. It may be argued, however, that, in respect at least of sheet E and the reading *tombe*, the reviser's copy very probably coincided with Q2 in showing the corrected state, so that it is the other reading of the pair (*ancient*, deriving from uncorrected *ausrent*) which is significant.

Of the evidence relevant to (b), the readings from sheet H cannot have derived from Q2, while those from sheet E remain unaffected except for *Turlygod*. The F reviser may have preserved *Tuelygod* from Qa copy without consulting the manuscript: *Turlygod* may be the contribution of Q2. As has already been mentioned, however, he is more likely to have been working on a corrected state of sheet E.

See Appendix C1, introductory note (p. 249 below), for an interpretation of the evidence respecting the state (whether corrected or uncorrected) of the variant formes in the reviser's copy of Q.

CHAPTER TEN
EDITORIAL PRINCIPLES

Since we now have before us a complete theory of the history of the text, it is time to ask how the conclusions we have arrived at would affect the editing of the play.

The goal of textual theory is, of course, to ensure the establishment of a text which shall be as nearly as possible a reproduction of the author's original. The guiding principle is very well defined by McKerrow: 'For scholarly purposes, the ideal text of the works of an early dramatist would be one which, on the positive side, should approach as closely as the extant material allows to a fair copy, made by the author himself, of his plays in the form which he intended finally to give them, and, on the negative side, should not in any way be coloured by the preconceived ideas or interpretations of later times.'[1]

This aim, it goes without saying, is not always pursuable with the same degree of confidence and security. In the case of *King Lear*, certainly, the 'extant material' is not encouraging. No procedure, we may feel sure, short of a discovery of the original manuscript, could now possibly lead to a faithful restoration of Shakespeare's play. The editor, however, may satisfy himself that his approximation will not be hopelessly remote from the original.

It must follow from the argument presented in the preceding chapters that the editor, in attempting his reconstruction, will derive very much more help from Q1 than from F. Q2, a wholly derivative text, he may safely discount. This is not to imply, however, that Q1 should serve as the 'copy-text', or even as the 'basic text', of a modern edition.

If he conforms to standard practice, an editor will choose one from amongst the early editions available to him as his 'copy-text'. This is the edition he will follow in respect of 'accidentals' (spelling, punctuation and other details of presentation). He should select the one which promises in his judgement to reflect most clearly the 'accidentals' of the original, or, if there is little chance of that, one which shows at least the forms (of spelling, and so on) characteristic of the time and locality to which the original belongs.[2]

1 R. B. McKerrow, *Prolegomena for the Oxford Shakespeare: A Study in Editorial Method* (Oxford, 1939), p. 6.

2 See Sir W. W. Greg, 'The Rationale of Copy-Text', in *Collected Papers*, ed. J. C. Maxwell (Oxford 1966), pp. 374ff., for a full exposition of the theory supporting the 'copy-text' principle. The subject has been much debated of recent years. The interested reader is referred for a

There is unfortunately no likelihood at all that any of the early editions of King Lear preserves the spelling or punctuation of the author's manuscript. One justification, therefore, for adopting a 'copy-text' is wanting. If, nevertheless, an old-spelling edition were thought desirable, the text of F would serve the purpose of 'copy' far better than that of Q, since it does at least display a certain normality and consistency in its system of 'accidentals'.

It would be still less to the purpose to make use of Q as a 'basic text'; indeed, it would be in principle wholly mistaken.

The doctrine of the 'basic text' has not, so far as I know, been formally defined. But there is such a doctrine implicit in the introductions and commentaries of numerous Shakespearean editors, including some of the most recent. From their statements its outlines are not difficult to infer. It applies to cases such as that of King Lear which confront the editor with more than one text of independent derivation, and is adapted to resolving the problem of variant readings. The editor is required to choose one of the texts (the most reliable one) as the 'basis' of his edition. The readings of this 'basic text' he will reproduce except where the variant in some other text is arguably superior. In cases of genuine doubt (when, that is, there is nothing to choose between the merits of one variant and another) he will prefer the reading in the 'basic text'.[3]

useful summary of Greg's views, and of the controversy arising from them, to G. T. Tanselle, 'Greg's Theory of Copy-Text and the Editing of American Literature', Studies in Bibliography, XXVIII (1975), pp. 167–229.

3   Recent English editions of King Lear have been prepared on these principles. 'The present text of the play . . . is based on F; but . . . we shall accept Q readings not only where the F readings are manifestly corrupt, but also where Q seems palpably superior' (The Arden Shakespeare (1952, reprinted with corrections 1972), p. xvii). 'The present text is based on the Folio; but all the variants to be discovered in the Quarto . . . have been considered, and have been admitted if a good enough argument for their superiority could be discovered' (The New Penguin Shakespeare (1972), p. 321). 'For the purposes of an old-spelling edition . . . it

seems reasonable to adopt Q as copy text and to correct from F . . . I have followed Q where it was not clearly wrong or where changes in F . . . seemed dictated more by the sophisticating tendencies of the compositors than by authoritative alterations in their copy [sc. where F is clearly wrong]' (The Fountainwell Drama Texts (1973), p. 13). The last-cited editor, it will be seen, has combined the principle of 'copy-text' with that of 'basic text'. I have said that the 'basic text' theory has never been formally defined. In fact it seems to me a vestigial remnant of the original copy-text theory, developed by McKerrow and Greg, and now discarded, which held that a copy-text should govern not only in the 'accidentals' but in the readings of a modern edition. There is a passage in the essay of Greg's cited above which shows that he himself never entirely forswore allegiance to the old

No doubt there is something to be said for this procedure on grounds of practicality and common sense. And no doubt it will on occasion produce good enough results. But if so, good results will be produced for bad reasons. For implicit in the procedure are at least three altogether false principles of critical method.

In order to bring the fallacies to light it will be necessary first to remind the reader of a distinction, very familiar to Classical critics, between the criterion which separates 'good' from 'bad' readings and that which distinguishes 'true' from 'false'. 'Good' readings are acceptable in their context; 'bad' are not. 'True' readings are original; 'false' are spurious. Given these definitions, it is easy to see that 'good' readings are not bound to be 'true', nor 'bad' readings (which may simply be errors) 'false'.

That being so, it may also be seen that it is highly uncritical to judge between variants by the simple process of comparing their merits. The better variant is by no means likely *ipso facto* to be the truer. An illustration may make this clear. At III.ii.58 in *King Lear* Q reads *centers* against *Continents* in F. No editor of the play, to my knowledge, has ever hesitated here over his choice: *Continents* is quite obviously the 'better' reading. Yet *centers* is merely an error: scarcely even that, but the anomalous form of a word which, in fact, conforms fully as well to the context as the reading in F (see Appendix A3, p. 196 below).

The important point is that until variants have been thoroughly examined and their origin understood there can be little purpose in appraising their respective 'merits'. It is true that editors of *King Lear* have traditionally offered a general justification for dismissing variants in Q: as a reported text it must, they have frequently claimed, contain a great many actors' substitutions which must clearly be rejected as spurious. But the assumption once made, they resort to a straightforward comparison and judgement of the variants, all too often condemning without further argument the 'worse' reading as the 'false' one. No one has ever asked what word the actor can have uttered which appears in the Q text as *centers*; let alone whether an actor could conceivably have thought of such a word *extempore* as a substitute for *Continents*.

theory. Having maintained that 'the choice between substantive readings belongs to the general theory of textual criticism and lies altogether beyond the narrow principle of the copy-text' (*op. cit.*, p. 382), he proceeds to lay down principles relating to that choice: two criteria are relevant, the relative intrinsic merits of the readings and the respective 'authority' of the texts in which the readings are found (*ibid.*, p. 385). Here are principles which have little to do with the general theory of textual criticism, and which appear to lead straight to the adoption of a 'basic' text, differing little if at all from a 'copy-text' in the old and repudiated sense.

Paradoxically, when it comes to the cases of genuine doubt, the opposite
argument must be directed against the 'basic-text' theory. Where the origin of
two variants is clearly understood, and where it is still open to question which of
the two is the true reading, or (though an error) contains the clue to the true
reading, then indeed there can be no recourse but to a comparison of merits. In
default of any other criterion, the editor is bound to fall back on the assumption
that the better reading is more likely to be the true one.[4]

But in cases of doubt the 'basic text' doctrine recommends an adherence to the
chosen text. Let us concede that the doubt envisaged in this case arises at a
further stage in the argument, from the question, precisely, which of the two
readings is the better one. The procedure recommended remains, in any case,
unsatisfactory.

It may appear to be justifiable on grounds of statistical probability. Where
doubt arises, it may be argued, the more generally reliable text (the 'basic' text)
is more likely to be correct since it has, on the whole, a better record of
correctness. The chances are in its favour. Let us examine this argument, too, in
relation to a particular problem.

At II.i.41 in *King Lear* the editor is faced with a choice between *warbling* (Q)
and *Mumbling* (F). Going by the theory presented in these pages, he would be
obliged to regard these variants as alternative interpretations of the manuscript
copy for Q: *warbling* represents what the Q compositor found there, *Mumbling*
(because of its graphical similarity to the other reading in secretary script) must
be considered a possible correction of the reviser's (whether right or wrong) from
the same source. Both readings make sense in the context, thus both have a
claim to be regarded as the true reading. Neither, on the face of it, is 'better'
than the other.

Were the editor to have adopted Q as his 'basic text' (because it is much more
reliable generally than F), he would, in these circumstances, give it the benefit
of the doubt: he would opt for *warbling*. In doing so, however, it is interesting to
note, he could no longer look for support to the argument from statistical
probability.

The argument would be difficult to sustain in the case we are considering, or
in others like it. The fact is that when it comes to readings from the manuscript
copy, Q is not more reliable than F, but less so. Taking into account every

---

4   To which principle the familiar
    maxim might serve as a corollary
    that in uncertain cases the more
    'difficult' reading should be
    preferred.

probable or possible instance of common derivation from the manuscript source, the record of F is better than that of Q, since it shows several certain corrections of Q misreadings and no single example of a certain miscorrection. This reveals immediately that it cannot be logical to prefer Q *warbling* to F *Mumbling* on the grounds that Q is *in general* the more trustworthy text.

Should we expect the editor, then, simply to be more careful in appealing to the argument from probability? Should we expect him, when in doubt, to prefer the more reliable text, but not until he has satisfied himself that it is more reliable in the relevant respect — which means that he will not always on principle give his preference to the same 'basic' text? That would certainly better preserve a show of reason. I am inclined to think, nevertheless, that to appeal thus implicitly to a principle of statistical probability is, more often than not, to clutch at a straw.

Let us revert to the variants we have been considering, either of which might represent a misreading of the other. No *a priori* arguments add weight to the probability on either side. It might be suggested that the reviser would be unlikely to alter an acceptable reading in Q unless he found positive encouragement for his correction in the manuscript. Against that it might be argued that the reviser is given to spurious substitutions, some of which are bound fortuitously to resemble (when written in manuscript) their counterparts in Q: there would be nothing, formally, to distinguish such substitutions from genuine corrections. The alternatives, then, are genuinely open: *prima facie* either F or Q might be correct. But in other instances of the same kind F is demonstrably more often correct than Q, and we are to take that demonstrable superiority as the deciding factor.

The appeal, in other words, is simply to the numerical frequency of F's successes in similar circumstances elsewhere. It can, as such, have very little force. The evidential value of the successful corrections in F must be estimated in relation to the total number of readings which the reviser may be assumed to have derived from the manuscript, or confirmed by reference to the manuscript (including, of course, those which show that he left Q errors uncorrected). However the computation is effected, it will have in reason to cover several hundred readings which show the text of Q to be neither more nor less accurate in reproducing the manuscript copy than that of F. Comparing, on this evidence, the reliability of the Q compositors with that of the F reviser, it will inevitably emerge that the latter revealed his superiority in a very small proportion of the given instances. To put it another way: were we to compute from the available data the odds in favour of F giving the right reading against Q in a doubtful case, we should find them very slightly higher than the even chance which an editor gives himself by making a guess.

Before resorting to statistics, or to guesswork, an editor faced with a problematical choice between 'good' variants would surely be well advised first to examine thoroughly their relative suitability to the context. It must rarely be the case that *no* objective argument is forthcoming from collateral evidence in support of a rational choice; and rarely, therefore, that he is thrown back on more or less mindless expedients.

There is a third, and more fundamental, reason for deprecating the 'basic-text' approach to editing: it begins from the assumption that an editor who finds two or more authoritative early texts at his disposal is bound to choose one of them on which to model, or 'base', his edition. Whether this necessary choice is believed to be dictated by expediencey, or by scholarly caution, the reasoning at work is fallacious. If an editor is interested, as he surely must be, in reconstructing the *original* as faithfully as opportunity allows he cannot regard the *unoriginal* extant editions before him as models. These, of course, will appear to him merely as imperfect replicas of the text he aims to restore, offering him no more than evidence, more or less obscured by the operation of chance and human fallibility, of the lost original.

Expediency and caution, therefore, both dictate that he should make use of the whole of the evidence to reconstruct, by careful inference, what in his judgement must have stood in the lost original. The result will not be 'based' on one of the existing editions rather than another; nor will it be a judiciously compiled amalgam of selections from each (as would, incidentally, follow from what used to be called the 'eclectic' method of editing). Rather will it represent an independent entity, the hypothetical reconstruction of a text which does not in fact exist, but which once did exist as the ancestor of the editions still surviving.

To this process of reconstruction no labour-saving rules-of-thumb can possibly apply. It scarcely needs stating that an infinite variety is possible in the kinds and combinations of data which different textual traditions present. The editor's approach must vary with the problems he meets and the solutions he is able to develop to them.

This is not to say that as he proceeds with the establishment of his text he will find himself at each encounter with a pair of variants in an entirely fresh dilemma. Obviously he will have started by seeking to form historical hypotheses to explain the peculiar features of the evidence at his disposal. From these hypotheses he may very readily abstract a set of editorial principles, a rationale to guide him through the innumerable decisions of detail which the editorial process requires. But, it goes without saying, the set of principles

164 which is applicable to one textual tradition will not necessarily be valid for any other.

I give below a list of the few principles it would be necessary to apply in the editing of *King Lear* on the theory presented in this book. It should be understood that in each instance the conditions stipulated by the rule will be fulfilled by the most likely inference from the evidence of the readings, and that the final decision will depend on a weighing of probabilities.

1. Where the variant in F corrects a misreading in Q, it should be accepted as deriving from the manuscript copy (e.g. Qa: *crulentious*, F: *contentious*, III.iv.6). The reviser's few successful corrections of phonetic errors in Q must, of course, be accepted likewise. The editor should be wary, however, of phonetic errors in Q 'corrected' in F as though they were misreadings (e.g. Q: *stale dull lyed bed*, F: *dull stale tyred bed* for *stale dull-eyed bed*, I.ii.13).

2. When the readings in F and Q are both possible, or both unsatisfactory, and where at the same time they would bear a graphic resemblance to each other in secretary script, they must be regarded as true variants, i.e. as offering alternative interpretations of the Q manuscript (e.g. Q: *warbling,* F: *mumbling*, II.i.41). Every such case must, of course, be decided on the editor's opinion of its merits. The procedure will be correct, or as good as correct, even where an unsatisfactory variant in F represents a misreading not of the reviser's but of the copyist's (e.g. Qa: *battero*, F: *Ballow*, IV.vi.247, where *Ballow*, a non-word, can only be a corruption of the reviser's original *Batton* marked as a correction on Q1 copy).

3. Additions in F should be carefully considered as representing, conceivably, recoveries from the manuscript of material which is absent from Q only because of the carelessness of the compositor. Small interpolations required by the sense (particles, pronouns, etc.) should obviously be given the benefit of the doubt. Corrections of this kind *may* not have been derived from the manuscript, but nothing is lost by assuming that they were. Longer additions may themselves reveal (e.g. by the presence in them of actors' gag) their origin in the Q 'copy'. In more doubtful cases it may be taken as a principle that (as long as their relevance is admissible) the less necessary such passages are the more trustworthy (e.g. the line at V.iii.76, *Dispose of them, of me, the walls is thine*, which repairs no fault of grammar, sense, logic or metre).

4. All other variants in F should be disregarded, with the possible exception of one less determinate category to be noted presently.

A somewhat ticklish editorial problem remains to be considered. It is less a particular problem than a general uncertainty which might be thought capable of raising difficulties. The existence of press-variants on certain pages of Q does not seriously complicate the editor's task. Since he may draw plausible inferences about the state, whether corrected or uncorrected, of the F reviser's copy for these pages,[5] he will be in a position to interpret the evidence with some confidence. We cannot exclude the possibility, however, that the remaining pages of Q, or some of them, may also have been subjected to correction in the course of printing. Of these corrections, if any were made, we cannot now, of course, hope to discover any direct evidence at all. The editor, it follows, will have to proceed through most of the text unaware whether he is dealing with 'corrected' or 'uncorrected' variants in Q, and entirely ignorant as to the state of the Q copy which may be reflected in the readings of F. Working in the dark, he will be likely, and this perhaps not infrequently, to be seriously misled by the evidence. How may he take this very significant possibility into account?

The problem, in theory very complex, may fortunately be reduced for practical purposes to a few simple considerations. First, in respect of Q. The editor will normally treat the text of Q as a naive reproduction, whether correct or incorrect, of its copy. He will not therefore be concerned at the possibility of encountering unidentified variants which thus 'faithfully' reflect their source, but will have only to mistrust press-corrector's sophistications, or other errors of a misleading kind, introduced — he will not know where — into 'corrected' pages of the text. The text of F, by contrast, he will not normally expect to provide reliable readings, except as he is able to infer from the evidence of Q that they represent true corrections incorporated from the manuscript copy. He will thus need to be wary of two possibilities: that true corrections in F may appear not against the errors in Q which reveal them as true corrections, but against Qb corruptions of a more or less plausible kind; and that errors in F may represent survivals of Qa copy which, if they appear not against true corrections in Q, but against plausible Qb corruptions, may not be recognised as affording the more valuable clue to the true reading of the copy.[6]

---

5   See introductory note to Appendix C1, p. 249 below.

6   If the reading in F represents a survival of Qa, the variant in Q must, of course, represent Qb. At the risk of tediousness, it should perhaps be added that survivals in F of Qb will either be mistaken for corrections from the manuscript (of the Qa error in Q) and rightly accepted; or if (as plausible press-corrector's sophistications) they differ markedly from the Qa reading, mistaken for reviser's substitutions, and rightly dismissed; or, if they do not differ markedly, mistaken for true variants and rightly considered as possible evidence of the manuscript. There exist among the known variants, to be sure, cases of obviously erroneous or nonsensical reading in both Qa and Qb: it is theoretically possible that obvious Qb corruptions have survived in F to be found against Qa errors in Q. I have noticed no

166   It will be seen that in every case the risk of possible misjudgement involves
the acceptance at face value of what is in fact a specious error in Q, introduced
into the corrected version of the text. Where both Q and F record such an error
(because both represent the Qb version of the text), the editor will be helpless. If
he had to choose, at IV.vi.230, between Qb: *to boot, to boot*, and F: *To boot, and
boot*, he might, though it seems very doubtful, suspect the transmission of a
press-corrector's revision, but he should certainly have no idea that the manuscript originally yielded: *to saue thee* (Qa). Where, on the other hand, F records a
true correction against a Qb sophistication in Q, much will depend on the
extent of the corruption in Q and the relative acceptability of its reading in the
context. Were the editor, in ignorance of the Qa reading, to discover Qb: *my
wracke* against F: *miracles* (II.ii.172), he would certainly be aroused to suspicion
of Q; but Qb: *tempestious* against F: *contentious* (III.iv.6) or Qb: *miscreant* against
F: *ancient* (II.ii.133) might place him in a quandary, since the Q reading,
though weakly pleonastic in both cases, is not impossible in either. Where the
sophistication in Q is wholly convincing (and is so unlike the true correction in F
that it will not appear as an alternative interpretation of the manuscript) the
editor will certainly be led into a mistaken decision. He will have no choice in
the circumstances but to dismiss the F reading as an unwarranted 'improvement'. His only consolation must be that he will not often be so deceived.
Judging from the known evidence, the press-corrector's capacity for manufac-
turing plausible readings was neither very great nor very often exercised. The
remaining eventuality presents still less of a risk. If F should happen to preserve
a relic of 'uncorrected' copy which coincides with a Qb sophistication in Q, the
variant in F will appear not only as an error but as an error strangely unrelated to
the ostensibly 'correct' reading in Q, from which it might be expected to have
derived. (We find an analogy at III.iv.6 in Qa: *crulentious*, Qb: *tempestious*,
III.iv.6 where *crulentious* might stand for the hypothetical reading in F.)
Circumstances so bizarre would at once alert the editor to the possibilities. So far
as I can judge, however, no such contrast is apparent anywhere in the text
between the readings of F and Q, the explanation for which must be that only
serious Qa corruptions provoked the press-corrector to inventing new readings,
and that it is precisely serious Qa corruptions which are most likely to have been
noticed and dealt with by the reviser, so that none has survived intact in the text
of F. We are left, therefore, with a single editorial principle to add somewhat
tentatively to those listed above.

likely instances, however. This
exhausts the possibilities of
misconstruction due to the
presence of undetected
press-variants.

5. Where an apparently correct reading in F appears against a Q error which
cannot easily be categorised as misreading, mishearing or trivial misprint, and
where, at the same time, the possibility of latent press-variants cannot be
dismissed (because no known variants appear on the same forme of Q), there
could be no strong argument against the assumption that F shows a true
correction from manuscript of a press-corrector's sophistication in Q. (Very few
pairs of variants satisfy these conditions, and all appear to me very doubtful
cases, e.g. Q: *accent teares*, F: *cadent Teares*, I.iv.307. See Appendix A5, p. 203
below, for a suggested emendation of Q.)

The assessment of variants according to these principles should not present
the editor with insuperable difficulties in practice. But he is likely to experience
some perplexity, it must be acknowledged, in attempting to repair the many
and serious deficiencies of Q, the text on which for the most part his assessment
of the evidence will oblige him to rely. Minor embarrassments abound: its
speech-prefixes are not wholly reliable, its stage directions inadequate, its
punctuation primitive and quite certainly unrelated to that which appeared in
the author's manuscript. Mislineation will present a worse problem, aggravated
by the large number of defective lines which lie concealed in passages of prose or
misaligned verse. But above all it is the verbal corruption pervading the text
which will tax the editor's resources. So constant is it, and so damaging, that he
will have no recourse but to adopt a policy of extensive and, where necessary,
radical emendation.

The difficulties, apart, this particular prospect is not likely to hold much
appeal in the present somewhat conservative climate of opinion: the practice of
conjectural emendation has long been regarded as subject to a strict, one might
say forbidding, code of regulating principles, and no editor impressed by the
necessity for these rules could wish, thus inhibited, to embark on the
thorough-going correction of a very corrupt text. Yet he would certainly be
justified in allowing himself greater liberties than are currently considered
permissible, and not only because of the unusual extent and difficulty of the
task.

In arguing this point I must impose on the reader's patience with another
digression into the realm of theory. The opinions which now prevail on the
subject of textual emendation were clearly defined some fifty years ago (if indeed
they were not then actually determined) by Sir Walter Greg. His celebrated
lecture 'Principles of Emendation in Shakespeare', delivered in 1928, has by
now acquired the status of a classic.[7] I do not think there can be many editors of

---

7   Reprinted (London 1928) from the
    Proceedings of the British Academy,
    XIV (1928), pp. 147–216.

168 the present day who would wholly dissent from the views propounded in it.

Its thesis is simple. Greg, acknowledging that no one can 'help great critics in making brilliant emendations' takes as his aim the discovery of 'some rules that should prevent little critics from making foolish ones'.[8] He proposes two canons, one establishing a criterion of acceptability ('By an acceptable emendation I mean . . . one that strikes a trained intelligence as supplying exactly the sense required by the context, and which at the same time reveals to the critic the manner in which the corruption arose'),[9] the other a criterion of consistency ('no emendation can, or ought to be, considered *in vacuo* . . . criticism must always proceed in relation to what we know, or what we surmise, respecting the history of the text . . . And if a critic is so bold as to propose several emendations in the same text, he may fairly be challenged to prove that they do not involve mutually contradictory theories of its origin').[10]

The criterion of acceptability stresses two conditions: the emendation must provide 'exactly the sense required by the context' and it must 'reveal to the critic the manner in which the corruption arose'. Greg admits that the standard of acceptance is 'high', but maintains that 'criticism should insist rigorously upon the conditions, for unless they are fulfilled there can be no certainty about the emendation, and there may be half a dozen, or half a hundred, with claims upon our attention'.[11] The corollary to this strict embargo upon uncertainty is, of course, that doubtful readings must be retained, and explained with as much conviction as may be, wherever they cannot be emended with the requisite degree of confidence.[12]

No one certainly, in demurring to these views, could wish for a revival of that spirit of scholarly dilettantism which Greg rightly deplored and did so much to discredit. We have learnt that ingenuity and literary taste do not suffice as qualifications for the critic, and that, when it comes to textual emendation, an editor must submit his freedom to proper regulation in the light both of relevant knowledge and of the logic of textual enquiry. It may not be too soon, however,

---

8 *Principles of Emendation*, p. 3.

9 *Ibid.*, p. 5.

10 *Ibid.*, p. 8.

11 *Ibid.*, p. 6.

12 As Greg writes eloquently elsewhere: 'Explanation is safer and less heady work than conjecture, and even when perverse it has served both to define the possibilities of interpretation and to help the formation of a severer code of emendation. Only through the discipline of endless trial and failure can be won the sure sense of where explanation becomes impossible and alteration of the text necessary. It is the fine flower of criticism and few attain it' ('Massinger's Autograph Corrections in *The Duke of Milan*, 1623', in *Collected Papers*, p. 118).

to ask afresh what constitutes the *proper* regulation of editorial freedom in this respect.[13]

We may start with a somewhat polemical point. Are we really still reluctant, and should we be, to discover half a dozen or even half a hundred conjectural emendations of a Shakespearean reading 'with claims upon our attention'? They are less likely nowadays, I fancy, to be ignorant and silly, and, if they are, their claims will not long importune us. Suppose them, however, to represent the speculations of judicious and well-informed scholars. Half a dozen intelligent guesses, though they fail in the end to win general approval, may stimulate a seventh man to the brilliant emendation of the great critic. Greg himself notes of one of the very emendations he cites as justly famous, Theobald's 'a' babled of green Fields' (for *a Table of greene fields, Henry V*, II.iii.17) that it was in fact suggested, on Theobald's own admission, by the previous conjecture of 'a Gentleman sometime deceas'd', *viz.* 'a' talked of green Fields'. We need to remind ourselves, perhaps, of the platitude that the constant circulation of fresh ideas is a stimulus to talent.

That may count, if at all, as a practical inducement to insist less rigorously on prudence and restraint. But there is a good theoretical justification as well for deprecating Greg's canons of emendation as altogether too absolute and narrow.

To his criterion of consistency there can be little objection. An editor's emendations must obviously conform to his textual theory. It is surprising, all the same, to find Greg stating that 'a sufficient number of acceptable emendations would form a good enough ground for the revision of any textual theory'.[14] Does this mean that, until the 'sufficient number' has been reached, inconsistencies will not signify? Surely even a single conflict between a convincing

---

13 In venturing to criticise Greg's essay I shall not, I believe, be invoking unfamiliar principles. The views I advance have long been common currency in the field of Classical criticism, if not universally accepted there. They have been eloquently championed in the still less distant field of medieval studies (by George Kane, 'Conjectural Emendation', in *Medieval Literature and Civilization: Studies in Memory of G. N. Garmonsway*, ed. D. A. Pearsall and R. A. Waldron (London, 1969), pp. 155–69). Yet, if these ideas are familiar to Shakespearean scholars, they are largely ignored or distrusted by them. Thus it seems to me that they deserve a more determined advocacy, in relation to Shakespeare's text, than (so far as I am aware) they have yet received. The 'probabilistic' character of textual-critical (and bibliographical) argument (see below, p. 172) has received much attention lately. The debate, summarised in G. T. Tanselle, 'Bibliography and Science', *Studies in Bibliography*, XXVII (1974), pp. 55–89, reflects general agreement on the main point at issue – and it is this agreed view which I apply to the problem of emendation.

14 *Principles of Emendation*, p. 8.

170   emendation and a textual hypothesis must be sufficient to cast doubt on the hypothesis? Surely too, therefore, we should assume that emendations of this order – it is otherwise with those conjecturally proposed on weaker grounds of probability – form part, in effect, of the evidence on which the editor founds his hypothesis?

Greg's rule of acceptability, by contrast, is very stringent. It is accompanied by an emphasis on 'certainty' as the aim in view ('unless [the conditions] are fulfilled there can be no certainty about the emendation').[15] It implies, too, that genuine errors are rarely even to be identified with any confidence – or so, at least, the drift of the argument might lead us to conclude.

From the definition of 'acceptability' we might deduce that those readings only are to be treated as erroneous which do not 'supply exactly the sense required by the context', but this would be to place too liberal an interpretation on Greg's intention. He is at pains to add that 'even the most careful authors do sometimes write sentences which it is impossible to regard as affording a perfectly satisfactory sense', and that 'if we were to cast out of Shakespeare's text all phrases which we should hesitate to admit into it as emendations, . . . we should leave some considerable gaps in the canon'. From this we are induced to conclude that it would not be safe to regard as erroneous any but the most clearly nonsensical readings.

This highly restrictive view need not detain us long. The belief implicit in it was once and for all discountenanced by a well-known Classical critic whose pronouncement on the question it is always a pleasure to recall: 'Chance and the common course of nature will not bring it to pass that the readings of a manuscript are right wherever they are possible and impossible wherever they are wrong: that needs divine intervention; and when one considers the history of man and the spectacle of the universe I hope it may be said without impiety that divine intervention might have been better employed elsewhere'.[16]

It may be added that, if Shakespeare's text is replete with phrases an editor would hesitate to introduce into it himself, that can only be because it is extensively marred by corruptions. We may observe, too, about the reminder that every author is liable sometimes to write less than perfect sense that, in so far as that tendency amounts to no more than an eccentric habit of thought or

15   *Ibid.*, p. 6.

16   A. E. Housman, 'Preface to Manilius I (1903)', in *Selected Prose*, ed. John Carter (Cambridge, 1961), p. 36.

style, it is the editor's business to know and recognise the indications, while, in so far as it is a question of unwitting solecisms, the editor should find it possible not to repine that occasionally, unbeknownst to himself or anyone else, he may correct an error which he should have preserved; by refraining whenever he feels he may be running that somewhat factitious risk he will almost certainly preserve many errors he should have corrected.

It is scarcely possible to rest satisfied even with the less cautious position implied by Greg's criterion of acceptability, namely that error is to be identified not only in impossible readings but in those which do not provide 'exactly the sense required by the context'. We should be wary of too narrow an insistence on 'sense'. It needs little thought to realise that a reading may supply a speciously acceptable sense and yet violate the logic of its context or destroy its rhetorical pattern or disrupt its metre. It may, though its sense is clear enough, prove entirely inconsistent with contemporary conventions of grammar or syntax or idiomatic usage. It may introduce an idea comprehensible in the immediate linguistic context, but incomprehensible in relation to the context of action or stage business or to the wider dramatic context of plot and character-relationship. And so on. An editor should surely be alive to the possibility that other purposes of importance to his author besides that of constructing intelligible sentences may be distorted by a corrupt or spurious reading.[17]

It might, of course, be argued that Greg was using the term without too fussy a concern for explicitness when he said that an emendation should restore the 'sense' required by the context. He doubtless meant that a good emendation should be compatible with the context in all its relations. The more material point, it might be urged, lies in his insistence that no emendation should be acceptable unless it fulfils the requirement with certainty.

To this argument two replies would, I think, be in order. One, that if 'sense' is understood in its widest acceptation the editor's chances of approaching certainty must be greater than Greg would have us believe. The standard of acceptance is not quite so formidably high. If a wide range of criteria may be recognised as applying to the identification of error, the same criteria apply as well to its emendation. It must often enough happen that a reading is condemned on several counts: it may happen that an emendation is approved on several. It is important in regarding such cases from a theoretical standpoint not

---

17   The argument, to be sure, might well be reversed. A reading unacceptable on grounds exclusively of 'sense' may fully justify itself on less narrow inspection. Instances occur in the text of *King Lear*. See, for example, comments on IV.ii.28, Appendix A7, p. 221 below.

172 to view them as failing or succeeding solely in regard of 'sense'. For when it comes to appraising the worth of emendations, it is obvious that, as the number, variety and stringency of the conditions to be satisfied increases, so may our confidence in accepting the conjecture which meets all of them successfully.

Secondly, it must be said that 'certainty' is a term admitted largely out of innocent vanity into the vocabulary of textual criticism. There can be very little certainty in textual matters. The largest part of an editor's determinations, which must certainly include the whole of his effort to identify and emend errors of reading, must be based on a balancing of probabiilities in the light of availble information. His conclusions may derive further strength from the support which they give to each other – the likelihood of a hypothesis must increase as it is found compatible with other likely and related hypotheses – but certain proofs are in the nature of things beyond his reach. That there is nothing irrational or unsound in this mode of proceeding is demonstrated by the not dissimilar methodologies of some of the non-experimental sciences, and by still more closely analogous procedures in the disciplines of history and archaeology. It is not, therefore, necessary to assume that only extremes of caution (the closest possible approach to 'certainty') can compensate for the ambiguous character of textual evidence and the fundamentally insecure structure of textual-critical argument. Indeed the critic must inevitably defeat his own purpose by distrusting the methods he is obliged in any case to use.

To be more explicit: if confidence in textual criticism is measured largely by the balancing of probabilities, it is only reasonable to argue that emendation should not be withheld from all but 'certain' cases of error, and that it should not be required itself to achieve 'certainty'. If an editor is convinced, on balance, that a reading is more likely to be erroneous than not, he is guilty of self-contradiction in attempting to explain it away as possibly what the author intended. And if the emendation he is prepared to offer in its place does not fully satisfy his sense of what is required, he should in consistency none the less propose it, since it must be closer, in his opinion, to the author's intention than the reading he rejects.[18]

---

18 To this a plausible counter-argument might be returned, that, since we can have no communication with the original version of a text except through the readings of the early editions, an editor should be extremely chary of severing the connection. He will, therefore, rightly be reluctant to replace an inferior reading which there is some slight chance may reflect the original with a doubtful emendation which there is some chance will misrepresent it. By yielding, however, to this natural reluctance on principle, regardless on every occasion of his honest appraisal of the alternatives before him, will he not subvert his own

I may, perhaps, repeat now with less appearance of wilful paradoxicality that 173 the text of Q requires frequent, and sometimes radical, emendation. In discounting the theoretical prejudices likely to discourage such an undertaking, I do not, of course, overlook the practical difficulties. The Appendices following this chapter (A1–6) represent an attempt to classify the erroneous readings in Q. Since I have been obliged in numerous instances, where accepted emendations (drawn mainly from F) are wanting or inadequate, to draw my own conclusions as to the kind of corruption exemplified, I have had necessarily to venture conjectural emendations of my own. In making the attempt I have hoped partly to show that the conclusions of this study do not necessarily leave the editor with counsels of despair, and partly to suggest, by my rather tentative answers to many of the problems, the way to better solutions.

It remains true, of course, that, with the utmost that editorial industry and ingenuity can do, a reliable reconstruction of the text of *King Lear* must lie well beyond the bounds of possibility. The all-important evidence of Q is woefully imperfect. There is good reason to suspect that, apart from its obvious irregularities and corruptions, it may have been mutilated in ways not now readily detectable: portions of the text may have been omitted by way of abridgement in the theatre, or accidentally dropped by the reporter, others perhaps travestied by nervous actors mangling their lines. Considering these probable defects, the many others more certain which resulted from the extremely hazardous means by which the text was transmitted, and the very limited help to be expected amid these perplexities from the text of F, the prospective editor might well feel a sinking of the heart. Yet if the outlook is not especially encouraging, the endeavour would certainly be worthwhile. The worst of Q's deficiencies must count as minor blemishes when it is considered that it undoubtedly reproduces more faithfully and more completely than any other of the early editions the play that Shakespeare originally wrote.

We are assuming, however, an editor committed to the scholar's aim of establishing a text which approximates as closely as possible to the original. Other aims there may well be, and perhaps ought to be: that, for example, of

aims and, by the same token, evade his responsibility to the reader? A reader will expect to find in the text what in the editor's best judgement most closely approximates to the original. He will not rejoice to be brought up short by every dubious reading, nor be gratified to discover in footnotes that the editor, while aware of the difficulties, has none the less thrown him upon his own speculations. It is not even as if he would otherwise be forbidden his own speculations, since in a critical edition all readings displaced by emendation are by sound tradition recorded in the apparatus.

174 continuing to provide the reading public and the theatrical profession with a version of the play which has been known, loved and revered for almost as long as the play has existed. There can, at any rate, be nothing wrong with such a purpose. The text of F has advantages beyond that of familiarity. Though a heavily edited text, it was skilfully revised, and by a contemporary of Shakespeare's, with the practical end in view, what is more, of theatrical production. If it ought not, as I believe, to satisfy the student and the scholar, it may better serve the turn (its more obvious lapses duly retrieved) of those whose interest in Shakespeare is not much affected by academic scruples.

APPENDICES

The following lists present a detailed review of evidence relevant to the discussion in the preceding chapters. The majority of this evidence has not been previously cited. The whole is now set out, with such additional comment as may be necessary to show its compatibility with the explanations given. At the same time, since the problems connected with the textual history of *King Lear* are interesting largely because they bear upon the problem of editing the play, it seemed desirable to demonstrate as far as possible the practicability of an edition in conformity with the theory here proposed.

The resulting classification represents a compromise. In Appendices A1–6 will be found lists of the substantive errors in Q1, errors which will constitute the main problem facing the editor of the play. They are classified according to type for clearer treatment and to facilitate reference from the text of this book. These lists show the correspondent readings in F, wherever they exist. Thus they serve also to illustrate the extent to which substantive errors in Q have been retained in F, further corrupted, replaced by editorial substitutes – or successfully corrected.

Variants printed in italics are those presumed to be correct. In a few cases correct readings are cited from Q2 or from the (contemporary) manuscript revisions in surviving copies of Q1.[1]

Wherever necessary I offer conjectural emendations. I need not, perhaps, emphasise that they are conjectural, and therefore offered with varying degrees of confidence. Especially tentative proposals are marked: '?Emend'.

Since every emendation implies a categorisation of the error corrected, an equal uncertainty attends the classification of emended readings. This is of material importance only in relation to the controversial category of phonetic errors. The reader must judge whether the evidence of mishearings collected in Appendices A3 and A4 – including or excluding, as he thinks proper, the readings which appear there by virtue of their conjectural correction – will support the degree of weight placed upon it by the argument in Chapter Two.

---

1   The copies I refer to, BM2 and Bod2, are held in the British Library (C.34.k.17) and Bodleian (Malone 35) respectively. See Greg, *Variants*, pp. 115ff., for a complete list of manuscript alterations in the extant copies.

176   For the rest, I may, perhaps, remind the reader that the preceding pages have argued the need to attempt the emendation of Q wherever Q is wrong and F fails to correct it; but that the argument does not − nor, obviously, could it − prescribe for certainty in the results.

In Appendix A7 appears a list of Q readings which, though acceptable, have been subject to 'correction' in F of a more or less specious kind.

Appendix A8 contains all those Q/F variants which, in my judgement, might be regarded as offering the editor a problematical choice. These are the readings which might be regarded as 'true' variants (i.e. those derived independently from the Q manuscript which yet show no clear superiority of F over Q).

The lists in this section do not pretend to exhaustiveness. I have omitted trivial Q errors, and have inevitably exercised my own judgement in deciding which are trivial, as inevitably, too, I have done in deciding what constitutes an error. I give no details of mispunctuation, mislineation or faulty stage directions in Q: lists of errors in these categories would be endless, and though they present a serious enough editorial problem it is not such as requires particular commentary.

Another kind of omission demands more particular notice. Excluded from the lists is an extensive category of Q/F variants which might easily be explained by the theory here proposed, but which might as easily be accommodated by an indefinite number of alternative theories. This is the class of 'indifferent' variants which, because of the equal admissibility of the readings in each pair, and at the same time the lack of any sign that one reading has derived from the other (or that both stem from a common source), can indicate only that one of the texts has undergone some radical form of alteration or corruption. Either reading in each such pair might be adjudged, with more or less conviction, 'superior' to the other, according to the text one wished to defend, but judgements of the sort are often little better than arbitrary assertions, and I have thought it better to avoid them. The status of these variants must be determined, I assume, by inference from evidence of a more informative kind.

Further data of importance to the editorial question are comprised in Appendices B1 and B2, which relate respectively to the ascription of speeches in Q and F and to the omissions and additions in the F text.

Appendices C1 and C2 contain evidence of particular features of the F text upon which part of the preceding argument has been based. In Appendices D1−4 will be found details illustrating the relationship of F with Q2.

All line references are to the Globe edition of 1864. All definitions are quoted, unless otherwise specified, from the *Oxford English Dictionary*.

APPENDIX A1

MISREADINGS IN Q1

Note: From the nature of the misreadings in Q, a large number of which are corrected either in Qb or in F, we may infer a fair amount about the handwriting in the manuscript copy. That its illegibility may have been due less to untidiness or crowding or wilful distortion than to the haste of the writer is suggested by much of the evidence. Most notably by those mistakes which show, some of them, that separate words were connected by a stroke of the pen (so that the compositor set them as one word) and, others, that a lift of the pen in the middle of the word left a larger gap than was intended (so that the compositor saw one word as two). These are signs of hurried writing. They are confirmed by the evidence of certain recurrent misreadings which appear to have originated in oversimplified outlines of the letters concerned. For example, 'o' is very often misread as 'a', 'r' or 'e', no doubt because the top of the letter was left open; equally often 'a' is taken for 'o', which seems to indicate that the descender on the right of the letter was left unformed, being assimilated, perhaps, with a horizontal link rightwards to the next letter. The letters 't' and 'l' are regularly confused one with another. Several times 'k' is read as 'b', from which the most plausible inference is that 'k' was written in one continuous stroke, the descender being looped up to the right to join with the cross-strokes. 'B', on the other hand, never mistaken for 'k', seems to have been left with an insufficiently pronounced loop at the bottom of the letter: it is sometimes read as 'l' or 't'. The 'r' was apparently not easy to distinguish from 'n', 'u' and 'o'.

We find besides, of course, no lack of the misreadings to which secretary hand customarily gives rise: the minim confusions, the mistaking of final 'e' for final 'd' and *vice versa*, the interchanging of 's' and 'f' and the failure to notice, or decipher correctly, the ligature of 's' or 'f' with a succeeding letter (e.g. 'c', 'l', 'r', 't').

On the other hand, one does not receive the impression of a featureless scrawl. It is, perhaps, not very significant that the letters never misread are 'h', 'p', 'q', 'x', 'y' and 'z': their secretary forms are sufficiently distinctive to remain recognisable in all but the most careless hands. Other letters, however, potentially much more liable to misconstruction, e.g. 'c', medial 'd', 'g', 'i' and 'w', must have been clearly formed on the whole, since they are rarely missed.

178

	Q1	F
I.i.41	Confirming	*Conferring*
I.i.84	confirm'd	*conferr'd*
I.i.172	straied	*strain'd*
I.ii.148	them of	*Tom o'*

(The name may have been spelt *Thom* in the copy.)

I.iv.168	a: lodes b: *Ladies*	(om.)
I.iv.284	list	*lyest*
I.iv.305	disuetur'd	*disnatur'd*
II.i.31	crauing	*cunning*
II.i.60	found	found

Emend: *sound* (= free from injury). The QF reading, generally retained in modern editions, entails a clumsy and unconvincing syntax: 'Not in this land shall he remain uncaught, / And, found – despatch!' (i.e. 'if he is found, despatch him!'). It is clear, moreover, from the succeeding lines that Edgar is not to be despatched as soon as found, but brought to the stake. The construction is surely simpler. Gloucester's menace is less specific, a *litotes*: 'Not in this land shall he remain uncaught / And sound'. 'Despatch!' is addressed to the attendants who have earlier been ordered to pursue Edgar. (Reiterated instructions of this kind – to apparently sluggish retainers – are a curious feature of the play. See esp. IV.iv.)

II.i.122	a: prise b: *poyse*	prize

Poise (= weight, gravity, importance) is required by the context. *Price* or *prize* (= value, worth) would be unidiomatic. F's *prize* was possibly inherited from Q2. (See p. 156, n.22 above.)

II.i.126	a: hand b: *home*	home
II.ii.83	stir	*fire*
II.ii.86	dayes	*dogges*
II.ii.130	flechuent	*fleshment*

Though *fleshment* is a nonce-word, it must be correct. 'Flesh' is spelt *fleach* elsewhere in Q
(V.iii.24); and surprisingly often elsewhere, too, 'm' is misread. An affected coinage, furthermore, is appropriate in the mouth of Oswald. I do not quite agree, however, with the sense
attributed to the word in *OED* and editorial glossaries: 'the action of "fleshing" [i.e. rewarding a
hound with flesh from the game killed so as to excite its eagerness in the chase]; hence, the
excitement resulting from a first success'. The extension of meaning to 'excitement' is not
required, though it remains, of course, a natural implication. 'In the fleshment of this dread
exploit' may quite well convey, 'On the rewarding of, on his receiving a reward for, this dread
exploit'. For 'in' = 'on' see Abbott §160.

II.ii.133	a: ausrent	*ancient*
	b: miscreant	
II.ii.139	a: Stobing	*Stocking*
	b: Stopping	
II.ii.141	a: set	sit
	b: *sit*	
II.ii.178	a: Late	Take
	b: *Take*	
II.iii.16	a: Pies	Pins
	b: *Pins*	
II.iii.17	a: frame	from
	b: *from*	
II.iii.17	seruice	*Farmes*
II.iv.1	hence	*home*
II.iv.8	heeles	*heads*
II.iv.35	men	*meiney* (= meinie)

Spelt, perhaps, *meyne* (see *OED*) in the copy.

II.iv.57	Historica	Historica

Emend: *Hysterica* (F4).

II.iv.90	Iustice	fetches

Emend: *justles*. (For comment see p. 49 above.)

180 II.iv.120 cry   crie

? Emend: *try* (= afflict). The verb *cry* seems entirely inappropriate to the sound of a drum, and as unsuitable in the transitive construction 'cry sleep to death'.

II.iv.139   a: diptoued   deprau'd
            b: depriued

Emend: *deplor'd* (= deplorable = lamentable, miserable. See Abbott §375 for the use of *-ed* in place of *-able*, and cf. IV.vi.21 *vnnumbred* for 'innumerable'). Since Lear's sentence is incomplete and the clues it provides, therefore, not very specific, *deplor'd* cannot be preferred to *deprau'd* on grounds of sense: both are possible. But the former is far more likely as the source of the misreading *diptoued*. Whereas 'l'/'t' errors are common in Q, the mistaking of 'r' for 't', intrinsically unlikely, is unexampled elsewhere in the text.

II.iv.278–9 foole me not   foole me not
            to much,   so much,
            To beare it lamely   To beare it *tamely*

? Emend: *school* (= teach [a person] his part). The construction in both texts involves an ellipsis which would be avoided in modern English – Q: 'Fool me not too much (for me) to bear it lamely'; F: 'Fool me not so much (as that I) bear it tamely'. Q says the opposite of what is meant, and that undoubtedly accounts for the emendation in F. It is arguable, however, that a misreading *schoole* (sp. *scole*?) / *foole* in Q would be more likely than the misreading *so/to* implicit in F's correction; and, more forcibly, that Lear in this speech would hardly see himself as duped ('fooled') by the Gods while invoking their support in his ordeal: 'You Heavens, give me that patience, patience I need!' But the reading *tamely* in F is surely correct.

II.iv.304   russel   *ruffle*

III.iv.6   a: crulentious   *contentious*
            b: tempestious

III.iv.52   fire   Fire

? Emend: *firth* (= arm of the sea, estuary of a river. Originally a Scottish word, introduced into English literary usage c. 1600). Since 'poor Tom' has been led by the 'foul fiend' through a series of watery ordeals (ford, whirlpool, bog, quagmire) it is odd to find 'fire' mentioned casually among them ('through fire and through ford'). The F editor, perceiving the anomaly, removed it by adding a phrase: *though* [sic] *Fire, and through Flame*. It is possible that in fact the Q compositor misread a phonetic spelling, *fird*.

III.iv.113 a: leadings   Lendings
            b: *lendings*

III.iv.120	a: Sriberdegibit b: fliberdegibek	Flibbertigibbet

Emend: *Fliberdigibbet*, the spelling in Samuel Harsnett's *A Declaration of Egregious Popishe Impostures*, from which this and other names were taken.

III.iv.122	a: he gins the web, the pin-queues the eye b: he *giues* the web, & the pin, squemes the eye	Hee giues the Web and the Pin squints the eye

? Emend: *skews*. Neither *squints* nor *squinies* (= squints; adopted in some editions) is quite convincing. Both are intransitive verbs, or transitive but with a reflexive implication: one may squint one's own eye, but it cannot be squinted by some other agent. The verb 'skew', meaning 'squint', but employable, too, in various transitive applications, seems more appropriate. This conjecture implies an extraordinary phonetic spelling (*squeues*) in the copy; on the other hand, a spelling which closely corresponds with the original reading in Qa. (The more attractive alternative that we are dealing here with a phonetic error, i.e. that the reporter originally heard and wrote *pins queues*, should perhaps be ruled out as the less likely possibility. Final 's' and initial 's' in secretary hand are entirely distinct letters and we should have to postulate a deliberate critical emendation on the part of the press-corrector in removing an 's' which clearly belonged to *pins* so as to place it at the beginning of *queues*.)

III.iv.126	a: a nellthu night more b: *he met the night mare*	He met the Night-Mare

III.iv.129	a: with b: *witch*	Witch

III.iv.135	a: wall-wort b: *wall-newt*	wall-Neut

III.iv.146	snulbug	Smulkin

Emend: *Smolkin* (Harsnett). The spelling in Q copy evidently terminated in a hyper-correct *-ing* for a sound heard as '-in'.

III.iv.149	modo	Modo

Emend: *Modu* (Harsnett).

III.iv.187	towne	*Tower*

III.vi.5	deserue	reward

Emend: *discern* (cf. below the identical error at IV.ii.52).

182   III.vi.7   Fretereto   Fraterretto

Emend: *Fraterretto* (Harsnett).

III.vi.27   broome   (om.)

Emend: *bourne* (Capell: boorne).

III.vi.57   store   (om.)

Emend: *stone* (Theobald).

III.vi.72   him   Hym

Emend: *lym* (Hanmer).

III.vii.10   festuant   festiuate
            (BM2: festiuant)   (F2: festinate)

Emend: *festinant* – as is obviously intended by the correction in BM2. No less or more of a coinage than *festinate*, it is equally acceptable as such – later coinages from the same root include 'festinance' and 'festinancy' – while being more acceptable as the origin of Q's *festuant*.

III.vii.17   questrits   Questrists
            (BM2: coystrills)

Emend: *questrels.* (For comment, see p. 50 above.)

III.vii.58   a: aurynted   Annointed
            b: *annoynted*

III.vii.59   a: of his lou'd head   *as his bare head*
            b: on his lowd head

Or, possibly, *bow'd head*, as the Q corrector must have intended.

III.vii.60   a: layd   buoy'd
            b: bod

Emend: *boil'd* (Warburton). Modern editions gloss *buoy'd* as 'rose, swelled', as does *OED*, but on the strength of this passage alone. Though no doubt the F editor had such a meaning in mind, as a metaphorical extension of the ordinary meaning of 'buoy'd' it is both feeble and strained. Warburton's emendation is convincing. Q copy must have shown *boyd*, as the result, perhaps, of a naive mishearing.

III.vii.61   a: steeled   Stelled
               b: *stelled*

III.vii.63   heard   *howl'd*

Written *hould* in the copy, or possible *howd*, since the 'l' may not have been heard, or, conceivably in this case, even pronounced (*cf.* Dobson, II. 988).

IV.i.39   bitt   *kill*

IV.i.44   here   *hence*

IV.i.64   Stiberdigebit   (om.)

Emend: *Fliberdigibbet* (Harsnett).

IV.i.73   vnder   *vndoo*

IV.ii.10   desire   dislike

Emend: *defy* (= set at nought, reject), likely to be misread *desire*, if the copy-spelling were *defie*. Cf. *As You Like It*, Epilogue, lines 20–1: 'complexions that liked me and breaths that I defied not'.

IV.ii.12   a: curre   terror
               b: terrer

? Emend: *tenor* (= quality, character . . . in non-physical sense: the way in which a thing continues; *esp.* habitual condition of mind). *Terror* seems too strong a word for the faint-heartedness in Albany 'that dares not undertake'; *cowish terror* is feebly pleonastic. A neutral word seems required to throw the emphasis on *cowish*. The Q copy spelt it, perhaps, *tenner*.

IV.ii.21   a: coward   command
               b: *command*

IV.ii.45   a: beniflicted   (om.)
               b: *benifited*

IV.ii.49   a: Humanly   (om.)
               b: *Humanity*

IV.ii.52   eye deseruing   eye-*discerning*

(F's hyphen, however, is an error.)

184 IV.ii.56   a: noystles   (om.)
                    b: *noyseles* (= noiseless)

     IV.ii.57   a: slayer begin threats   (om.)
                    b: state begins thereat

? Emend: *slyre* (= a fine kind of linen or lawn) *biggin* (= a cap or hood for the head) *threats*. It is safe to assume that the compositor, as so often elsewhere, accepted uncritically what he found in the copy. If so, the corrector's (Qb) version is pure sophistication, and has not the merit, in any case, of making better sense. The emendation I suggest makes credible the misreading in Qa and provides, as seems called for, the image by which Goneril contrasts Albany's unpreparedness with the armed menace of France: 'France spreads his banners in our noiseless land, / With plumed helm thy slyre biggin threats, / Whilst thou, a moral fool, sits still and cries: / Alack, why does he so?' But, whereas I place some confidence in *biggin* (*cf.* the use of 'quoif' in a closely analogous context, *2 Henry IV*, I.i.147–9), I am less certain of *slyre*, which is a Scottish word.

     IV.ii.60   a: seemes   seemes
                    b: *shewes*

The copy-spelling was doubtless *sewes*, misread as *semes*.

     IV.ii.73   thrald   *thrill'd*

     IV.iii.18   streme   (om.)

Emend: *strove* (Pope)

     IV.iii.31   beleeft   (om.)

Emend: *beleft* (past tense of 'beleave' = abandon).

     IV.iii.33   moystened   (om.)

Emend: *master'd* (= overcame), on the assumption of a copy-spelling *maystered*, which would be consistent with the invariable Q spelling *maister*. Modern editions are right, if not, as I think, for the right reasons, to omit the succeeding *her*, which must have been introduced to justify *moystened*. The effect of the omission is to make *clamour* (which we must take to mean 'outburst of grief', as it does at V.iii.208) the object of *master'd*, and *she* (Cordelia) the subject – exactly what is required to clarify the sense.

     IV.iv.3   femiter   Fenitar

Emend: *fumiter* (Theobald), properly *fumitory*. Probably a misreading, but possibly a phonetic spelling in Q (see Kökeritz, p. 210, for spellings suggesting the pronunciation of '-ew-' as '-ee-').

IV.vi.23   the deficient sight   the deficient sight   185

Emend: *thy*. The one objection to reading 'thy' is that Edgar addresses Gloucester as 'you' throughout this part of the scene. On the other hand, the succeeding episode (following Gloucester's 'fall') finds Edgar calling him first 'thou', then 'you', then 'thou' again, while Gloucester, for his part, uses 'thou' and 'you' apparently indiscriminately. In other respects *thy* strongly recommends itself. Edgar, in saying: 'Lest my brain turn and the deficient sight / Topple down headlong', seems very oddly to speak of his sight as a part or appendage of his brain: such is the implication of the definite article where one would expect a repetition of 'my'. Furthermore, the word 'deficient' must in the circumstances mean 'fainting, failing': it is so glossed in *OED*, but on the slight evidence of this line and an equally questionable citation dated 1632. It is much more satisfactory to assume (a) that 'deficient' has its normal meaning here of 'wanting'; (b) that, if Edgar says 'thy deficient sight' will 'topple down headlong', he must nevertheless mean himself and not Gloucester, since the context makes it clear that Gloucester is still standing some way from the supposed edge of the imaginary cliff; and (c) that we may find an explanation of the difficulty in the ambiguous logical status of certain types of adjective in Elizabethan English. 'Thy deficient sight' might mean 'the sight which supplies your deficiency'. Compare 'your needy bread' (*Pericles*, I.iv.95), which can only mean 'the bread which supplies your need'. See Abbott §§ 3, 4 for numerous examples of a similarly paradoxical usage of adjectives in Shakespeare and other Elizabethan writers.

IV.vi.57   sommons   Somnet

Emend: *somnets* (= summits). The difficulty is to explain the reading in Q. (1) The use of plural forms as a means of amplifying (in the rhetorical sense) singular conceptions is common in this play, especially in the Q text, and indeed is common in Shakespeare generally (see Abbott § 338). The singular *Somnet* in F very probably represents an editorial alteration (as at I.i.37 *purposes/purpose*; 138 *additions/addition*; 223 *affections/affection*, and *passim*). (2) The form *sommons* is only explicable on the hypothesis that in the copy the tittle representing 'm' or 'n' was misplaced, so that the compositor found not *soṁets* (= somnets) but *soṁēts* (= soments), which either he or the press-corrector then further corrupted into *sommons*.

IV.vi.247   a: battero   Ballow
             b: bat

Emend: *batoon* or *baton* (= a staff or stick used as a weapon). The Q copy-spelling was probably *battoon*, the F (a manuscript correction of Qb) *Batton*. *OED* notes that *batoon* was the usual English (as distinct from Scots) form in the seventeenth and eighteenth centuries. Qb's *bat* is, of course, a mere expedient of the press-corrector's. *Ballow* is repudiated by *OED*.

V.i.52   Hard   *Heere*

V.i.52   quesse   guesse
          (Q2: *guesse*)

V.i.56   sting   *stung*

186 V.iii.28   a: And   One
                   b: *One*

     V.iii.46   a: saue   send
                   b: *send*

     V.iii.49   a: coren   common
                   b: *common*

     V.iii.123   yet are I mou't   Yet am I Noble as the
                   Where is the aduersarie   Aduersary
                   (Bod2: *ere*)

?Emend: *moot* (= speak). The word is appropriate in the formal context of a trial by combat, since it is especially associated with pleading, or other forms of address, in a court of law. Any such change depends, of course, on the acceptance of *ere* for *are*, itself less likely to be a misreading than a printing slip. F's alteration, in any event, though it makes sense, does not convince one as an accurate reflection of the original.

     V.iii.132   fortun'd   *Fortune*

     V.iii.135   Conspicuate   Conspirant
                   (BM2: Conspirator)

? Emend: *Conspirate* (Capell). Harsnett uses 'conspirant', but as a noun (= conspirator). The context here requires an adjective parallel with *false* in the preceding line. Capell's emendation is superior to F's both logically (since it derives, as befits the context, from *conspiratus* rather than *conspirans*) and on grounds of resemblance to the reading in Q. *Conspirate* has no lexicographical status, *conspirant* hardly any (*OED* quotes F, Harsnett and Swinburne).

     V.iii.143   being   *tongue*

     V.iii.291   foredoome   *fore-done*

APPENDIX A2

MISREADINGS IN Q1 IMPLYING THE MISDIVISION OR MISPLACEMENT OF WORDS IN THE COPY

	Q1	F
I.ii.147	mine	*my Cue*
I.iv.125	Ladie oth'e brach	the Lady Brach

Emend: *Lie the Brach* (Archibald Smith conjecture). An image antithetical to Truth the dog is clearly required, and no other possibility presents itself. The misreading in Q may be explained as the misconstruction of a hiatus in the copy between the *Ly* of *Lye* (mistaken for an abbreviation of 'Lady') and a detached 'e' resembling, because linked to the succeeding word, an 'o'.

II.i.72–3	no. what I should denie, as this I would	No, what should I denie, (As this I would . . .)

Emend: *Nowhat* (= nothing). (*OED* gives as a meaning of *What*, 'Something; anything: only OE exc. as surviving in phrases in which *what* is qualified by a quantitative or identifying word . . . e.g. ANYWHAT, ELSEWHAT . . . MUCHWHAT . . . NOWHAT . . . SOMEWHAT'.) It is likely that F is badly mispunctuated and that the reviser intended a rhetorical question: *No, what should I denie, / As this I would, though thou didst produce / My very Character?* But this creates an awkwardness in that it is tangential to the previous question, when its opening *No* leads one to anticipate a direct contradiction. 'Nothing', or its equivalent, is the word one naturally expects as the object of 'deny'.

II.ii.170–7

b:	
Approach thou beacon to this vnder gloabe, That by thy comfortable beames I may Peruse this letter, nothing almost sees my wracke But miserie, I know tis from *Cordelia*, Who hath most fortunately bin informed Of my obscured course, and shall find time From this enormious state, seeking to giue Losses their remedies	Approach thou Beacon to this vnder Globe, That by thy comfortable Beames I may Peruse this Letter. Nothing almost sees miracles But miserie. I know 'tis from *Cordelia*, Who hath most fortunately beene inform'd Of my obscured course. And shall finde time From this enormous State, seeking to giue Losses their remedies.

188 It was first noticed by Jennens that the sentence 'Nothing almost sees miracles but misery' forms part of Cordelia's letter. This piece of insight has found no favour with later critics, doubtless because they regard F as confirming the testimony of Q, which incorporates the words with Kent's speech. F, however, is merely copying Q in an error of misplacement, which the disruption of the metre makes obvious, if it were not sufficiently obvious from the sense, or lack of it. The sentence should have been printed clear of the speech, in italics, and with the direction '(reads)'. The half-lines before and after (*Peruse this letter . . . I know tis from* Cordelia) would then have appeared, as is evidently intended, to constitute a complete line broken by a quasi-aside in prose. It is not at all implausible, given Kent's situation at this juncture, that Cordelia should communicate with him in somewhat cryptic terms which she could none the less rely upon him to understand. Indeed, the ensuing lines of his speech indicate that he has taken her drift. Of the lines quoted above the last three have caused difficulties. I gloss them as follows: 'and [*sc.* she] shall find time [= people, society, as very often in Shakespeare; see Onions, *Glossary*] From [= away from, outside] this enormous [= disorderly] state seeking to give Losses home [= effective, for which emendation see Appendix A4, p. 201 below] remedies'. Kent has inferred, in short, that the French will be eager to support Cordelia by force of arms in claiming the restitution of her inheritance.

II.ii.172   a: my rackles   *miracles*
                      b: my wracke

II.iv.103   a: come and tends seruise   commands, tends, seruice
                      b: commands her seruice

Qb's reading is the most satisfactory from the point of view both of metre and of sense. Yet it is clearly a sophistication of what stood in the copy, as the reading of Qa shows. See the discussion of this passage above (pp. 86ff.). If my analysis of the difficulty is correct, the lines, duly emended and re-arranged, should run:

> *Glou.* Aye, my good Lord.
> *Lear.* The King would speak with Cornwall;
> The dear father would with his daughter speak.
> Command the fiery duke, tell the hot duke
> That Lear tends service . . .
> No, but not yet. Maybe he is not well . . .

Command = order to come; *tends service* = awaits 'duty' (in the complimentary sense, i.e. a payment of respects). The rearrangement of lines requires that *dear* be pronounced as a disyllable, but this is common in Shakespeare (see Abbott §480), and is probably necessitated in any case by the QF arrangement as reproduced in modern editions.

III.iv.149   ma hu   Mahu

Emend: *Maho* (Harsnett).

III.vi.102   a: Take vp to keepe   *Take vp, take vp*
              b: Take vp the King

IV.i.10   a: poorlie, leed,   poorely led?
              b: parti, eyd,

Emend: *purblind?* (= quite, or totally blind). *OED* is doubtful of the modern (sixteenth- and seventeenth-century) use of the word in this acceptation, but Shakespeare so uses it no fewer than four times (*Love's Labour's Lost*, III.i.181; *The Winter's Tale*, I.ii.228; *Troilus and Cressida*, I.ii.31 (Q); *Romeo and Juliet*, II.i.12). Editors have observed that Edgar ought to notice his father's blindness rather than the poverty of his attendant. Indeed neither common sense nor dramatic principle could justify any other reaction from him at this point. Qa and Qb between them give us the necessary clues to the reading in the copy. It may have commenced with *por-* or *poor-* (various spellings were current); *ti* (Qb) and *li(e)* (Qa) represent *b*, after which appeared a misleading gap; *leed* (Qa) reflects *-lind*, sophisticated into *eyd* in Qb. (I have no doubt that the corrector had in mind the bizarre emendation *parti-ey'd*.)

IV.vii.35   Per du   (om.)

Emend: *perdu* (Warburton).

V.iii.147   With the hell hatedly,   With the hell-hated Lye,
              oreturnd thy heart   ore-whelme thy heart

Emend: *With the hell-hated lie return'd to thy heart.* Q makes no sense and F involves a contradiction: if 'the lie' is to overwhelm Edgar's heart how may it be said in the next line to 'glance by and scarcely bruise'? (I take it that it would be grammatically impossible for *they* in this line to refer to *Treasons* alone.) The emendation suggested explains itself: Edmund is returning the lie to Edgar, who has called him 'false' (*cf. Richard II*, IV.i.39–40: 'And I will turn thy falsehood to thy heart, / Where it was forged, with my rapier's point'). *Lie* is represented by *ly* and *o-*: a final 'e' in secretary hand, if linked by a horizontal stroke to the succeeding word is not unlikely to be mistaken for 'o' (*cf.* the note on I.iv.125 above, where the identical mistake has occurred). The omission of *to* after [o]*returned* may be due to compositorial oversight, or to the reporter's mishearing: an unstressed 'to' between the sounds -d and dh- would be very liable to disappear.

APPENDIX A3
PHONETIC ERRORS IN Q1

Note: I have not thought it necessary in recording Elizabethan pronunciations to employ the phonetic alphabet, since the exact quality of the sounds is less important here than considerations of similarity, identity or difference. Readers will be more familiar with the phonetic scheme current in the smaller Oxford dictionaries, which serves the purpose sufficiently well. It distinguishes the relevant vowel-sounds as follows: māte, mēte, mīte, mōte, mūte, mōōt; răck, rĕck, rĭck, rŏck, rŭck, rŏok; *italics*, vague sounds.

One sound existed in Elizabethan English – a broad *e* similar to French *è* – for which we have no approximate equivalent. For this I have used the French notation.

Some difficulty arises over the notation of preconsonantal and final *r* which have vanished from modern English, but which, according to Dobson (II. 992), had not yet done so in Elizabethan times. Preconsonantal *r* was sometimes dropped (especially before *s* and *sh*, occasionally before other consonants), but for different reasons and with different effect, i.e. leaving the value of the preceding vowel unaltered (so that *burst* might be pronounced bŭst). Kökeritz, on the other hand, argues (pp. 315–16) that the modern habit was already established in Shakespeare's day. I am inclined to follow Dobson, so that *r* in the notations given below should be taken as sounded.

The sounded *r* apart, where I append no comment to the readings below on the pronunciation or pronunciations at issue, it should be assumed that they do not differ significantly from those of standard English today.

	Q1	F
I.i.60	As much a child ere loued, or father friend,	As much *as* Childe ere lou'd, or Father found.

? Emend: *faitour feign'd*. The word 'father' did not acquire its present pronunciation until the late seventeenth century. In Shakespeare's day it was pronounced either fādhĕr or fădhĕr (see Dobson, II. 467, and Kökeritz, p. 169), i.e. not very differently, in the latter guise, from 'faitour'. The reporter seems to have made the same substitution at V.iii.192 (see below). Such a mistake was all the more likely, perhaps, because the word 'faitour' (= impostor, cheat) was already obsolescent or obsolete. Shakespeare, however, uses it in another play (*2 Henry IV*, II.iv.171). The emendation proposed must be justified, if it can be at all, by a somewhat oblique argument. It is easily seen that Q is meaningless and that F's *Father found* permits, at best, a rather strained interpretation. An equally serious difficulty tends to go unremarked in editorial comments on the passage: the succeeding line, *A loue that makes breath poore, and speech vnable*, is entirely at odds syntactically with the rest of the speech. The pattern is one of adverbial clauses of degree qualifying a simple main statement: 'more than . . . Dearer than . . . Beyond . . . No less than . . . As much as . . . Beyond all manner of so much I love you'. The noun clause in line 61, quoted above, has no place in this series and is left, as the text stands, syntactically disjunct. It is difficult to avoid the inference, therefore, that it, too, is part of an adverbial clause and that it must be linked to the preceding 'As much as' by a verb concealed under the suspect reading *friend*. What that verb is must be partly determined by the nature of its subject, represented by *father*. At first sight, indeed, there is no reason to distrust *father*, since it stands as a natural antithesis to *child*. Given, however, the syntax we have assumed, it produces a logical absurdity. Goneril cannot intelligibly tell her father that she loves him as much as a *father* has ever loved (or inspired love, or received it, etc.). 'Faitour' is the one alternative I can conceive to *father*, and 'faitour' readily suggests 'feign'd', which, if spelt *feind* or *faind* in the copy might well be misread as *friend*. If my conjectures have any force, the lines should run: 'As much as child e'er loved, or faitour feign'd / A love that makes breath poor and speech unable, / Beyond all manner of so much I love you'.

I.i.76   square of sence   square of sense

Emend: *quar* (an abbreviated form of *quarry* = [*fig.*] any object of chase, aim . . .). *Quar* must have been pronounced, on the analogy of 'far', 'bar', etc., approximately as it would be now (see Dobson, II. 518–19). That the reporter heard *square* is explained by the facts that the preceding word ends with 's' (*precious*) and that educated speakers continued until 1650 or thereabouts to pronounce *square* as squăr (with lengthening of the vowel), although the modern pronunciation had already become current in vulgar speech early in the century (see Dobson, II. 95ff.). If the word *sense* is taken, as it may legitimately be, to mean 'the senses', it will immediately be seen that the substitution of *quar* for *square* satisfactorily clarifies the sentence. It is, perhaps, needless to add that *square of sense* never has been, nor, I think, could be, adequately explained.

I.i.112   mistresse   miseries
                                            (F2: *mysteries*)

I.i.193   with a King   with this King

Emend: *with the King*.

I.i.230   murder   murther

Emend: *mother* (= dregs, scum). The word was applied in its literal significance to the dregs or scum of vinegar, oil, etc. In a figurative sense it sorts much better with *blot* and *foulness* as generic images for stained virtue than does *murder* which is non-metaphorical, too specific and too strong (no one could imagine Cordelia capable of murder). *Mother* was pronounced more or less as now, *murder* as mŭrdher or mŭrder, or, if the *r* before *d* were not sounded, mŭdher (i.e. as a homonym of *mother*).

192   I.i.281   almes   almes

Emend: *arms*. Editors seem little troubled by the violation of idiom in 'at Fortune's alms', but seek, as well they might, to explain why Regan should regard Cordelia as *alms* (= a charitable gift) conferred by Fortune upon the French king. There is, by contrast, no strain either upon grammar or upon sense in the phrase: 'Who hath receiv'd you at Fortune's arms (= from the arms of Fortune)'. The phrase 'Fortune's alms' occurs in *Othello* (III.iv.122), where it strikes me as equally implausible, indeed another instance of the same mistake. 'Alms' was pronounced awms (where the older pronunciation ălms did not still prevail: see Dobson II. 553 and 604); an identical pronunciation existed for 'arms' (see Dobson II. 519–20), though polite speakers would pronounce it with long *a* and articulated *r*.

I.i.282   worth   want

Emend: *words*. The choice between Q and F is poor: all editions recognise the problem. The clue lies in the logic of Regan's gibe. Clearly she is intended to say that Cordelia is worth nothing, and to convey the idea of 'nothing' by referring to a conspicuous default in Cordelia's previous behaviour ('the . . . that you have wanted'). This can only be Cordelia's silence (*cf.* 'How, nothing can come of nothing', line 92). It is true that this way of putting it, '[You] well are worth the words that you have wanted', comes perilously close to saying the opposite of what is obviously meant. But the fault could not be remedied by any other choice of reading after *worth*: it lies in the confused structure of the sentence, which is not untypical of Shakespeare in expressing a negative idea. The assumed phonetic confusion involves the loss in hearing of '-dz' from *words* before 'dh-' of *that*, or rather the mergence of the two as '-th dh-': not improbable, granted a less than meticulous articulation.

I.ii.3   stand in   Stand in

Emend: *Stand on* (= to value, set store by [something external to oneself]). I can find no suitable meaning for *stand in*. According to *OED* the sense 'to rest or depend upon [something] as its ground of existence' relates only to things.

I.ii.13   a stale dull lyed bed   a dull stale tyred bed

Emend: *a stale dull-eyed bed*. (For comment, see pp. 51–2 above.)

I.ii.21   tooth'legitimate   to'th'Legitimate

? Emend: *tew th'legitimate* (= *taw* = [fig.] to treat . . . with contumely; to vex, torment; to harass, afflict). *Tew* might well be misheard as the commoner word, though its pronunciation (tū or tèō̄: see Dobson II. 799ff.) differed somewhat from tō̄. The context demands a monosyllabic verb: editors normally accept Capell's emendation *top*.

I.ii.83   I apprehend   Ile apprehend

Emend: *aye, apprehend*. (For comment, see p. 52 above.)

I.ii.99   aurigular   *Auricular*

I.ii.162   Cohorts   (om.)

Emend: *courts* (Steevens), pronounced evidently cōerts (i.e. with a glide before *r*), as would not be inconsistent with what is known from other sources about the contemporary pronunciation of the word and others like it. (The evidence is not, however, of the clearest. Dobson, II. 688 §(a), 689 n. 1, 739 §(iii), seems to leave it an open question whether the word at this date would be pronounced cōōrt or cōrt. Though the evidence for a glide before *r* in such words, *viz.* those incorporating ME *ū* before *r*-plus-consonant, is scanty, Dobson says (II.762) that 'we should expect the glide to be fairly frequent' and that 'the extreme paucity of evidence . . . may be accidental'.)

I.iv.236   beit   *by it*

'By' was pronounced beī (see Dobson, II. 451).

I.iv.305   thourt   *thwart*

Judging by variant spellings listed in *OED*, the pronunciation was thawrt or thawt.

I.iv.366   a: y'are much more alapt   Your are much more at task
                 want of wisedome, then   for want of wisedome,
                 praise for harmfull mildnes   Then prai'sd for harmefull
                 b: . . . attaskt for want . . .   mildnesse.

Emend: *You were* or *You're . . . ill-happ'd to want . . .* The phrases *attaskt for* and *at task for* are unknown to the language. Greg's coinage *attax'd,* adopted in some editions, though it is more consonant with the original reading *alapt,* is scarcely of more genuine manufacture. The problem resolves itself if *alapt* is regarded not as a misreading but as an error of the ear. The main verb must in consequence be converted to a subjunctive, but *praise* may be left unchanged. The emended reading may be explained: 'You were (= would be) much more ill-happ'd (= unfortunate) to want of (= lack) wisdom / Than [to want of] praise for harmful mildness'. The phonetic mistake may be easily accounted for as a failure to catch the 'h' of *happ'd* (because, perhaps, it was dropped), and the loss of an unemphatic *to* between words which respectively repeat and anticipate its component sounds. The mishearing *y'are* for *you're* or *you were* is, it must be admitted, less intelligible; but it may be that *y'are* is rather to be seen as a misreading.

I.iv.369   ought   *oft*

II.i.121   Thus   Thus

Emend: *This,* so as to read: *This out-of-season, threatening, dark-ey'd night.* One cannot feel easy about *threatening* in Q as a misreading of F's *thredding* (always accepted in modern editions). Still less satisfactory is the association of 'thread' (= to make one's way through [a narrow place, a forest, a crowd, or the like]) with 'night': the primary idea of passing through a gap or series of gaps virtually disappears. That in addition *threading* supports a pun on *ey'd,* as some editors aver,

194   is incredible: (a) a reminder here of the eye of a needle would be irrelevant to the point of unintelligibility, (b) *dark-ey'd* is already laden with metaphorical meaning ('dark' = sightless; hence 'dark-ey'd' = blind; hence further – as applied to 'night' = moonless). This is not to say that *ey'd* may not have suggested *thredding* to the F editor, who, accepting *Thus* at the beginning of the line, and reading *out of season* as an adverbial phrase, looked to replace *threatening* with a verb implying motion. The emendation proposed does, however, raise a difficulty; or rather is implicated in a difficulty raised at several points in the course of Act II: how are we to understand the passage of time during its four scenes and the intervals between them? Regan's description of the night is, I believe, intended as a portent of the coming storm: yet the storm does not break, it is clear, until the *following* night. If there is an inconsistency here, however, it is not the only one of its kind. Though the night, according to Regan, is *dark-ey'd*, we find the moon shining in the next scene (which must follow without break, since it opens with an enquiry from Regan's steward about shelter for her horses). Whereas, again, Regan and Cornwall are evidently roused at Lear's behest the following *morning* ('Good morrow to you both', II.iv.129), they are scarcely up before night falls again ('Alack, the night comes on', II.iv.303). The play, however, as is well known from A. C. Bradley's analysis, is riddled with minor anomalies and contradictions of this kind. The time of year, at least, causes no perplexity. Though the night of the storm is cold (III.iv.80), the season is summer (*cf.* the 'high-grown field', IV.iv.6), hence the epithet *out-of-season*.

II.ii.1	a: deuen	dawning
	b: *euen*	

Qb is certainly correct (though it was possibly a variant spelling – perhaps *good deven* on the analogy of *good-den* – rather than a phonetic confusion which the corrector emended). The scene takes place at night and not at dawn (*cf.* lines 33–4, 'though it be night, the moon shines'), the action probably intended to be continuous with that of the preceding scene. The shining moon contradicts Regan's 'dark-ey'd night' (see preceding note), but this may be overlooked as the kind of careless, and not immediately obvious, inconsistency discoverable throughout the play. F's *Good dawning* was possibly invented (it is not an expression known to *OED*) to suit Oswald's euphuistic style.

II.ii.81   to intrench, to inloose   t'intrince, t'vnloose

Emend: *too entrench'd to unloose*. (For comment, see pp. 52–3 above.)

II.ii.115   dialogue   *dialect*

The final t of *dialect* would be dropped in vulgar speech (see Dobson, II. 961–2), and evidently was by the actor.

II.ii.146   speake   speakes

Emend: *spake*. The sound of *speake* (spèk) was closely similar: see Dobson, II. 623ff. For comment on the reading in its context, see p. 54 above.

II.ii.153   hee's so   *he so*

II.iii.10   else all   elfe all

? Emend: *ensnarl* (= to catch or entangle in . . . a 'snarl' or ravelled knot). Modern editions adopt the reading in F. The verb 'elf', however, is unknown outside this passage, if we leave out of consideration an eighteenth-century etymological dictionary which very probably copies it from here. The undoubtedly genuine expression 'elf-locks' (= a tangled mass of hair, superstitiously attributed to the agency of elves) lends it some colour which, however, one may feel inclined to discount on considering the very unusual extension of meaning involved: 'to elf = to tangle or twist (hair) as an elf might do. (Personal nouns converted into transitive verbs do not normally carry the sense 'behaving as a . . .' unless constructed with 'it', e.g. 'to lord it'; but instead imply 'turning (the object) into a . . .'. Shakespeare so uses 'to coward', 'to fool', 'to god', etc.) *Ensnarl*, at all events, is an obvious substitute, and not impossible as the cause of the error in Q. Were the accented syllable pronounced awl and interpreted as *all* (*cf. arms / alms* at I.i.281 above), the more serious confusion at the beginning of the word might well have occurred.

II.iii.20   a: poore Tuelygod   poore Turlygod
                 b: poore Turlygod

? Emend: *tirly-gaud* or *tirlery-gaud*. *OED* defines 'tirlery' as: '? Whirling, flighty, trifling, trumpery'. It is used only in combinations. Those cited (under various spellings of the word) include *tyrlery trashe, turlery-ginkes, tirlery-puffkins*. All derive from the period c. 1550–c. 1650 and all are used, judging from their respective contexts, as terms of mild contempt for frivolous or insignificant things or persons. The *English Dialect Dictionary* cites *tirly-toy,* an exactly analogous expression. Though the first and only citation is dated 1809, this parallel is interesting since the meaning of 'gaud' is 'toy' or 'gewgaw'. It does not, at any event, seem too far a step from this evidence to the conclusion that *Turlygod* may represent *tirlery-gaud*, and that the expression *poor tirlery-gaud* might mean, as is quite appropriate to the context, 'poor good-for-nothing'.

II.iv.213   owle   Owle

Emend: *howl* (Collier). The dropping of initial aspirates in stressed syllables is said by Dobson (II. 991) to have characterised vulgar speech only. We must assume that the actors were not above reproach in this respect (*cf.* the name *Obidicut* at IV.i.62 – *Hoberdicut* in Harsnett). Collier's emendation is convincing. It is clear that the succeeding phrase, 'Necessity's sharp pinch', must stand as the object of a verb: it has otherwise no grammatical relation to the sentence. *Howl* is exactly appropriate to the context, besides being entirely plausible as the origin of *owl*.

II.iv.248   chanc'st   *chanc'd*

196 III.i.18   Arte   note

? Emend: *heart*, on the assumption of a dropped aspirate. All editors concur in adopting *note*, yet it cannot, I feel, sustain the meaning they are obliged to attribute to it, *viz.* 'knowledge'. Shakespeare does, indeed, very frequently use the word in a similar sense, but it is the more particular sense of 'notice', i.e. either 'attention' or 'intelligence, news' (= 'knowledge' considered as information imparted). Examples cited in *OED* confirm this interpretation, though the relevant definitions given are (a) 'Notice, regard, or attention'; and (marked 'rare') (b) 'knowledge, information; intimation' – the latter a vaguer definition than seems warranted by the accompanying citations. From the contextual point of view, it seems to me more in keeping with the situation, with Kent's character, and with the implied sentiment of the passage if he says, 'Sir, I do know you, / And dare upon the warrant of my heart / Commend a dear thing to you'. If this is right, some explanation is still required of the not wholly meaningless, but awkward and irrelevant, reading in F. It is perhaps enough to point out that *Arte* makes no sense at all, that *know* might suggest *note*, and that the manuscript copy might go some way to justify the reviser in his emendation.

III.ii.4   Thought executing   Thought-executing

Emend: *thwart-executing* ('thwart' = across; 'execute' = of a thing: to perform its functions, 'work'). *Cf.* IV.vii.35: 'quick cross-lightning'. *OED* lists the following spellings of *thwart*: *thort*, *thaught*, *thought* and (presumably reflecting a pronunciation determined by the latter false spelling) *thoft*.

III.ii.58   centers   Continents

Emend: *centures* (= cinctures). The reading in Q represents a variant spelling and doubtless reproduces the word as the actor pronounced it. Yet *centures* must be correct since the metre requires a trisyllable. The ending *-ure* was still in polite speech pronounced with a long vowel – either ū or ui, as in Scots 'guid' (see Dobson, II. 850–1) – followed optionally by a glide before the *r*, hence an extra syllable (see Dobson, II. 761). But the pronunciation -er (unstressed, with indeterminate vowel) was already common.

III.iv.23   one   *owne*

'One' was normally pronounced ōn (see Dobson, II. 994).

III.iv.79   a lo   alow: alow

Emend: *Hollo* (Warburton: *Halloo*).

III.iv.104   caese   Sesey

Emend: *sess* (= a call to a dog when giving him food). The reading in Q is apparently a misprint for *cease* (pronounced sĕs, see Dobson, II. 475). It is hard to account for the substitution in F unless it represents a compositor's sophistication of the variant spelling *sesse*, for which see the *English Dialect Dictionary*.

III.iv.127	O light	*a-light*
III.vi.26	at tral	(om.)

Emend: *A trial*. Only *at* for *a*, of course, indicates mishearing: *tral* is a printer's error. I take it that Edgar falls in at this point with Lear's delusion, as the Fool does later, and pretends to be reproving one of the arraigned daughters as if for disrespectful inattention to the proceedings: 'Look where he stands and glares! Want'st thou eyes? A trial, madam!'

III.vi.32	Hoppedance	(om.)

Emend: *Hoberdidance* (Harsnett).

III.vii.43	answerer	answer'd

Emend: *answer her*. The argument for this correction entails a re-ascription of speeches which is discussed (together with the correction) in Appendix B1, p. 232 below.

III.vii.62	holpt the	*holpe the*
III.vii.65	else subscrib'd	else subscribe

Emend: *I'll subscribe*. Unstressed vowels are easily confused, though it is odd to find a comparatively elaborate word such as 'else' emerging from the confusion. Perhaps the reporter was unconsciously prepared to hear it as part of a phrase beginning with *all*. I gloss the passage as follows: 'All cruels [= cruel people or creatures] I'll [= I am, if necessary, willing to] subscribe [= countenance], but [sc. come what may] I shall see / The winged vengeance overtake such children'. An exactly parallel construction occurs in *The Taming of the Shrew*, II.i.14–15: 'If you affect him, sister, here I swear / I'll [= I am, if necessary, willing to] plead for you myself, but [sc. come what may] you shall have him'.

IV.i.1	and knowne	and knowne

Emend: *unknown* (Johnson conjecture). It is understandable that Edgar should prefer to be despised when unknown than to be flattered as a lord and still despised. Q and F afford neither grammar nor sense, and their faulty punctuation makes things worse. A full stop should stand after *flatter'd* and the passage read: 'Yet better thus unknown to be contemn'd / Than still contemn'd and flatter'd. To be worst, / The lowest and most dejected thing . . .' etc. The phonetic confusion, involving an unstressed syllable, is easily understood.

198   IV.i.41   angring it selfe and others   Ang'ring it selfe, and others

?Emend: *anchoring itself on others.* The implied phonetic confusion needs no comment. The sentence might be glossed: 'Bad is the trade [= course of action] that must play the fool to sorrow [i.e. counterfeit insensibility], / Anchoring itself [= fixing its attention] on others'. Edgar has just heard with dismay his father's bitter remark: 'As flies to wanton boys are we to the gods: / They kill us for their sport'. He is clearly meant to announce the intention here, which he subsequently carries out, of curing his father's despair by dissimulation and trickery – and, incidentally, to reassure the audience that his apparent callousness has a humane object. The use of 'anchor' in this figurative sense is, but for the omission of the reflexive pronoun, exactly paralleled in *Measure for Measure*, II.iv.4, and *Cymbeline*, V.v.394.

IV.i.62   Obdicut, Hobbididence   (om.)

Emend: *Hoberdicut, Hoberdidance* (Harsnett).

IV.iv.6   a centurie is sent forth   *A Centery send forth*

IV.iv.26   important   inportun'd

Emend: *importunate* (Capell). *Important* is possibly merely a variant spelling.

IV.iv.27   in sight   incite
             (BM2: *incite*; Q2: insite)

IV.v.25   aliads   Eliads

Emend: *oeillades* (Rowe: *oeiliads*).

IV.vi.80   Bare   *Beare*

IV.vi.163   a dogge, so bade   *a Dogg's obey'd*

IV.vi.201   and laying   (om.)

? Emend: *in laying*, to avoid the awkward ellipsis and pointless distinction otherwise implied: 'To use his eyes for garden water-pots, / Aye, and [*sc.* for] laying autumn's dust'.

IV.vi.276a   for Venter   (om.)

Emend: *forfender* ('forfend' = secure or protect by precautionary measures). In her letter Goneril represents the projected murder of Albany to Edmund as a deed of *rescue*: 'If he return the conqueror, then am I the prisoner, and his bed my gaol, from the loathed warmth whereof deliver me'. Hence in closing she is careful to reassure Edmund that the anxiety she expresses to be rid of Albany is not purely selfish ('for *you* her own forfender'). The mishearing of *t* for *d* would be encouraged by the pronunciation of *r* immediately after the latter. The word 'forfend' is again associated with Goneril later in the play when Regan asks Edmund (V.i.10–11): 'But have you never found my brother's way / To the forfended place?'

IV.vii.16   hurrying   iarring

Emend: *erring*. *Iarring* in F has clearly been prompted by *untun'd* and *wind up*, and seems satisfactorily consistent with the image of a viol or lute with strings grown slack. But it is not, in fact, very appropriate to the substance of the metaphor: Lear's madness. His senses might well be described as 'untuned' and therefore 'erring', but I do not see how Cordelia could refer to them intelligibly as 'jarring' (with each other, or upon her feelings?). The mishearing could have been produced by a pronunciation of *erring* as ărin[g] (see Dobson, II. 563): *OED* records a variant spelling *arr*. *Hurrying* would be heard as [h]ŭryin[g].

IV.vii.80   to make him euen ore the   (om.)
             time hee has lost

? Emend: *have in ure*. No one has satisfactorily explained *euen ore* and it seems not satisfactorily explicable. 'In ure' is defined by *OED* as follows: 'In or into use, practice, or performance. Often with vbs., as *bring*, *come*, *have*, and esp. *put* (freq. c. 1510–1630)'; and further: 'In remembrance or recollection. Only *to have . . . in ure*'. The phrase is much less frequently found in this latter acceptation, and only fifteenth-century examples of it are cited, but while the expression 'to have in ure' remained current presumably this remained a natural extension of its meaning. 'To make him have in ure' thus meant 'to recall to his mind'. If the actor dropped the aspirate in 'have', an easy mishearing is involved: ĕvn or èvn for ăvn (see Dobson, II. 634 for the various pronunciations of 'even' current during the period). It is even possible that 'ure' was heard as [y]ōr. (Dobson, II. 802, finds no evidence for this development from the standard yūr until the late seventeenth century, though Kökeritz, pp. 211–12, discovers comparable examples in Shakespearean texts). But if the reporter took down 'ure' correctly, it is not beyond the bounds of credibility that the compositor misread it as 'ore'.

V.i.26   bolds   (om.)

? Emend: *beholds* (= concerns). Both *bolds* (emboldens) and *beholds* were already archaic, the latter in use till the fifteenth century, the former recorded by *OED* to c. 1540. But whereas *bolds* makes poor sense, *beholds* seems to be demanded as a counterpart to *touches* ('It touches us as France invades our land, / Not beholds the King'), and as providing the sense clearly intended: 'It is our fault, not the King's'. Albany is anxious to have it frankly acknowledged that the King's defection was not part of a conspiracy, and that the French invasion cannot be laid at his, the King's, door.

V.iii.150   trumpets speake   Trumpets speake

Emend: *Trumpet, speak!* (Only one trumpeter has so far appeared, and it is unlikely, from what one is able to surmise of Elizabethan theatrical economy, that supernumeraries would be held in the offing.)

200   V.iii.185   with the   *we the*

V.iii.192   Neuer (O Father) reueald   Neuer (O fault) reueal'd
                 my selfe vnto him   my selfe vnto him

? Emend: *faitour*. Q's *O Father* makes an unconvincing melodramatic aside, as the reviser apparently felt. His substitution is much better. But the original reading must have borne a closer similarity to *father*, either phonetically or visually. *Faitour* (= impostor, cheat) seems to meet all the requirements. See note on I.i.60 above for comment on the phonetic confusion involved.

V.iii.280   or   and

Emend: *ere*. Q makes no sense, and F no point. The point, I think, is the fickleness of Fortune who changes her mind with a turn of the wheel. That usage permitted the ellipsis after *ere* of repetitions now strictly required ('two she loved ere [she] hated [them]') is confirmed by Abbott §386.

V.iii.306   a rat of life   *a Rat haue life*

In addition a number of minor errors may be due to mishearings registered in the copy, though they may as easily have resulted from compositorial carelessness. These include:

I.iv.104	their's	*there's*
I.v.8	where	*were*
II.iv.149	on you	*in you*
II.iv.174	The	*Thy*
II.iv.270	life as	*life is*
III.iv.14	their	*there*
IV.ii.47	this (Emend: *these*)	(om.)
IV.vi.214	here's	*heares*
V.iii.139	As bent	are bent (Emend: *is bent*)[1]

1   See Abbott §333 for the very common use in Shakespeare of the singular inflection with plural subjects, especially (as here) with multiple singular subjects or plural subjects of quasi-singular significance (e.g. *spirits*).

APPENDIX A4
COMPLEX ERRORS IN Q1

(involving both misreading and phonetic confusion)

	Q1	F
I.iv.363	a: after	hasten
	b: *hasten*	

After can only have been prompted by a phonetic mis-spelling *asten*.

II.ii.150	a: belest and contaned	(om.)
	b: basest and temnest	

? Emend: *batedst and contemned*. It is obvious that the Q corrector intended not *temnest* but *contemnedst* and that the compositor misconstrued his markings on the proof. It seems, however, equally clear that the copy must have read *conte[m]ned*: the compositor could hardly have overlooked a final -*st* in the first instance. *Contemned* requires no alteration: Elizabethan English, possibly for reasons of euphony, permitted the omission of '-[e]st' in either one of a pair of superlatives (see Abbott, §398). It is hard to see in *belest* a misreading of *basest*. Of words similar in form and suitable in sense *batedst* ('bate' = to cast down, humble) seems the likeliest candidate, if it were imperfectly heard and recorded as *batest*.

II.ii.177	a: Losses and remedies	Losses their remedies
	b: Losses their remedies	

Emend: *home* (= that strike home . . . effective, appropriate). Qa's *and* is impossible; the reading in Qb, on the other hand, is weak, besides is far from convincing as an authoritative correction: it is scarcely credible that the compositor would mistake a *their* in the copy for an *and*. I assume that the copy contained a naive mishearing caused by a dropped aspirate (*ome*) which gave rise to the misreading (*and*): a not unwarrantable assumption in view of the analogous case at I.iv.363 (*asten*, read as *after*). The *ome/and* misreading is exactly paralleled at II.i.126, where *home* (Qb) was originally printed *hand* (Qa).

II.iv.133	a: fruit	F: Tombe
	b: tombe	

Emend: *vault*. Though -*ruit* may conceivably reflect -*omb* in the copy, it is nearly impossible to imagine a *t* in secretary hand which would look at all like *f*. There is certainly no evidence elsewhere in the text of any such anomaly. *Vault* is the only possible alternative: if it were misheard as *fault*, and appeared thus in the copy, the transformation to *fruit* is much easier to explain.

IV.i.64   Mobing, & Mohing   (om.)

Emend: *mocking and mowing* (Duthie). Theobald's *mopping* for *Mobing* is generally accepted. But 'mock' was equally often connected with 'mow' (e.g. *The Tempest*, III.iii.83 *s.d.*); and *Mobing* for *mocking* finds an exact parallel in *Stobing* for *stocking* at II.ii.139.

IV.vi.53   at each   at each

Emend: *alength* (= lengthwise). The expression 'at each' does not exist in the language, despite the meaning for it found by some editors. Plainly a word is needed to show that Edgar has in mind ten masts set end to end, one on top of the other. *Alength* would have been heard, and therefore presumably spelt, *alenth*; and if, as frequently elsewhere (see Appendix A2, p. 187 above), the word was badly spaced in the copy (i.e. as *al enth*), the misreading is satisfactorily explained.

APPENDIX A5
MISCELLANEOUS ERRORS IN Q1

(Misprints and other minor errors due to carelessness, excluding those too trivial
to obscure grammar or sense)

	Q1	F
I.i.148	man	mad
	(BM2, Q2: *mad*)	
I.i.175	made	made
	(Q2: *make*)	

Since it is in this very passage that Lear reasserts his will over Kent, a reference in the past tense ('Our potency made good') to the maintenance or enforcement of his power (whatever 'made good' may be taken to mean) makes little sense. The fact that the construction with nominative absolute strongly implies in the context the fulfilment of a condition ('Our potency made good' = 'Now that our potency has been made good') adds to the trouble. In the present *make good* is a simple imperative, parallel with *take*, meaning 'prove to be true or valid' (with the threatening implication 'prove the reality and feel the weight of').

I.iv.227	put on	*put it on*
I.iv.266	make	Makes it
	(BM2: *make it*)	
I.iv.307	accent teares	cadent Teares

Emend: *accens'd* (= *incensed* = kindled, set on fire. In figurative use, as here, = enraged, exasperated). *Cf.* 'these hot tears that break from me perforce' (I.iv.320), 'mine own tears / Do scald like molten lead' (IV.vii.47–8). It is necessary to suppose that the compositor, intending to print *accenst*, accidentally omitted the *s*. *Accent* is otherwise inexplicable: it could hardly be a mishearing, and is equally unlikely, on the evidence, to represent a naive misreading. Not inconceivably the press-corrector sophisticated some such misprint as *cacent*, which the F reviser then restored to its true form, *cadent*. But F's *cadent*, besides giving too weak a meaning, savours of elegant euphemism – most implausibly in the context of a passionate speech.

I.iv.321	fogs vpon	*Fogges vpon thee*
I.iv.325	you cast	*cast you*
I.iv.339	the foole with	*the Foole with thee*

204 II.i.38   no, helpe?   no helpe?
                 (Q2: no helpe?)

Emend: *Ho! Help!* The note of surprise, or desperation, in *no helpe?* might be attributed to
Edmund's clever play-acting, but I should be sceptical of any such interpretation. One expects
cries of 'Ho!' in situations of this kind (*cf.* 'Help, ho!' at II.ii.43 and 46), and the comma after *no*
in Q1 confirms, I think, a misprint. Foul case might well result in the mis-setting of *n* for *h*. The
question mark is not, of course, significant since it might well stand, as is frequently the case
elsewhere in Q, for a point of exclamation. Whether the reading in F was inherited from Q2 (the
compositor's copy at this point) or whether F reviser and Q2 editor were tempted coincidentally
to the same sophistication, it would be difficult to decide.

II.i.125   a: defences   differences
             b: *diferences*

II.ii.100   That   *Then* (= Than)

II.ii.174   a: not   most
             b: *most*

II.iii.15   a: numb'd mortified   num'd and mortified
             b: *numb'd and mortified*

II.iv.103   a: the   his
             b: *his*

II.iv.267   deed   *need*

III.ii.65   demaunding after me   *demanding after you*

III.iv.12   a: the   the
             b: *this*

(*The* is a possible reading, and the corrector would surely not have troubled to alter it had he not
found *this* in the copy.)

III.v.14   treason were   *Treason were not*

III.vi.24   no   (om.)
             (Q2: *now*)

IV.ii.27   a: womans   a Womans
             b: *a womans*

IV.ii.29   a: whistle   whistle
             b: *whistling*

Goneril's phrase 'I have been worth the whistling' makes allusion to a proverb: 'It is a poor dog that is not worth the whistling'. Editors cite the proverb in their commentaries without explaining its meaning; *OED* records it under WHISTLING, together with other phrases which imply the sense 'call, summon' for 'whistle', but offers no further clarification; and the standard modern dictionaries of English proverbs provide a wealth of references to early printed sources – but no word of elucidation. Yet the proverb is not, so far as I am aware, now current, nor is its drift altogether unambiguous. From its uses in early printed books, those, at least, which supply a context, I should judge that it means: 'You cannot much value what you take no pains to get'. The derivative phrase 'to be worth the whistling' is cited several times in the reference books. It appears to bear a more general sense: 'to be worth the trouble'. We may accordingly gloss Goneril's speech on the appearance of Albany: 'So you have thought me worth some effort after all!' (It must be recalled from earlier in the scene that, on Goneril's return home, Albany has neglected to 'meet her on the way', IV.ii.2.) A different (but related?) saying, 'not worth a whistle', appears to have distracted the Q compositor on first setting the passage. The resulting amalgam *worth the whistle*, reproduced in F, finds no parallel in recorded usage.

IV.ii.47   a: the vild   (om.)
               b: this vild

Emend: *these vile* (Jennens).

IV.ii.79   a: your Iustices   You Iustices
               b: *you Iustisers*

IV.iii.13   I say   (om.)

Emend: *Aye, sir* (Theobald: *I, sir*).

IV.iii.51   Tis so   (om.)

Emend: *'Tis said* (Warburton). If it were not, in any case, unidiomatic, ''Tis so' would confirm the negative in Kent's question ('you heard not?') – the opposite of what is intended.

IV.iv.2   vent   vext

? Emend: *vehement* (= of natural forces: operating with great strength or violence; *OED* comments as follows on the etymology: ' . . . usually regarded as f. *vehe-* . . . lacking, wanting + *mens* mind'). *Vext* is a good reading; yet *x* could not have been misread as *n* in Q, and it would be strange if *n* were substituted inadvertently. Foul case seems even less likely. Haplography is possibly responsible: the inadvertent reduction of *vement* (a phonetic spelling: see Dobson, II. 878; and Kökeritz, p. 375, who lists a number of disyllabic uses of the word in Shakespeare) to *vent*.

IV.vi.2   it vpnow   *vp it now*

206	IV.vi.73	made	*make*
	IV.vi.107	argue-proofe	*Agu-proofe*
	IV.vi.188–9	shoot . . . fell	*shoo . . . Felt*

(A curious spoonerism which may have been perpetrated by the actor rather than the Q compositor.)

IV.vi.231	a: was framed	was first fram'd
	b: *was first framed*	
V.i.9	I, honor'd loue	*In honour'd Loue*
V.i.65	his mercy	*the mercie*
V.iii.24	good	good yeares

? Emend: *gorcrows* (= carrion crows). F's reading has been much discussed. There did, indeed, exist a word 'goodyear', used, according to *OED*, 'as a meaningless expletive, chiefly in the interrogative phrase *What a* (or *the*) *goodyear*', and later 'App. from the equivalence of this phrase with *what the devil* . . . etc., the word came to be used in imprecatory phrases as denoting some undefined malefic power or agency'. Indeed the many examples quoted all show optative constructions − except that from *Lear*, which is not an imprecation but an asseveration. It is noticeable, too, that the reference in this passage is scarcely to an 'undefined' power or agency, but to one capable of devouring 'flesh and fell': a predatory animal is strongly suggested. The metre makes it clear that the line in Q contains a gap, and that a dissyllable is required beginning with *good* or a syllable which might be mistaken for *good*. Perhaps no further explanation is required for the emendation suggested except to say that *gorecrows* was a common alternative spelling, and that *r/o* and *e/d* errors are frequent in Q. It may well be that *crows* was separated in the copy from the rest of the word, since it was overlooked in Q. Its omission in Q may have caused the reviser to overlook it as well in collating his copy with the manuscript, so that on returning to the passage to revise it he would be thrown back on invention.

V.iii.47	a: (om.)	(om.)
	b: *and appointed guard*	
V.iii.49	of his side	*on his side*
V.iii.85	bare	bare

Emend: *bar* (Rowe).

V.iii.145   By right   By rule
             (BM2: *my right*)

(For comment, see above, p. 69.)

V.iii.213   threw me   (om.)

Emend: *threw him* (Theobald).

V.iii.300   you to   you to

Emend: *to you* (Pope).

APPENDIX A6

CRUXES

	Q1	F
II.i.102	a: To haue these - - and wast of this his reuenues b: To haue the wast and spoyle of his reuenues	To haue th'expence and wast of his Reuenues

Greg argues (*Variants*, p. 155) that the compositor 'was evidently unable to read his copy, since he inserted hyphens in place of illegible letters'; that the true reading behind *these* — may have been *the spoyle*; but that it is more likely to have been *the spence*, sophisticated in F to *th'expence*. I do not find any part of his argument altogether convincing. Double or multiple hyphens in Q invariably represent dashes, and a dash is presumably what the compositor saw after *these*. The alteration of the word-order in Qb betrays the arbitrariness of the press-corrector's emendation, and F's is, on the face of it, scarcely more credible. Abbott says (§ 338) that the Folio occasionally prints a dash or hyphen in place of final *s*, and quotes two examples. He accounts for the phenomenon by explaining that final *s* was 'indicated by a mere line at the end of a word in MS'. If the dash here represents final *s*, the correct reading might be *the seise*. ('To have seise or seisin of' = to have possession of.) That elsewhere in Q final *s* was mistaken for a hyphen is perhaps borne out by *sheep-coates* (II.iii.18), for which F, it may be on the authority of the manuscript, substitutes *Sheeps-Coates*; and *pin-queues* in Qa (III.iv.122), revised in Qb as *pin, squemes* (see Appendix A1, p. 181 above). Though in this latter case the Qa hyphen occurs at the end of a line, two unhyphenated words, and the missing *s*, must certainly have stood in the copy. I am at a loss, however, to explain by what conceivable distortion of the final *s* in secretary hand it could come to be confused with a hyphen or dash.

III.iv.103	hay no on ny	Sayes suum, mun, nonny

It is highly likely that the phrase in Q represents a substitution of the press-corrector's for what was originally a more extensive reading. One notices not only that the word 'nonny' has been split into three elements, but also that these syllables are separated in the print, both from each other and from the words which precede and follow, by an inordinate amount of space. This unusually generous spacing in a line which required no special effort to 'justify' it (the following line begins with two three-letter words which might easily have served to fill the gap) strongly suggests correction after setting. The inference is almost irresistible that F supplies the longer form of words (discounting, perhaps, *Sayes*) which was 'corrected'. The reviser may have retrieved from the manuscript exactly what we find in F, or the reading may have been rescued from the manuscript in somewhat more comprehensible form, only to be corrupted again by copyist or compositor. If it accurately reproduces the original, the reviser may have added *Sayes* to suggest that the following words render onomatopoeically the sound of the whistling wind: Edgar has just been talking (or singing) about 'the cold wind', and it must be that which 'says' *suum, mun, nonny*. It is now traditional to accept this, to my mind wholly unconvincing, interpretation in the editions (who has ever, I wonder, heard the wind say 'nonny'?); *faute de mieux*, however, it must do.

III.iv.126   a: a nellthu night more and   He met the Night-Mare, and
                  her nine fold   her nine-fold
                b: he met the night mare and
                    her nine fold

OED somewhat recklessly decides, on the strength of this passage, that 'ninefold' may be used as a substantive with the meaning 'An attendant company of nine'. Editors embroider the definition: the company consists of 'offspring' or 'imps or familiars'. But it is surely less arbitrary to suppose that *nine fold* is the adverb which it appears to be. Where the subject is exorcism, indications of ritual repetition are entirely what we should expect (*cf. thrice* in the preceding line). Unfortunately, if this is so, the verb modified by *ninefold* has been accidentally omitted. It must have been a monosyllable in the past tense placed between *and* and *her*; but the context supplies no clue to its probable meaning.

IV.iv.4   hor-docks   Hardokes

The context makes it clear that 'hordocks' are weeds of a kind. No species of that name, however, has ever been recorded. Of many emendations suggested, *burdocks* (Hanmer) is the most plausible. Yet, aside from the *u/o* error, which is trivial enough, it presupposes either that *b* was misread as *h* or that, because of foul case, an *h* supplanted a *b* in the compositor's stick – neither eventuality very probable.

IV.vi.187   this a good blocke   This a good blocke

Blocke is usually associated with hats. It might mean 'a mould for a hat', hence also 'shape, fashion (of a hat)'. Since the phrase (or sentence if, as is usually explained, *this* = this is) occurs in one of Lear's 'mad' speeches, it should, perhaps, occasion no surprise when, among other things, he suddenly and irrelevantly refers to his hat. On the other hand, one cannot escape the impression that, on the whole, Shakespeare is at pains to avoid portraying Lear's madness as mere delirium: the associative links between his apparently disjointed utterances are generally quite clear. Edgar has indeed just exclaimed in this very scene: 'Oh, matter and impertinency mix'd, / Reason in madness!' One strongly suspects, therefore, that *blocke* has nothing to do with hats but bears some closer relationship to the context. The punctuation in Q suggests that it is connected with what precedes: *When we are borne, we crie that wee are come to this great stage of fooles, this a good blocke.* If this is correct, *blocke* must mean 'a block of wood', and *a good* represent a (phonetic?) corruption concealing some appropriate epithet. The punctuation in F emphasises by contrast a connection with what follows: *This a good blocke: / It were a delicate stratagem to shoo / A Troope of Horse with Felt*, etc. The relevant association here seems to be with the verb 'to block' (= to lay out, plan). The corresponding noun 'block', however, which *OED* defines: 'a scheme, contrivance; generally used in a bad sense', seems to have passed current only in Scotland, so that its appearance here arouses suspicion. I am inclined, on balance, to judge that Q's syntax is correct, and that the problem would be solved if a convincing emendation of *a good* were forthcoming; that, notwithstanding, an association between *blocke* (i.e. 'to block') and *stratagem* was probably also intended.

210 IV.vi.217–18 Neere and on speed fort the
                     maine descryes,
                     Standst on the howerly
                     thoughts.

                     Neere, and on speedy foot:
                     the maine descry
                     Stands on the hourely
                     thought.

This is easily the most complex and baffling textual difficulty in the play. Though we may gratefully rely here on such authority as the F revision can claim (it was, at least, the work of a contemporary), the meaning it yields is no very great improvement on the nonsense in Q (see my comments on p. 47 above). It presupposes, besides, and one may think unrealistically, that the Q compositor added or dropped letters no fewer than four times in two lines: compare *speed/speedy; descryes/descry; Standst/Stands; thoughts/thought*. Paradoxically, it would be easier to accept the possibility of quite radical error (e.g. the mishearing of a whole phrase) than that of a series of such trivial slips. In tackling the problem without reference to F the main difficulty lies in determining the structure of the sentence. Where is the main verb: do we find it in *descryes* or *Standst*? The sentence seems to fall into two sections: does it divide after *fort* (= plausibly, *foot*, as in F), or before (so that *Neare and on speed* should read *Nearing in speed*, and *fort* either *for* or *forth* or *for't*, changes which, if appropriate to the sense, would be justifiable on phonetic grounds)? *Thoughts* seems to represent *thwarts* (= checks), as a mishearing or irregular phonetic spelling (see my comments on III.ii.4, Appendix A3, p. 196 above). The only two readings of which we may feel fairly sure are *Neere* (supported by the context) and *howerly* (which is scarcely open to doubt as misreading or mishearing). The latter must mean 'continual'. But one cannot ponder the problem thus analysed for very long without suspecting a more serious textual deficiency. It is only too likely, unfortunately, that a line or two may be missing between the two quoted.

IV.vi.228–30 a: Hartie thankes, the bornet
                 and beniz of heauen to saue
                 thee.
              b: Hartie thankes, the bounty
                 and the benizon of heauen,
                 to boot, to boot.

              Heartie thankes:
              The bountie, and the
              benizon of Heauen
              To boot, and boot.

Qb supplies a good reading, but comparison with Qa raises serious doubt whether it is the true reading. The phrase *to saue thee* ('to-save thee'? – *cf.* 'to-bless', *Pericles*, IV.vi.23), which must have stood in the copy, has entirely disappeared. Though, furthermore, *beniz* is intelligible as a mistake for *benizon*, it is less easy to regard *bornet* as a misreading of *bounty* or even *bountie*.

V.i.30   domestique dore particulars

              domesticke and particurlar
              broiles

The word 'domestic' at this date was most likely to mean: 'of or pertaining to one's own country or nation; internal'. The meaning now more familiar ('of or belonging to the home, house or household') is not recorded before 1611. Though, of course, the word might well have been used in this sense less than a decade earlier, it is *a priori* more probable that the meaning then customary was intended. Hence to *domestic-door particulars*, the clumsy and unidiomatic expression generally offered as an emendation, one ought perhaps to prefer *domestic dower-particulars*. 'Dore' is recorded in *OED* as a contemporary spelling of 'dower'. Unfortunately the context almost, but not quite, justifies this change. The tenor of Goneril's speech is 'Stop bickering: unite against the enemy', but it is not altogether clear what the bickering is about. Albany avers that the French invasion is not to be laid at the King's door but at their own (his, Goneril's, Regan's): Edmund approves the sentiment, Regan does not, at which point Goneril intervenes. Possibly Albany has alluded to the expropriation of Cordelia's inheritance in saying that the invasion 'touches us', so that Goneril would understand him as making a fuss about 'domestic dower-particulars'. The connection, however, is far from clear. The speeches in this brief episode (a meeting between Goneril and Albany, Regan and Edmund) are almost without exception unusually laconic and elliptical, consequently cryptic. I think it highly probable that the text has been heavily and clumsily cut to shorten the scene. If so, there is little hope of resolving the textual difficulty here with any confidence.

| V.iii.129–30 | Behold it is the priuiledge of my tongue, My oath and my profession, | Behold it is my priuiledge, The priuiledge of mine Honours, My oath, and my profession. |

The substitution in F (if the redundant *my priuiledge* be removed, as modern editors agree is necessary) makes satisfactory sense. Edgar, having declined to divulge his name, proffers his drawn sword as the 'privilege' (= prerogative) of his 'honours' (= position or title of rank) and of his (*sc.* knightly) 'oath' and 'profession', thus establishing his 'quality' or status, and, therefore, his right to challenge Edmund to combat. The reading *mine Honours*, however, offers no clue to the mistake in Q – if *my tongue* constitutes a mistake. It cannot, however, be a phonetic mistake, and there seems little scope for deducing a misreading. If it is not an error, *tongue* can only mean, in the context, 'words, discourse' (*my tongue* = what I am about to say); and, if that is so, the word 'privilege' requires a different gloss. The verb 'privilege' could mean: 'To authorize, license (what is otherwise forbidden); to justify, excuse', and Shakespeare so uses it elsewhere (see Onions, *Glossary*). The noun is not, in *OED*, supplied with an equivalent general meaning, 'authority, licence'; nevertheless, Shakespeare employs it in this sense at least twice (*The Two Gentlemen of Verona*, III.i.160; *Sonnets*, xcv.13). Assuming that he does so again here, 'the privilege of my tongue' must mean 'the licence or sanction for what I am about to say'. It is less easy, however, to connect 'privilege' in this sense with 'my oath and my profession'. No reference to the knightly oath and profession could be intended, since Edgar could not intelligibly be seeking to justify his knightly status. It is just possible that we should infer an allusion to the oath, accompanying a declaration or 'profession' of the justice of his cause, which each of the participants in a trial by combat was required to swear before entering the lists (*cf. Richard II*, I.iii, which portrays the formal preliminaries to a judicial duel). There is no trace, it must be admitted, of an oath in Edgar's speech. On the other hand, after formulating the charge of treason against Edmund, he does, in the last words of the speech, declare the truth of his cause, invoking his sword as the sanction of this 'profession': 'Say thou no, / This sword, this arm and my best spirits / Is bent to prove upon they heart, whereto I speak, / Thou liest'. The anachronisms involved do not, of course, present any difficulty: the encounter between Edgar and Edmund is presented throughout as an affair of medieval chivalry. (Indeed many allusions in other parts of the play make it plain that Shakespeare imagined a feudal society in pre-Roman Britain.)

APPENDIX A7
Q1 READINGS UNNECESSARILY ALTERED

Note: All the substantial alterations in Q1b are listed which appear, on balance, to be wrong.

From the innumerable variants in F which correspond to 'good' readings in Q a selection has been made of those which wear the most plausible appearance of being 'corrections' (because, that is, they resemble emendations of misreadings, of minor omissions or transpositions etc., or simply because they offer more immediately intelligible and attractive alternatives to their counterparts in Q). With certain exceptions mentioned below, I omit the rest as non-significant evidence. These 'indifferent' variants, which may be counted by the hundred, and which range from trivial substitutions of *which* for *that* through doublets such as *pleated/plighted* (I.i.283) to more substantial, but no less imponderable, alternatives such as *transforme/transport* (I.iv.242), do not offer grounds for reasoned judgement. They are readily explained on the theory advanced in this book; but they cannot be held to count either in its favour (as they would do if the alterations in F were not only unnecessary but clearly erroneous) or against it (as they would do if, conversely, the changes were both requisite and clearly correct).

The succeeding appendix (A8) gives a list of those readings in F, which, although they correspond to 'good' readings in Q, may derive from a common source in the manuscript copy for Q, and may, therefore, represent authentic variants.

(a) *Alterations in Q1b only (F omitting or following Qa)*

	Q1	F
II.i.125	a: *best*	best
	b: lest	

The Qb correction *lest* (= least) probably stems from a misunderstanding of the ambiguous phrase *from our home* in the next line. The corrector must have taken the phrase in its most obvious sense and altered the apparently contradictory *best* accordingly. But *from* here is quite clearly intended to have the meaning 'away from'.

III.vii.104   a: *rogish madnes*   (om.)
              b: madnes

Probably the result of accident rather than deliberate correction, though there is no sign of typographical disturbance in Qb.

IV.ii.32   a: *it origin*   (om.)
              b: ith origin

As Greg suggests (*Variants*, p. 173), *ith* probably stands for *i'th'*. The genitive *it* is not unexampled elsewhere in the play (*cf.* I.iv.236), and Qa is certainly correct, although *its* or *his* would be less unusual in the context.

IV.ii.68   a: *now*   (om.)
              b: mew

Greg (*Variants*, p. 175) considers *mew* an 'excellent emendation'. Yet (since 'mew!' is an exclamation of disgust) it makes, in my view, Goneril's reaction to Albany's outburst too crudely dismissive. It is much more consistent with her contemptuous attitude towards him generally, and with the scorn, particularly, which she has just heaped upon his timidity, that, hearing him now at last roused to anger, but anger directed at herself, a mere woman, she should say with sarcasm: 'Marry, your manhood now!'

V.iii.57   a: *sharpes*   (om.)
              b: sharpnes

Sharpes = sharp edges. Accordingly, *those that feele their sharpes* = those who actually receive the wounds. The meaning given by *sharpnes* (= harshness, painfulness) is rather weak.

(b) *Alterations in Q1b (F following) or in F only*

I.i.5   *equalities*   qualities

Gloucester cannot be citing as evidence for Lear's impartiality ('it appears not which of the Dukes he values most') that impartiality itself ('qualities are so weighed'). The evidence lies in the apportionment of the kingdom into exactly equal shares ('equalities are so weighed').

I.i.151   *Reuerse thy doome*   reserue thy state

In Q Kent refers to Lear's judgement (*doome*) on Cordelia, and this is obviously right in the context of a speech which concludes with a defence of Cordelia: 'Thy youngest daughter does not love thee least, / Nor are those empty-hearted whose low sound / Reverbs no hollowness'. The phrase in F, by contrast, can only relate to Lear's decision to abdicate ('reserve thy state' = preserve thy power). This is consistent neither with the immediate context nor with the more

214   general context of Kent's quarrel with the King, a quarrel which is provoked by Lear's treatment
of Cordelia and has reference solely to that. A later 'correction' in F, *reuoke thy guift* for *Reuoke thy
doome* (I.i.167), is clearly prompted by the same wish on the part of the reviser to alter, or
elaborate, the motivation of Kent's protest. It is difficult to imagine the reason for it, but the
result is, in any case, unconvincing.

I.i.223–4   *or you for voucht affections*   Or your fore-voucht affection
             Falne into taint   Fall into taint

Q is perfectly intelligible and correct, though the construction exploits a logical ambiguity.
Cordelia's offence, if real, must be so unnatural as to make it monstrous, or, if imagined by Lear,
so unnatural as to make *him* monstrous 'for [= because of] vouch'd [= declared] affections / Fall'n
into taint [= decay]'. F alters the construction so as to obviate the slight, but somewhat
confusing, change of focus on the word *or* – and not unsuccessfully, except that the ensuing
relative clause *which to beleeue of her* follows much less naturally than in Q.

I.i.229   *may know*   make knowne

Q's *may know* is a subjunctive after *beseech* (see Abbott, § 369 on the use of the subjunctive after
verbs of command and entreaty, esp. the quotation from *1 Henry IV*: 'I do beseech your majesty
may serve', III.ii.155). F's *make knowne* implies, very strangely, that Cordelia is anxious about
her reputation at court.

I.i.244   *She is her selfe and dowre*   She is herselfe a Dowrie

The reading in F is not more correct. Q expresses in equally acceptable form the idea: 'she is her
own dowry' (see Abbott, §20 for the use of 'self' as a noun).

I.i.251   *respects / Of fortune*   respect and Fortunes

Respects = considerations, the meaning required. F comes close to nonsense.

I.i.283–4   *Time shall vnfould what*   Time shall vnfold what
             pleated cuñing hides,   plighted cunning hides,
             Who couers faults, at   Who couers faults, at
             last shame them derides   last with shame derides

Though it involves awkward inversions, the Q construction is clear: 'Who (= whoever) covers
faults, shame derides (= mocks) them at last'. In F, less happily, 'Time' is made the subject of
both 'covers' and 'derides'. Since the latter verb is deprived of its object it must mean 'laughs
scornfully', while 'with shame' implies 'together with Shame (personified)'. The result may be
considered rhetorically more stylish. Nevertheless syntactically it is confused: 'Who', if it is to
have (as it does not in Q) an antecedent in the preceding line, should properly refer back to
'cunning'.

| I.i.308 | *lets hit together* | let vs sit together | 215 |

Hit together = agree together. F's reading is probably to be ascribed to the compositor, and if so, to a lapse of aural memory. (It may be worth adding here, in view of the importance attributed to phonetic errors in Q, that no other instance of one is apparent in F.)

| I.ii.24 | *subscribd his power* | Prescrib'd his powre |

Prescrib'd (= limited) cannot be right, since Lear has not retained limited power: he has surrendered it all (*cf.* 'only we still retain / The name and all th'additions to a King', I.i.137–8). 'Subscribe' (= yield) gives the right meaning, and must be the true reading, though no other instance is known of its use in this sense as a transitive verb.

| I.iv.102 | *you haue wisedome* | haue you wisedome |

'You know better': a piece of sardonic encouragement to the chastened Oswald. F's version, framed as a question, is not impossible, but does not follow as naturally from the rest of the speech.

| I.iv.183 | *They know not how their wits doe weare* | And know not how their wits to weare |

'They' are the 'wise men' of the preceding line, not the 'fools' from the one before; *weare* = diminish, fade. F, not very clearly intelligible, misses, in any case, the point – which is not simply that 'wise men' have 'grown foppish' but that they are unaware of having done so. 'Apish' in the next line means, I take it, not 'imitative' but 'silly, affected', the target being the extravagance and empty-headedness of courtiers. The original target, that is to say: the squib was presumably imported into the play from some other source.

| I.iv.267 | *great pallace* | grac'd Pallace |

Editors attribute, illegitimately, the sense 'dignified, honourable' to *grac'd*. But it means neither more nor less than 'graced'; and here, in the mouth of the sarcastic Goneril, addressing Lear, must imply, if anything, 'graced by the presence of the King'. The contrast, however, which concludes the sentence requires no more meaning or weight in its second term than is given by *great pallace*: the added emphasis of *grac'd* is superfluous, and its meaning (if any) irrelevant. *Grac'd* was possibly suggested to the reviser by an untidily written *greate* in the manuscript he consulted; it may, on the other hand, represent compositor B's misreading of manuscript copy.

| I.iv.279 | *We that too late repent's* | Woe, that too late repents |

Repent's = repent us. The ellipsis in F, 'Woe [to him] that . . .', for which no precedent has yet been found, is doubtfully idiomatic. See Appendix B1, p. 231 below, for further comment.

216 I.iv.320–1 *that these hot teares that breake* That these hot teares, which
                 from me perforce, should make the breake from me perforce
                 worst Should make thee worth
                 them.

The passage in Q should be followed by a dash to indicate that Lear interrupts himself to break into impotent cursing in the next half-line: 'Blasts and fogs upon thee!' Bitter frustration that he is not capable of any more serious reprisal than the 'hot tears that break from [him] perforce' explodes in anger. F (as often) completes a sentence deliberately left unfinished: in this case to very poor effect.

I.iv.322 a: *the vntender woundings* Th'vntented woundings
          b: the vntented woundings

A wound may be untented, i.e. untreated by means of a tent (= a roll, or pledget, usually of soft absorbent material, often medicated . . . formerly much used to search and cleanse a wound, or to keep open or distend a wound); but it is hardly possible to speak of an untented *wounding*. There is no doubt that the *action* of wounding is implied by the context. Why then did Qa's *vntender*, right as it obviously is, fail to satisfy the corrector? It may well be that he was unfamiliar with the word. It is a curious fact that *OED* records no examples of its use before *Lear*. If the corrector rejected the word as spurious, he would readily be reminded, by the association with wounds, of 'untented'.

I.iv.364 a: *mildie* milky
          b: milkie

Either word is acceptable. But *mildie* is the rarer, hence may not have been recognised by the corrector, who may simply then have substituted what he expected to see. It is doubtful, to say the least, that a compositor would misread *k* as *d* in a fairly common word; and not *a priori* likely that foul case would produce such an error.

I.v.16 *yet I con, what I can tel* yet I can tell what I can tell

Con = know; citations in *OED* show that the word was in use until at least 1674.

II.i.19–20 *and I haue one thing of a* And I haue one thing of a
            quesie question, which must queazie question
            aske breefnes and fortune helpe Which I must act, Briefnesse,
            and Fortune worke

There is no fault in Q's syntax. We may even now say: 'I asked him a favour'. Elizabethan English permitted, more than does our own, the dropping of prepositions before the indirect objects of certain verbs (see Abbott, §201). Q's line from *which* to *helpe* is, of course, a foot short: no doubt the chief reason for F's 'correction'. It is possible that 'I' has been omitted from Q before *must aske*: in that event, *which* = 'as to which' (see Abbott, §272 for this usage).

II.i.54   lancht   latch'd
           (Q2: *launcht*)

'Launched' = pierced, wounded; 'latched' = grasped, seized. Q is unquestionably correct. F's reading cannot have derived from Q2 (the copy at this point): it suggests nothing so much as a misreading of *lāch'd* in manuscript (see above, pp. 147ff., for further comment).

II.i.56   *quarrels, rights*   quarrels right
           (Q2: quarrels right)

The comma in Q1 is manifestly wrong, but there is no other reason for the alteration in Q2, which is followed by F, here derived from Q2 copy.

II.i.58   *but sodainly he fled*   Full sodainely he fled

Q's *but* appears clumsily to repeat the *but* three lines further up: *but when he saw*. It serves a different function, in fact: that of introducing a certainty to set against the uncertainty implied in the previous clause. The construction should be read: 'but when he saw . . . , or whether ghasted . . . , (*sc.* I cannot tell), but suddenly he fled'. If 'whether . . . whether' stood in place of 'when . . . whether', no difficulty would be felt. Both 'but's are removed in F.

II.i.78   *spurres*   spirits

F's reading makes no discernible sense in the context. It is very probably a misreading from manuscript copy (see above, pp. 147ff.).

II.i.79   *Strong and fastned villaine*   O strange and fastned Villaine

Strong = resolute. Though *strange* is just possible (in the sense 'surprising, unaccountable', if hardly in the sense 'unfriendly'), it gives, one might consider inappropriately, a colouring of wonder or puzzlement to Gloucester's indignation. More probably it is evidence of misreading from manuscript (see above, pp. 147ff.).

II.i.81   *why*   wher
II.i.89   *strange newes*   strangenesse

The two readings in F could scarcely be defended. They are almost certainly manuscript misreadings (see above, pp. 147ff.).

II.ii.84   *Reneag*   Reuenge

If the reviser altered the spelling of *Reneag* to *renegue* in his copy of Q, *Reuenge* is quite possibly a copyist's misreading.

218 II.ii.85 *gale*   gall

All modern editors recognise the necessity of *gale*. One is tempted to see *gall* as a manuscript misreading, but it is more probably a compositorial slip (see above, pp. 149–50).

II.ii.112 *graund aspect*   great aspect

The reading in Q is consistent with the stilted phraseology Kent affects in this speech, hence the 'correction' in F is unusually obtuse. *Graund*, it should perhaps be added, is merely an old-fashioned spelling of 'grand' (*cf.* elsewhere *commaund, auncient*, etc., modernised in F).

II.ii.125 *coniunct*   compact

The two words are virtually synonymous, meaning 'joined' or 'associated', 'in league'. But *OED*, interestingly, adds to the definition of 'conjunct' '*esp.* in a more or less subordinate capacity', an appropriate nuance here, since the word is applied to Kent in his relation to Lear. (It is later applied, V.i.12, to Edmund as conspirator with Goneril. The line is omitted from F.)

II.ii.167   a: *say*   saw
            b: saw

Another synonymous pair (= saying, proverb). It is scarcely likely that the Q compositor misread *saw* as *say*.

II.iv.26 *purpose*   impose

Purpose = resolve upon the performance of.

II.iv.142 *slacke*   scant

Slack = to be slack or remiss in respect of (some business, duty, etc.).

II.iv.170 *To[-]fall and blast her pride*   To fall, and blister

That F omits *pride* is almost certainly accidental. The substitution of *blister* for *blast her* was very possibly prompted by the interpretation of *to fall* as an infinitive implying purpose: 'fogs drawn by the powerful sun / To fall and blister pride'. The Q text cannot be so construed without absurdity. Indeed *to* in Q is an intensive particle, and *to-fall* an imperative, the last of the series which makes up the speech. Abbott (§§28, 350) is responsible for persuading Shakespeare scholars that the intensive 'to-' was obsolete in Shakespeare's day, and that it is therefore nowhere to be found in the plays. He does indeed succeed in explaining on other grounds a number of plausible instances; but he omits from the list not only the reading in question here but several others which are scarcely more open to doubt: 'Mine innocency and Saint George to-thrive!' (*Richard II*, I.iii.84); 'Rain, to-lay this wind, or my heart will be blown up by the

root!' (*Troilus and Cressida*, IV.iv.55–6); 'Now the gods to-bless your honour!' (*Pericles*,
IV.vi.23); and, very possibly, the Qa reading in *Lear* at IV.vi.230: '[The bounty and the benison
of Heaven} to-save thee!' It is scarcely likely that the verb in any of these cases is a simple
infinitive. Exclamations depending on an infinitive absolute are confined to expressions of
'astonishment, indignation, sorrow, or (after *O* or other interj.) longing' (*OED*: examples cited:
'My own flesh and blood to rebel!', 'Oh, to be in England!', etc.). There is thus no alternative
but to suppose that, at least in optative exclamations (blessings, imprecations, adjurations) of a
particularly emphatic kind, the intensive 'to-' survived in Shakespearean English.

II.iv.174	*tēder hested*	tender-hefted

Though editors frequently adopt the F reading, it makes very poor sense, besides wearing every
appearance of a graphic error. *Hested* derives from 'hest' (= will): the formation of quasi-
participial adjectives from nouns is, of course, common in Shakespeare (see Abbott, §294).

II.iv.191	*Gon. Who struck my seruant*	Lear. Who stockt my Seruant?

The change of reading and prefix in F is very plausible since Lear has a few moments previously
asked, without receiving an answer: 'Who put my man i'th'stocks?', and is shortly to revert to
the question: 'How came my man i'th'stocks?' On the other hand, it is an encounter between
Lear and Oswald which immediately precedes the line in question here. Lear greets Oswald's
appearance with hostility, and then presumably strikes him ('Out, varlet, from my sight!') as he
has done before (*cf.* I.iii.1 and I.iv.93). If so, Cornwall's 'What means your Grace?' is ruffled
protest rather than polite deprecation. Goneril, who enters immediately, would need no
explanation of what had just occurred.

II.iv.215	*the hot bloud in France*	the hot-blooded France
		(press-correction: hot-bloodied)

Blood = 'A hot spark, a man of fire' (Johnson). The word is used in *King John*, II.i.278. *Hot* =
ardent, passionate, eager.

III.ii.33	*shall haue a corne cry woe*	Shall of a Corne cry woe

Though the F editor did not, it seems, approve of the construction in Q, it is perfectly sound: 'to
have something happen to one' is good English idiom.

III.iv.10	a: *the raging sea*	the roaring Sea
	b: the roring sea	

There seems no good reason for the change in Qb. This in itself might be considered a guarantee
of its genuineness, except that (a) the compositor is most unlikely to have read an *r* as a *g* and (b)
the raging sea was not yet a cliché, and is the more appropriate expression here, since the context
requires an image representing mortal danger.

III.iv.53   *through foord*   through Sword

The reviser cannot be held responsible for the absurd reading in F. But the compositor (E), if he was to blame, was misreading printed, not manuscript, copy (Q2 repeats the spelling *foord* discovered in Q1).

III.iv.83   *keep thy word[s] iustly*   keepe thy words Iustice

Pope's emendation (*word* for *words*) is clearly necessary. The reading in F has so little to recommend it that *Iustice*, we may conclude, is a misreading of *iustlie* in the manuscript copy.

III.iv.140   *stock-punisht and imprisoned*   stockt, punish'd, and
                                                         imprison'd

F implies confusingly that being stocked is something other than being punished.

III.vi.73   *Bobtaile tike*   Bobtaile tight

Since *bobtail* = either a dog with its tail cut short; or (used attributively as in Q) having the tail cut short, F's reading makes no sense. *Tight* must represent a misreading of manuscript *tike* as *tite*, a common alternative spelling of the former word.

III.vi.73   *trūdletaile*   Troudle taile

Another manuscript misreading in F, involving once more an alternative spelling *trondletaile*.

III.vii.12   *intelligence*   intelligent

Intelligence = convey intelligence. No other instance is recorded of the use of 'intelligent' to mean 'bearing intelligence', a meaning which does not in any case strike one as a natural extension of the normal one. The reading in Q presents no difficulty.

III.vii.63   *dearne*   sterne

Dern = dark, drear, dire; an unusual word, hence presumably the substitution in F – about which modern editors agree that it is of suspect origin (*cf. sticke* for *rash* a few lines earlier, III.vii.58).

IV.i.54   *I cannot dance it farther*   I cannot daub it further

Daub = to put on a false show. Since Edgar none the less continues to put on a false show the reviser felt it necessary to add to his next speech: *And yet I must*. This, if it does not necessarily discredit the reading *daub*, casts grave doubt on it. Q's version bears no obvious relevance to the

context, but is quite intelligible: 'mad' Tom has been dancing his way along, like the clown   221
Kempe on his famous journey from London to Norwich.

IV.i.71   *stands*   slaues

Stands = withstands. The 'ordinance' (= dispensation) of the Heavens which Gloucester
supposes the 'superfluous and lust-dieted' man will withstand is that providing for the equitable
distribution of riches: it is, of course, a projection of Gloucester's desires ('Heavens deal so
still!'). F gives a less clear and satisfactory meaning: 'slaves your ordinance' may be taken to
signify 'enslaves (? lords it over) the order of things created by you', but whether the allusion to
order, not to mention that to enslavement, is wholly relevant here remains doubtful.

IV.i.77   *firmely*   fearfully

Firmly = fixedly, steadily; *fearfully* = so as to cause fear. Q's reading is more suited to the image
of a cliff 'with high and bending head' looking into the deep.

IV.ii.17   *armes*   names

Goneril goes on to mention the 'arms' she must exchange at home: she will, she says, 'give the
distaff / Into [her] husband's hands'. The reading in F is very likely a misreading from
manuscript copy.

IV.ii.28   a: *My foote vsurps my body*   My Foole vsurpes my body
             b: A foole vsurps my bed

It is extremely unlikely that the Q compositor could have mistaken *A* for *My, bed* for *body*. A
misreading of *foote* for *foole* would be more credible, though we need not assume it. The Qb
reading is certainly a thoroughgoing sophistication of the corrector's, who was evidently doing
his work here as elsewhere in a somewhat near-sighted way. The development of the action
makes it clear what is meant by the line in Qa. Goneril has bestowed a favour and a kiss upon
Edmund, with hints of greater rewards in future. His reaction is an extravagant affirmation of
loyalty ('Yours in the ranks of death!'), which is both a vassal's profession of fealty and a courtly
lover's vow. With this, it is natural to suppose, he throws himself at her feet. A man of his rank
would not, of course, go to the lengths of prostration, but make a low reverence on one knee. If
he were at the same time to kiss his hand and place it on Goneril's foot as a further gesture of
obeisance, her next words to him are explained. She replies to his act of homage by insinuating
that the relationship he is dramatising should be reversed: 'My most dear Gloucester, / To thee a
woman's services are due: / My foot usurps my body'. If this is correct, Edmund cannot, of
course, leave the scene (as he does in F) before hearing this reply. It must be Oswald's warning of
Albany's approach ('Madam, here comes my Lord') which prompts him to a hurried exit.

IV.ii.75   *thereat inraged*   threat-enrag'd

Q's reading needs no defence: F's shows the reviser sorrily misapplying his ingenuity.

222

IV.iv.18	*distresse*	desires
IV.vi.71	*enridged*	enraged
IV.vi.83	*coyning*	crying

Modern editors concur in preferring Q. F's readings, though the first is not altogether impossible, are very probably the product of manuscript misreading.

IV.vi.168–9	*through tottered raggs, smal vices do appeare, robes & furd-gownes hides all*	Thorough tatter'd cloathes great Vices do appeare: Robes, and Furr'd gownes hide all

F misses the point, which is that *even* small vices will show through tatters, and seems to make a less plausible one: that seen through tatters all vices appear great.

IV.vi.262	*I am only sorrow*	I am onely sorry

Cf. 'I am sorrow for thee' (*Cymbeline*, V.v.297), and see Abbott §230 for comment.

IV.vi.267	*Let your reciprocall vowes bee remembred*	Let our reciprocall vowes be remembred

F assumes the meaning 'mutual' for 'reciprocal', Q the meaning 'given in return'.

V.iii.13	*heare poore rogues*	heere (poore Rogues)

An extraordinarily obtuse error in F, which has led to a further blunder in the addition of brackets. It is unlikely that the same person was responsible for both mistakes. If the brackets were introduced by the compositor (E), it is probable that *heare* had already been altered to *heere* in his copy of Q2, perhaps because *heere* stood in the manuscript prompt-book from which corrections to the copy were drawn. (For further comment, see above, p. 150.)

V.iii.155	*stople* (Q2: stop)	stop

F's reading was derived from Q2 copy.

V.iii.170–1	*The Gods are iust, and of our pleasant vertues, Make instruments to scourge vs*	The Gods are iust, and of our pleasant vices Make instruments to plague vs

In Q the word *vertues* has the sense 'powers, capacities'. See Onions, *Glossary* (*virtue* 6) for several parallels elsewhere in Shakespeare. (*OED* recognises only the more particular meaning 'accomplishments' in relation to persons.)

V.iii.288   *from your life of difference*   from your first of difference
              and decay   and decay

In Q, Kent refers to the fact that he has last seen Lear in circumstances of 'difference and decay'; in F he emphasises that he has been with him from the start of his misfortunes. I do not think it can be objected against Q's reading (as, perhaps, the F editor was tempted to do) that it has Kent refer back, paradoxically, to a 'life of difference and decay' which continues in the present. 'Difference and decay' refers surely to the loss of worldly standing, and Lear's life has improved in this one respect at least: he has been restored to honour and dignity, if nothing else.

V.iii.293   *He knowes not what he sees*   He knowes not what he saies

Both readings make sense, though Q's is by far the apter in the context. *Cf.* Lear's remarks earlier at lines 278–9, 'Who are you? Mine eyes are not o'the best'. Because Lear 'knows not what he sees', Albany says it would be vain to 'present us to him': the point is that Lear has failed to recognise Kent, and pays no heed even to the bodies of his elder daughters when Kent attempts to draw his attention to them.

APPENDIX A8
Q1/F 'TRUE' VARIANTS

Note: I include all those variants in F which, acceptable themselves, correspond to acceptable readings in Q; and about which, furthermore, it might be argued that they must derive from the manuscript copy of Q, and that they offer more convincing readings than their Q equivalents. As my comments will show, however, I do not regard the reasons for preferring F as equally strong in every case.

	Q1	F
I.i.39	first	fast
I.i.102	Happely (= haply)	Happily

But *happily* here = haply. It cannot mean 'fortunately'.

I.i.177	diseases	disasters

Diseases = inconveniences, troubles. It is, perhaps, the harder reading and the apter, and not, besides, very easily dismissible as a misreading of *disasters*.

I.ii.40	your liking	your ore-looking
I.ii.133–4	Trecherers by spirituall predominance	Treachers by Sphericall pre-dominance

Treacherer = *Treacher* = traitor; *spiritual* = of or pertaining to Spirit; *spherical* = of or pertaining to the celestial spheres. The weaker reading, *spirituall*, may well be traceable to a phonetic spelling *spericall* in the copy. It is known that 'sphere' was pronounced in the same way as 'spear' (see Dobson, II. 1010).

I.iv.127	A pestilent gull to mee	A pestilent gall to me

It is not clear whether Lear's remark is a retort to the Fool's saying about Truth the dog and Lie the brach, or whether it is a protest applying generally to the Fool's taunting. In the former case *gull* may well be correct, and in a double sense: (a) (= deception) as denominating 'Lie the brach', (b) (= simpleton) as applying to the Fool, on whom the King, perhaps, retorts his own observation by making out that he it is, after all, who will be allowed to 'stand by the fire and stink'. *Gall* (= something galling or exasperating) is acceptable if Lear is referring to the Fool's behaviour generally. If this is the case, however, it is a little odd to find an unattached sentence (which is something more than a mere exclamation) lacking a main verb.

I.iv.248–9   his discernings are   his Discernings   225
                lethergie   Are Lethargied

Lethargy = a disorder characterised by morbid drowsiness or prolonged and unnatural sleep. The construction in F is more natural. Though the use of 'lethargy' as a verb is almost unknown (*OED* citing only one eighteenth-century example besides the reading in F), the practice of converting nouns into verbs is common enough in Shakespeare. Q might be defended on the grounds that a phrase such as 'nothing but' or 'no more than' is understood after the verb, the main emphasis falling on *lethargy*: 'his discernings are [mere] lethargy'.

II.i.9   eare-bussing   eare-kissing

The misreading of *k* as *b* is frequent in Q.

II.i.41   warbling   Mumbling

II.i.47   reuengiue   reuenging

Revengive is not recorded elsewhere. But against F it might be argued that a form approximating to 'revengeful' would be preferable to 'revenging' in the context, and that this passage in F contains an unusual number of misreadings from manuscript copy (see above, p. 147), of which *revenging* might be one.

II.i.75   pretence   practise

Practice = machination, artifice. Hence, in respect of sense, there is little if anything to choose between the readings. It may be relevant that *practise* in F occurs in the course of a passage marked by several compositorial misreadings (see the preceding note and above, p. 147).

II.ii.83   Bring   Being

Q's *bring* is the stronger reading, and the more suited to the image conveyed by the context.

III.ii.49   force   feare

Feare is more consonant with the preceding *affliction*. On the other hand, perhaps a distinction is intended: psychological *affliction*, physical *force*.

III.iv.114   a: come on bee true.   Come, vnbutton heere.
              b: come on

We must eliminate the reading in Qb which is merely the result of an accident to the type. The full stop after *bee true* in Qa having disappeared in Qb along with the words, it is unlikely that the compositor removed them deliberately. We should also probably discount *heere* in F as an

226   interpolation. The remaining *Come, unbutton* may easily represent a more accurate decipherment of the manuscript reading which yielded *come on bee true* in Q. The latter, however, makes sense and is perfectly consistent with the idea expressed in the context. Lear, exhorting himself, and perhaps his companions, to the honesty of 'unaccommodated man', may well say: 'Off, off, you lendings! Come on, be true!'

III.vii.86   vnbridle   enkindle

An example, perhaps, of the misreading in Q of *k* as *b*. The word 'enkindle' does, indeed, seem the more properly applied to *sparks of nature*. Yet if the latter is considered as a set-phrase meaning 'natural feelings', 'unbridle' does not jar; it gives, besides, more force to the sentence as a whole.

IV.i.4   experience   esperance

The fact that the metre requires a stress on the first syllable does not disqualify Q's reading (see Dobson, II. 448 for variability of stress in polysyllables with prefixes).

IV.v.14   army   Enemy

IV.vi.131   consumation   consumption

Both words mean 'the action of consuming, destruction'.

IV.vi.215   sence   sound

Here *sense* probably = meaning.

IV.vi.278   wit   will

IV.vi.289   fenced   seuer'd

IV.vii.36   iniurious   Enemies

Injurious = wilfully inflicting injury. The word in F, though 'easier', reads more plausibly in the context.

V.i.3   a: abdication   alteration
            b: alteration

Abdication = resignation, surrender, renunciation: the stronger and more appropriate reading, although Qb's is perfectly consistent with the context.

V.iii.65   imediate   immediacie   227

Immediate = (in feudal language) holding directly of the sovereign or lord paramount; *immediacy* = the condition of being the immediate . . . vassal. *OED*, however, quotes the F reading to illustrate the primary meaning of *immediacy*, 'the quality or condition of being immediate; freedom from intermediate or intervening agency', as is doubtless necessary since Regan is speaking of Edmund not as her vassal but as her deputy. The choice between the readings depends upon whether we judge that 'the which' refers to Edmund, in which case it qualifies *immediate* used as a substantive, or whether we take 'commission' as the antecedent of 'the which immediacy'. An awkwardness arises in any case: either Edmund or the commission must 'stand up / And call itself your brother'.

V.iii.269   murderous   Murderors

APPENDIX B1
ASCRIPTION OF SPEECHES IN Q1 AND F

(a) *Errors in F*

	Q1	F
I.iv.110	*Kent.* Why Foole?	*Lear.* Why my Boy?

It is clear that in the preceding and ensuing speeches the Fool is addressing Kent, not Lear.

	Q1	F
II.ii.158	*[Reg.]* Come my good Lord away?	*Corn.* Come my Lord, away.

Since Regan and Cornwall make their exit on this line it is properly given in Q to Regan. Cornwall could speak it only to Gloucester, who is, however, to remain on stage for the rest of the scene.

	Q1	F
II.iv.191	*Gon.* Who struck my seruant . . .	*Lear.* Who stockt my Seruant?

See Appendix A7, p. 212 above, for arguments on behalf of the reading *struck*, hence of the ascription of the speech to Goneril.

	Q1	F
IV.vii.21	*Doct.* I madam . . .	*Gent.* I Madam . . .
23	*Gent.* Good madam be by . . .	Be by good Madam . . .

The change in F, not strictly an error, follows from the suppression of the Doctor's role in this scene. His other speeches are either omitted or re-ascribed to *Gent*.

V.iii.160   *Gon.* Aske me not what I know. *Bast.* Aske me not what I know.

F, by ascribing the speech to Edmund, commits a double violation of dramatic logic: (a) the violent interchange between Albany and Goneril is interrupted two lines before Goneril's exit, depriving her of an exit line, (b) Edmund is made to appear recalcitrant only two lines before he declares his readiness to confess everything: 'What you have charg'd me with, that have I done / And more, much more: the time will bring it out'. The change in F was possibly prompted by the fact that Albany has already taxed Goneril with the letter, and received a dusty answer (*'Alb.* I perceive you know't. *Gon.* Say if I do . . . '). This, however, is perfectly consistent with his returning more openly to the attack: 'Know'st thou this paper?', so that Goneril is betrayed into petulance ('Ask me not what I know!') and retreat.

(b) *Unnecessary alterations in F*

(In each of the following instances no objection can be raised to the change in F, except that there is no need for it.)

	QI	F
I.i.279	*Gonorill.* Prescribe not . . .	*Regn.* Prescribe not . . .
	Regan. Let your study . . .	*Gon.* Let your study . . .
I.iv.141	*Lear.* This is nothing foole.	*Kent.* This is nothing Foole.

The remark occurs in the course of a protracted exchange of dialogue between Lear and the Fool: there seems no reason why Kent should intervene.

| I.iv.251 | *[Lear.]* *Lears* shadow? | *Foole.* *Lears* shadow. |

In Q Lear answers his own question, *who is it that can tell me who I am?*, with another, *Lears shadow?* In a speech largely consisting of rhetorical questions there is nothing untoward in this.

| II.ii.66 | *Glost.* Speake yet, how grew your quarrell? | *Cor.* Speake yet, how grew your quarrell? |

Though it is Cornwall who heads the enquiry into the dispute between Kent and Oswald, so that the F reviser may have felt Gloucester should play no part in the interrogation, nevertheless it is Gloucester (in both Q and F) who asks the same question several lines later: 'How fell you out? Say that.' (II.ii.92).

II.iv.296	*Duke.* [i.e. *Corn.*] So am I puspos'd . . .	*Gon.* So am I purpos'd . . .
II.iv.298	*Reg.* Followed the old man . . .	*Corn.* Followed the old man . . .
II.iv.301	*Re.* Tis good . . .	*Corn.* 'Tis best . . .
V.iii.70	*Gon.* That were the most . . .	*Alb.* That were the most . . .
V.iii.81	*Bast.* Let the drum strike, and proue my title good.	*Reg.* Let the Drum strike, and proue my title thine.

More than the prefix is altered in F: *my title*, used by Edmund, must mean 'my title to Regan'; used by Regan, 'my title as sovereign' or 'my title to soldiers, prisoners, patrimony', powers made over to Edmund. But either sense is appropriate in the context.

230 V.iii.222–3   *Alb.* What kind of helpe, what   *Edg.* What kinde of helpe?
                   meanes that bloudy knife?   *Alb.* Speake man.
                                                  Edg. What meanes this
                                                  bloody Knife?

V.iii.251   *Duke.* {i.e. *Alb.*} Hast thee for   *Edg.* Hast thee for thy life.
                   thy life.

Edgar's previous speech implies that it is he who is preparing to run to the castle to save Cordelia. The line ascribed to Albany in Q must therefore be addressed to him. The re-ascription in F suggests that an anonymous soldier is to carry the reprieve, since no one else is available. The change was made doubtless because Edgar speaks again within the next fifteen lines: the reviser may have assumed that he was required to remain on stage. It is very probable, however, that Edgar is intended to leave the stage at line 251 and to return almost immediately with Lear, who enters carrying the dead Cordelia in his arms. It would thereby be implied, of course, that Edgar had met them on the way, thus realising the fruitlessness of his mission.

V.iii.323   *Duke.* {i.e. *Alb.*} The   *Edg.* The waight of this sad
                   waight of this sad time . . .   time . . .

(c) *Errors in Q1*

                       Q1   F
V.iii.109   *Cap.* Sound trumpet?   (om.)

Read *Her.* (Herald).

V.iii.115–17   *Bast* Sound? Againe?   *Her.* Againe.
                                             Her. Againe.

F's ascription is obviously correct.

V.iii.312   *Lear.* Breake hart, I prethe   *Kent.* Breake heart, I
                  breake.   prythee breake.

F must be correct since Kent expresses the same sentiment, or something very close to it, in his next speech: 'Vex not his ghost. Oh, let him pass . . .'. The attribution to Lear is, in any case, highly implausible: he has clearly spoken his last words by this time.

	Q1	F
I.iv.279–81	*Lear.* We that too late repent's, O sir, are you come? is it your will that wee prepare any horses, ingratitude! . . .	*Lear.* Woe, that too late repents: Is it your will, speake Sir? Prepare my Horses. Ingratitude! . . .

The questions in Q (*O sir, are you come? is it your will that wee prepare any horses?*) should surely be given to one of Lear's gentlemen. It is clear that the King is accompanied during this scene not only by the Fool but by one or more of his followers. It is to them he has just delivered the orders 'Saddle my horses! Call my train together!', and to them that he later says 'Go, go, my people!' (line 294 and, Q only, line 311). Assuming that one of the gentlemen speaks at this point, we have a much more intelligible sequence of events. As Goneril is elaborating her complaint against Lear's household ('your disordered rabble make servants of their betters'), Albany enters, whereupon one of the household gives her the lie by politely – if, perhaps, somewhat desperately in the circumstances – requesting permission to saddle the King's horses, as he has commanded. The point is not lost on Lear, nor does he mean it to be lost on Goneril. His passionate outburst, 'Ingratitude! Thou marble-hearted fiend! . . .', serves only to introduce a triumphant rejoinder to her accusations: 'Detested kite, thou liest! / My train are men of choice and rarest parts / That all particulars of duty know, / And in the most exact regard support / The worships of their name.' Without the rearrangement suggested the text is very nearly incoherent, while the revision in F, it hardly needs adding, is entirely unconvincing. We are left with the problem of *We that too late repent's* (= repent us). I am inclined to think that these are the last words of Goneril's speech, interrupted by Albany's entrance. She is about, one may suppose, to voice some hypocritically despairing sentiment. *We* must refer to herself and Albany; uttered by Lear it could only be taken as the royal 'we', which would be odd in the circumstances and altogether inconsistent with his references to himself elsewhere in the scene. It is doubtless for this reason that the reviser changed *We* to *Woe* (see Appendix A7, p. 215 above, for comment on this reading).

III.iv.25	[*Lear.*] but ile goe in	[*Lear.*] but Ile goe in

There are two reasons for suspecting that these words should be attributed to the Fool: (a) Lear has only just refused an invitation to enter the hovel, so that (unless a line or lines are missing in Q which explain that he will go in later) he appears now to be contradicting himself; (b) it appears in the next speech that the Fool is already in the hovel ('Come not in here, nuncle'), though his entering it has not been marked, as one would have expected, in the dialogue. F deals with the difficulties by adding two lines in which Lear urges the Fool to take shelter, and says *Ile pray* (presumably outside), *and then Ile sleepe* (presumably inside), thus explaining the apparent contradiction in what he has said earlier. The explanation, however, creates a new difficulty since, although Lear continues speaking for nine lines after the Fool's exit in F, he cannot be said to pray.

232   III.iv.130   *Kent.* How fares your Grace?   *Kent.* How fares your Grace?

This is surely Gloucester's entrance line. There is no dramatic reason why Kent should, at this particular point, express his concern for the King, and every reason why Gloucester, on entering, should do so before he turns to Kent and Edgar ('What are you there? Your names?')

III.vii.42–7 *Corn.* Come sir, what letters	*Corn.* Come Sir.
had you late from *France*?	What Letters had you late from
Reg. Be simple answerer, for we	France?
know the truth.	*Reg.* Be simple answer'd, for we
Corn. And what confederacy	know the truth.
haue you with the tratours late	*Corn.* And what confederacie
footed in the kingdome?	haue you with the Traitors,
Reg. To whose hands you haue	late footed in the Kingdome?
sent the lunatick King speake?	*Reg.* To whose hands
	You haue sent the Lunaticke
	King: Speake.

It seems likely that *answerer* is a phonetic error for *answer her*: F's emendation, at all events, sounds too high-flown in a context of very forthright utterances. If this is so, the speech 'Be simple [= honest]. Answer her; for we know the truth' must be ascribed to Cornwall. This resolves rather than creates other difficulties. The first speech follows Gloucester's protest to Regan (who has plucked him by the beard): 'You should not ruffle thus. What will you do?' It is, therefore, more natural for Regan to respond than Cornwall. The third and fourth speeches contain a single question, not two, hence are more plausibly ascribed to one speaker – which must again be Regan.

APPENDIX B2
OMISSIONS AND ADDITIONS IN F

Note: Only substantial cuts or interpolations of a half-line or more are listed.

(a) *Omissions*

1   I.i.106   to loue my father all.

A half-line necessary to the sense. Its omission must be accidental.

2   I.ii.103–5   *Bast.* Nor is not sure.
                           Glost. . . . heauen and earth!

The lines are not strictly essential, though there seems no special reason for omitting them. The reviser, perhaps, failed to notice that Gloucester is concluding a sentence begun in his previous speech ('He cannot be such a monster'), and so failed to make sense of its syntax.

3   I.ii.157–65   [*Bast.*] as of vnnaturalnesse . . .
                           [*Edg.*] . . . sectary Astronomicall?

Gloucester has previously (I.ii.115ff.) expatiated on the effects of the eclipses. Though Edmund is here addressing Edgar, not Gloucester Edmund, and though he discusses the subject in somewhat different terms, and certainly for different motives, the reviser very probably felt that there was something too much here of the same ideas.

4   I.iii.16–20   [*Gon.*] not to be ouerruld . . .
                           . . . when they are seene abusd

Inessential, the last two lines more than somewhat obscure.

5   I.iii.24–5   [*Gon.*] I would breed from hence occasions, and I
                           shall, that I may speake

This appears to contradict what Goneril has said shortly before: 'I will not speak with him', I.iii.8.

6   I.iv.154–69   *Foole.* That Lord that counsail'd thee . . .
                           [*Foole.*] . . . they'l be snatching;

234 The cut shortens a long series of exchanges between Lear and the Fool, all of which bear upon the same point: Lear's want of wisdom. But it would be impossible to guess why this passage was chosen for omission rather than another. The cut should have begun at line 151. As the text stands in F, the Fool propounds a riddle (lines 151–2), Lear asks for the solution (line 153) but none is forthcoming. Since this page in F (qq4ᵛ) was set by compositor E, it is possible that the mistake occurred in miscalculating the length of the marginal line marking the deletion in Q2 copy. On the other hand, the lines (151–3) which should have been deleted but were instead retained do not follow Q2 word for word. A single editorial change (the substitution of *one* for *foole*, line 152) is enough to indicate that they were in fact discovered in the manuscript copy. The misleading marginal mark of deletion must therefore have appeared there. It follows that the passage was omitted neither by the compositor nor even by the reviser but cut by the book-keeper in the theatre.

7   I.iv.252–6   [*Lear.*] I would learne that . . .
                          [*Foole.*] . . . an obedient father.

The reviser may well have had difficulty in following the drift of this passage: modern editors have been puzzled by it. Yet it is not corrupt, or particularly complicated, and should, I think, be understood as follows: 'I would learn that [i.e. that I am Lear's shadow], for by the marks [= criteria] / Of sovereignty [*sc.* man's sovereignty over the animals] – knowledge and reason – / I should be false persuaded I had daughters [= I ought to be wrong in thinking I had daughters]'. Lear argues, in other words, that, because knowledge and reason inform him that he has no daughters, he would as soon believe (for sanity's sake) that he does not exist. The next line, however, (the Fool's speech) betrays some corruption. Both sense and metre require the addition to it of 'thee': 'Which [= as to which, see Abbott §272] they will make [thee] an obedient father.'

8   I.iv.279   [*Lear.*] O sir, are you come?

An omission associated with the re-casting of the following line, both procedures being prompted (as is argued in Appendix B1, p. 231 above) by a faulty ascription of the speech in Q.

9   I.iv.326   [*Lear.*] yea, i'st come to this?

Obviously an accidental omission, for which the scribe who prepared the prompt-book must have been responsible. The *additional* half-line *Ha? Let it be so*, intended to supply the gap in line 327, has wrongly replaced the last half of line 326. The compositor (B) might have been guilty of omitting one half-line, but would not compound the error by misplacing the next, given that he was setting, as we have assumed, from clearly lineated manuscript copy.

10   II.i.80   [*Glost.*] I neuer got him

A strange omission, since the phrase is perfectly intelligible and the one substituted for it – *said he?* – is not only much weaker, but also leaves the metre deficient. Some confusion of the reviser's or copyist's may be responsible.

11   II.ii.148–52   [*Glost.*] His fault is much . . .

                              . . . are punisht with

12   II.ii.157   [*Reg.*] For following her affaires, put in his legges

Probably theatrical rather than editorial cuts, since the lines raise no serious textual or contextual difficulties. It seems to have been found desirable to shorten the episode of Kent's 'stocking'.

13   III.i.7–15   [*Gent.*] teares his white haire . . .

                              . . . bids what will take all.

Abbreviates a description of Lear 'contending with the fretful element'. What is here described is, of course, enacted in the following scene.

14   III.i.30–42   [*Kent.*] But true it is . . .
                      Offer this office to you.

An accidental omission, immediately following an insertion of eight lines. The omitted matter, the first four or five lines of it at least, is essential: without it indeed, the interpolation is incomplete in grammar and sense. So that this was certainly no deliberate deletion of the reviser's. Nor is it very likely that the copyist would make such an error. But if the insertion were not part of the original revision, and were written on a slip pasted to the margin of the prompt-book, it is quite likely that the compositor, B, was to blame. If the lines omitted were actually covered by the slip containing the interpolated material, the mistake is easily explained. (We have, in the prompt-book of *The Second Maiden's Tragedy*, extant specimens of this method of incorporating *addenda* into a theatrical manuscript.)

15   III.vi.18–59   *Edg.* The foule fiend . . .
                      [*Lear.*] . . . why hast thou let her scape.

The mock trial of Regan and Goneril: undoubtedly a theatrical cut, the first of several in this part of the play, designed, it would seem, to hasten its pace towards the climax. Not an entirely judicious omission here, since it leaves expressions of deep concern from Kent and Edgar (lines 61–4) not unmotivated, certainly, but somewhat disproportionate to the occasion – which has now become Lear's reply to the Fool's riddle (lines 16–17).

16   III.vi.104–22   *Kent.* Oppressed nature sleepes . . .
                      [*Edg.*] Lurke, lurke.

Reflective comment at the close of a scene: the motive is once again retrenchment.

236 17 III.vii.99–107   *Seruant.* Ile neuer care . . .
                               [*2 Ser.*] . . . now heauen helpe him.

See preceding note. An additional motive for this cut may have been the need to economise on minor speaking-roles: the passage creates two.

18 IV.i.61–6   [*Edg.*] Fiue fiends . . .
                        . . . blesse thee maister.

As at III.i.7–15, the reviser very probably felt that there was more in this speech than was dramatically justified.

19 IV.ii.31–50   [*Alb.*] I feare your disposition . . .
                        [*Alb.*] . . . monsters of the deepe.

20 IV.ii.53–9   [*Gon.*] that not know'st . . .
                        Alack why does he so?

21 IV.ii.62–8   *Alb.* Thou changed, and selfe-couerd thing . . .
                        Gon. Marry your manhood now - - -

Clearly a deliberate attempt to abbreviate the quarrel between Albany and Goneril.

22 IV.iii   (Omitted in entirety.)

23 IV.vi.201   [*Lear.*] I and laying Autums dust.
24 IV.vi.276a   [*Edg.*] and for you her owne for *Venter*
      [om. from Globe edition]

Both lines omitted very probably by the reviser on grounds of obscurity.

25 IV.vii.33–6   [*Cord.*] To stand against . . .
                       With this thin helme

On the same theme as III.i.7–15 (Lear in the storm), and doubtless omitted for the same reason.

26 IV.vii.79–80   [*Doct.*] and yet it is danger to make him euen ore
                       the time hee has lost

The reviser may have been, as modern editors are, puzzled by the reading *euen ore* (see Appendix A3, p. 199 above).

27   IV.vii.85–98   *Gent.* Holds it true sir . . .
                          [*Kent.*] . . . as this dayes battels fought.

The conclusion of the scene: a cut precisely analogous to those at the end of III.vi and III.vii.

28   V.i.11–13   *Bast.* That thought abuses you . . .
                          [*Reg.*] . . . as far as we call hirs.
29   V.i.18–19   *Gono.* I had rather . . .
                             . . . loosen him and mee.
30   V.i.23–8   [*Alb.*] where I could not be honest . . .
                          Bast. Sir you speake nobly.
31   V.i.33   *Bast.* I shall attend you presently at your tent.

Evidence of deliberate pruning as in II.ii and IV.ii. Edmund's speech at V.i.33, however, may have been inadvertently dropped by copyist or compositor.

32   V.iii.38–9   *Cap.* I cannot draw a cart . . .
                             . . . ile do't.

An amusing touch of characterisation which was perhaps thought superfluous or out of place.

33   V.iii.47   [*Bast.*] and appointed guard
                          (omitted also from Qa)

There are reasons for assuming that the reviser was working at this point from Qb copy (see Appendix C1, introductory note, p. 249 below), hence that this omission was not inherited from Qa, but constitutes a deliberate deletion. It is noticeable that, placed in its context, the phrase appears to produce a false relation between *guard* and the relative pronoun immediately following:

(Qb:) *Bast.* Sir I thought it fit,
              To send the old and miserable King to some retention,
                 and appointed guard,
              Whose age has charmes in it, whose title more . . .

The reviser may well have thought it advisable to remove the temptation to understand *appointed* not as the participial adjective it is evidently intended to be but as a second main verb, parallel to *thought* and sharing its subject *I*. Or indeed he may so have understood it, encouraged by the punctuation in Q, and therefore read *guard* as the (absurd) antecedent of *Whose*. The deletion of the phrase produces a metrical anomaly, but the reviser's procedures elsewhere do not always leave the metre intact. It might seem, perhaps, a little too markedly coincidental that he should delete the same phrase that Qa has accidentally omitted. But it may appear less so in the light of the fact that the words in question spill over the edge of a very long line in the Qb version of the

238 printed copy, and that they would positively have invited the pen of an editor who happened to be dissatisfied with them on other grounds.

34   V.iii.54–9   [*Bast.*] at this time . . .
                          Requires a fitter place.

There seems no particular reason for this omission: it is not strictly necessary for Edmund to advance his specious arguments for delay in 'the question of Cordelia and her father', yet the lines are no less necessary than others preserved in this scene.

35   V.iii.102   *Bast.* A Herald ho, a Herald.
36   V.iii.109   *Cap.* Sound trumpet?

Repetitions of Albany's orders, doubtless relayed by supernumeraries on the stage at the performance or performances attended by the Q reporter. His attributions of them to *Bast.* and *Cap.* are unconvincing, as is his ascription to *Bast.* of the second and third commands to the trumpeter (*Sound? Againe?*). These last are in F more plausibly given to the Herald. Line 109, if it belongs in the text, must also be spoken by the Herald, as Albany's command makes clear: 'Come hither, Herald: let the trumpet sound / And read out this.' Line 102 is clearly extra-metrical, and appears to be merely a record of stage business. If retained, it should be allotted to an attendant or attendants, certainly not to Edmund who would not, one feels, be moved to officiate as Albany's master of ceremonies.

37   V.iii.204–21   *Edg.* This would haue seemd . . .
                            [*Ed.*] Improper for a slaue.

Edgar's account of Kent's last meeting with Gloucester: an obviously dispensable 'messenger-speech', though its omission leaves unexplained Kent's premonition of approaching death at the end of the play.

(b) *Additions*

1   I.i.41–6   [*Lear.*] while we / Vnburthen'd . . .
                       May be preuented now.

This (a) completes a line left short in Q and (b) serves to call attention to Albany and Cornwall soon after their entrance. They do not speak at all in the course of the scene, and are not identified in Q until addressed by Lear a good deal later (I.i.129).

2   I.i.50–1   [*Lear.*] (Since now . . .
                          . . . Cares of State)

Repeats what Lear has previously said (lines 39–40), but in more precise terms. The reviser may have thought the earlier announcement too vague.

3 I.i.65–6   [*Lear.*] and with Champains rich'd
                   With plenteous Riuers

If this is an interpolation, there is no particular reason for it: the text of Q needs no repair at this point. It may, therefore, represent a genuine recovery of what stood in the manuscript copy for Q. Since the following phrase, too, begins with *and*, it is possible that the Q compositor jumped from one *and* to the other, omitting what lay between. Against this it might be argued that the reviser's additions and omissions at the beginning of the play tend to be more frequent and fussy than they are elsewhere, so that the apparent superfluousness of the two half-lines is not necessarily significant.

4 I.i.86–7   [*Lear.*] The Vines of France, and Milke of
                      Burgundie,
                   Striue to be interest.

The previous line, though entirely acceptable in Q, has been modified to suit this elaboration of the sentence: evidence that it is not a retrieval of the original text.

5 I.i.90–1   *Lear.* Nothing?
                   Cor. Nothing.

Another redundant interpolation; though it might be thought, and perhaps was thought, to emphasise a point of dramatic importance.

6 I.ii.118–24   [*Glou.*] This villaine of mine . . .
                      . . . disquietly to our Graues.

Despite appearances, it cannot safely be inferred that these lines represent a recovery (from the Q manuscript) of the original text. The following considerations apply. (a) The train of thought in Q is perfectly connected. There is a natural link between the last example given by Gloucester of the 'sequent effects' of heavenly portents (*the bond crackt betweene sonne and father*) and his command to Edmund (*find out this villaine*): it is clear that he has Edgar in mind. The additional lines in F merely make the connection more explicit: *This villaine of mine comes vnder the prediction*; *there's Son against Father.* (b) It is not quite plausible that the Q compositor, if the additional lines did indeed stand in his copy, should have skipped accidentally from a sentence beginning *This villaine* (line 118) to one beginning *find out this villaine* (line 124). The additional words, it is reasonable to suppose, would have jogged him into consciousness of error. It is, on the other hand, perfectly plausible that the reviser, if he wished to elaborate on *the bond crackt betweene sonne and father*, should begin to do so in terms suggested by the text before him (*find out this villaine*) – *This villaine of mine comes vnder the prediction.* (c) The interpolation appears to be associated with the omission, further down, of I.ii.157–65, lines which treat the same theme. It might seem perversity in the reviser to expand on one page the kind of material he proceeded to strike out on another – but only if he were working with more conscientiousness and forethought than (I believe) we should give him credit for. It is quite likely that, discovering, in a speech of

240 Edmund's, the re-opening of a vein he had just deliberately extended in a speech of Gloucester's, he cancelled original matter rather than undo his own work. (d) It is perhaps significant that the word *machination* (line 122) appears in the course of another addition (V.i.46) – and nowhere else in Shakespeare.

7 I.ii.149   *[Bast.]* Fa, Sol, La, Me

The reviser has seen a pun in the preceding word, *divisions*. In the context of Q it means, simply, 'dissensions', but he has taken the opportunity of making Edmund play facetiously on the musical significance of the term ('rapid melodic passages') by adding a snatch of solfa. Although this is suitably sardonic, it is hardly appropriate that Edmund burst into song here if Edgar is to say in the very next line: 'How now, brother Edmund, what serious contemplation are you in?'

8 I.ii.181–7   *[Edm.]* I pray you haue . . .
 Edg. Arm'd, Brother?

The passage introduces two circumstances not alluded to in Q: (a) Edmund invites Edgar to take refuge in his 'lodging', to which he gives him the key; (b) he promises to bring him 'to hear my Lord [Gloucester] speak' – a counterpart to his earlier promise to Gloucester: 'I will place you where you shall hear us confer of this'. Neither the invitation nor the promise is relevant to the plot, nor are they referred to again. They do, however, help to explain why Edgar, who at this point presumably goes into hiding, should later reappear so conveniently (II.i) at the very moment his brother requires him. If this were the motive for interpolating the lines, they must have been introduced as an afterthought, perhaps in the theatre. It is highly improbable that they were missed out accidentally by the Q compositor. Q has: Bast. *Thats my feare brother, I aduise you to the best, goe arm'd.* The additional matter appears between *feare* and *brother*, the latter word starting, in F, a new speech (Edm. *Brother, I aduise you to the best*), while the words *goe arm'd*, transposed to an earlier point, are supplied with an entirely different context.

9 I.iv.283   *Alb.* Pray Sir be patient.

This brief speech interrupts Lear's tirade, 'Ingratitude! thou marble-hearted fiend!' There were possibly two reasons for introducing it. It gives Albany something to say between his entrance at line 279 and line 295, the first opportunity allowed him in Q. And it justifies, *qua* interruption, an apparently pointless discontinuity in Lear's train of thought. As the speech stands in Q, Lear's ideas are indeed very confused: after a false start on the subject of repentance, he notices Albany's arrival, asks his permission to prepare horses, rages for a space on the theme of ingratitude and then abruptly reverts to Goneril's earlier complaints about his 'disordered rabble': 'Detested kite, thou liest!' (line 284). The reviser, having done his best to unravel the confusion of the earlier part of the speech, felt evidently that an interruption would best excuse this last and apparently most arbitrary change of direction. But see Appendix B1(c) (p. 231 above) for a clarification of the problems raised by this speech. That Albany's half-line is an interpolation is further demonstrated by the facts that the line of verse it interrupts needs no metrical adjustment and that its intrusion creates a half-line gap in line 283. Most editors, following the Globe edition, place the speech in fact at the end of line 283 – with awkward effect: *Than the sea-monster.* Alb. *Pray, sir, be patient.* The reviser, I am inclined to think, intended it for the first half of line 284: Alb. *Pray, sir, be patient.* Lear. *Detested kite, thou liest!*

10   I.iv.345–56   *Gon.* This man hath had good Counsell . . .
                             How now *Oswald?*

This addition, which is very likely to have been recovered by the reviser from the manuscript copy for Q, is fully discussed above, pp. 76ff.

11   II.iv.46–55   *Foole.* Winters not gon yet . . .
                             . . . as thou canst tell in a yeare.

These proverbial sallies (for the most part in doggerel) doubtless have their relevance to the dramatic situation, but have been very clumsily misplaced here between Kent's account of his mistreatment by Regan and Cornwall and Lear's vehement reaction to it ('Oh, how this mother swells up toward my heart!'). An obvious interpolation, though not in the style of the reviser. Its banality suggests theatrical origin, as does the fact that F prints the verse incorrectly, each pair of lines being strung out as one: if the passage appeared thus in the prompt-book copy, that was very probably because it had been added, written sideways, in the margin, i.e. as an after-thought.

12   II.iv.99–100   *Glo.* Well my good Lord, I haue inform'd them
                             so.
                             Lear. Inform'd them? Do'st thou vnderstand me
                             man.

Lear has just ordered Gloucester angrily to summon Regan and Cornwall. In Q Gloucester replies (line 101): *I my good Lord*, but without making any move to comply – clearly because he is persuaded that the errand would be hopeless (*cf.* lines 92–5), while at the same time, since the King is beside himself with rage, he is anxious to avoid an open refusal. The reviser must have thought this implausible or insufficiently clear and has Gloucester demurring explicitly ('Well, my good Lord, I have informed them so'), letting his 'Aye, my good Lord' remain as the simple answer to a question ('Dost thou understand me, man?'). That these lines did not belong to the original text is shown by their association with the next addition (see below): to suppose that both passages were omitted from Q would be virtually to assume a method and purpose in the omissions.

13   II.iv.104   *[Lear.]* Are they inform'd of this? My breath and
                             blood:

Related to the above. In Q Lear rages on, repeating his commands ('The King would speak with Cornwall . . .') to an embarrassed Gloucester, who makes for the present no move to obey them. As did the previous one, this interpolation evades the problem of Gloucester's inaction, or what the reviser evidently saw as a problem. Lear, having asked (see above) 'Dost thou understand me, man?', repeats his wishes – not as fresh commands, but by way of reminder – and adds 'Are they inform'd of this?'

242   14   II.iv.142–7   *Lear.* Say? How is that?
                            [Reg.] . . . from all blame.

Regan has been saying that Lear misappreciates Goneril, but in a form of words which seems to imply the opposite of what she intends: *You lesse know how to value her desert, / Then she to slacke her dutie.* Lear's request for clarification comes in with unintentionally comic effect, but it does enable the reviser to add a longer speech in which Regan makes her meaning perfectly plain. It is impossible to regard this clumsy proceeding as original. The wonder is that the reviser did not simply substitute the new speech for Regan's original one. One is tempted to infer from this, as from one or two other minor additions (see no. 27 below), that he did not object to exposing, while apparently covering up, the occasional absurdity in which he judged he had found his author out.

15   II.iv.299–300   *[Glo.* The King is in high rage.]
                        Corn. Whether is he going?
                        Glo. He cals to Horse, but [will I know not
                            whether.]

Q has simply: Glo. *The King is in high rage, & wil I know not whether*; but, the line being hypermetrical, the reviser has split it in two and, with the interpolated matter, makes two good pentameters. Since the plot involves frequent journeys on horseback, he probably felt it safe to introduce the detail of Lear's calling to horse (*cf.* for instance, 'Saddle my horses! Call my train together!' at I.iv.274). Subsequent events, however, make it obvious that on this occasion Lear departs on foot – rashly, since he is overtaken by the storm.

16   III.i.22–9   *[Kent.]* Who haue, as who haue not . . .
                            . . . these are but furnishings.

This addition is fully discussed above (pp. 70–75). It is quite likely to have been written on a separate slip and pasted into the prompt-book: the succeeding lines (which may have been covered by the slip) are missing in F (see 'Omissions' above, no. 14). This circumstance, together with the peculiar nature of the mistakes and misunderstandings the additional lines betray, strongly suggest that they were added to the text *after* it had been revised and the prompt-book prepared.

17   III.ii.79–96   *Foole.* This is a braue night . . .
                            . . . I liue before his time.

The style, the irrelevant subject-matter, the clumsy rupture of dramatic illusion (*This prophecie Merlin shall make, for I liue before his time*); the printing of lines 91–2 as one and their apparent misplacement (suggesting a misreading of marginal addenda) – all indicate a theatrical interpolation for which the reviser cannot be held responsible.

18   III.iv.17–18   [*Lear.*] . . . in such a night,   243
                             To shut me out? Poure on, I will endure:

Q's metre is defective, yet the passage should evidently be aligned as follows:

> . . . but I will punish sure,
> [No] I will weepe no more, in such a night as this!
> O *Regan, Gonorill,* your old kind father
> Whose frank heart gaue you all,
> O that way madness lies, Let me shun that,

(This is based on the assumption that *No* in the second line is actor's gag, and that the fourth line is – perhaps designedly – incomplete.) F substitutes:

> But I will punish home;
> No, I will weepe no more; in such a night,
> To shut me out? Poure on, I will endure:
> In such a night as this? O *Regan, Gonerill,*
> Your old kind Father, whose franke heart gaue all,
> O that way madnesse lies, let me shun that:

If this is a revision, it is easily seen that the accommodation of *No* at the beginning of the second line necessitated the loss of *as this* at the end of it, and that the (interpolated) third line was devised to piece out the sense as required until the whole phrase *In such a night as this?* could be repeated in the fourth. The repetition of the phrase compensates for the missing half-line in Q: a neat enough solution, except that it causes difficulties in the following line (the fifth). In spite of the fact that the perfectly satisfactory reading in Q has been modified (*gaue all* for *gaue you all*), the rhythm remains clumsy. It might, nevertheless, be tempting to regard the passage as a case not of revision in F but of accidental omission in Q: the compositor's eye might well have jumped from *in such a night* (F's second line) to *in such a night as this* (F's fourth line), leaving out what lay between. What lies between, however, is extremely suspicious. Was Lear 'shut out' from Gloucester's castle, in the sense that he returned to ask for shelter and was refused? Did he even know that he *would* be refused if he asked? III.ii ends (in Q) with Lear's words: 'Come bring us to this hovel', and III.iv opens with Kent's 'Here is the place [the hovel], my Lord', so that the two scenes are, to all intents and purposes, continuous. In III.ii Lear has deliberately ignored the Fool's entreaties that he should 'in, and ask his daughters' blessing' (III.ii.12). At III.ii.63–6 Kent tells Lear that he has asked after him at Gloucester's castle, but was refused entrance, and that he will now (having led Lear to the hovel) return there to 'force their scanted courtesy'. But he has not yet started upon his mission before Lear speaks (in F) of being 'shut out' (III.iv.18). In fact, Lear does not know that he has been 'shut out' until Gloucester appears, anticipating Kent's errand, to say: 'Go in with me. My duty cannot suffer / To obey in all your daughters' hard commands. / Though their injunction be to bar my doors / And let this tyrranous night take hold upon you, / Yet have I ventur'd to come seek you out / And bring you where both food and fire is ready.'

19   III.iv.26–7   *[Lear.]* In Boy, go first. You houselesse pouertie,
Nay, get thee in; Ile pray, and then Ile sleepe.

On being invited by Kent to enter the hovel, Lear demurs with the words: 'Prithee go in thyself. Seek thy own ease. / This tempest will not give me leave to ponder / On things would hurt me more'. He then adds, surprisingly: 'But I'll go in', without, however, making any move to do so. The Fool, however, must exit into the hovel at about this point, since his next speech begins: 'Come not in here, nuncle. Here's a spirit.' The additional lines in F solve this problem by having Lear change his mind again in taking thought for the Fool. (F, unlike Q, marks an exit for the Fool against line 26.) It is conceivable, therefore, that these lines are original and were carelessly omitted from Q. They are by no means, however, free from suspicion. There is no dramatic reason for Lear's wavering. He must be kept on stage, but his initial reply to Kent provides as much motivation as is needed for his remaining out of doors. His distraction of mind needs no emphasis at this point: rather the contrary since, as the remainder of his speech makes obvious, this is one of his moments of renewed apprehension and self-perception. One or two details are dubious, too. The unusual word 'houseless' is repeated within a very few lines (line 30). Though Lear is made to say *Ile pray, and then Ile sleepe* (which implies, however oddly, that he will remain outside to pray before going in to sleep), he utters no prayer, and shows no disposition to prayer beyond mentioning 'the Heavens' in the last line of the speech. It seems on balance likely that these lines were contrived by the reviser both to mark the Fool's exit and to resolve the problem posed by Lear's self-contradictions. Furthermore, it is possible, at least, that, if the phrase *but ile goe in* belongs rightly to the Fool, the reviser's attentions were quite unnecessary.

20   III.iv.37–8   *Edg.* Fathom, and halfe, Fathom and halfe; poore *Tom.*

Though this short speech (evidently to be spoken off-stage) precedes the Fool's sudden, and terrified re-emergence from the hovel, it is not necessary to an understanding of the situation, which is quite sufficiently explained by what follows. It *may*, therefore, be an interpolation, though it fits smoothly enough into the context.

21   III.vi.13–15   *Foole.* No, he's a Yeoman . . .
. . . a Gentleman before him.

One of the more intrusive interpolations; see above, p. 67.

22   III.vi.92   *Foole.* And Ile go to bed at noone.

A witticism which plays on the association between the words just uttered by Lear, 'We'll go to supper i'th'morning' (*sc.* and so, possibly, to bed at noon) and the current proverb, 'You would make me go to bed at noon'. Beyond the making of this neat connection, there seems to be no point to the joke. The proverb means: 'You are trying to deceive me', so that the Fool's modification of it must mean: 'I shall, or am willing to, be deceived'. But he has no motive at this juncture for saying any such thing. I suspect an interpolation, on the grounds that the reviser elsewhere interjects pointless or inappropriate quips (*cf.* no. 7 above). This may seem too summary a dismissal of a speech which, as the last given to the Fool (in the F text), has attracted considerable critical attention. It has been alleged to convey no fewer than seven meanings, one or two of which, at least, are accepted by most commentators. I do not think such interpretations (e.g. that which finds a prophecy here of the Fool's own death) are warranted by anything but a sense that the Fool must surely say something important before departing finally from the scene – together, perhaps, with an impression that the line is oddly cryptic and must surely conceal more significance than it reveals. It is only, in other words, an assumption of the pregnancy and importance of the speech, *a fortiori* its authenticity, which supports such interpretations. They cannot, therefore, be used in turn as arguments in favour of its authenticity.

23   IV.i.6–9   [*Edg.*]   Welcome then,
                          Thou vnsubstantiall ayre that I embrace:
                          The Wretch that thou hast blowne vnto the
                               worst,
                          Owes nothing to thy blasts.

This passage appears at first sight to offer better evidence of a deliberate cut in Q than of deliberate interpolation in F. The lines, though more histrionic in tone than those which have preceded, merely echo – somewhat indistinctly at that – the same meaning. There seems no motive for introducing them except to prolong Edgar's speech and to raise it from the level of introspective musing to that of brave declamation – unless the reversion to elemental imagery is significant. Did the reviser take it into his head that this out-of-doors scene, the first since III.iv, should open with some reference to the continuing storm? If so, he failed to notice that the storm is said later to have occurred 'last night' (IV.i.34).

24   IV.i.56   *Edg.* And yet I must:

Prima facie an intrusion, since it disturbs the regularity of the metre. It appears to have been called forth by the alteration, two lines earlier, of Q: *I cannot dance it farther* to *I cannot daub it* (= to put on a false show) *further*. Edgar cannot announce in this way that he means to stop pretending unless he immediately withdraws his remark, since it is quite clear that throughout the rest of the scene he maintains his pretence.

25   IV.ii.26   [*Gon.*] Oh, the difference of man, and man,

This serves to clarify the sense of the two succeeding lines: *To thee a Womans seruices are due,* / *My Foole vsurpes my body.* We should be puzzled by the abrupt reference to 'my fool' unless we realised that Goneril was comparing one man with another, Edmund with Albany. There are good reasons, however, for supposing that Qa's reading *My foote* is the correct one (see Appendix A7, p. 221 above). If it is, the additional line stands exposed as irrelevant.

246   26 IV.vi.169–74   *[Lear.]* Place sinnes with Gold . . .
                                    . . . to seale th'accusers lips.

See p. 68 above for a discussion of the inappropriateness of this passage to its context, and pp. 122ff. for remarks on its possible reference to contemporary events.

27 IV.vii.61   *[Lear.]* Not an houre more, nor lesse:

Metrically intrusive, though the line it interrupts (*Fourescore and vpward, and to deale plainly*) is not of the smoothest. More suspicious, however, is the inanity of the extra half-line (not an hour more nor less than fourscore and upward?). Lear, of course, as he presently says, is 'not in [his] perfect mind'. It is a question, however, of dramatic propriety. Lear's madness is not elsewhere portrayed as a matter of ridiculous logical solecisms, but (much more convincingly) in terms of extreme emotional excitement, moral disorientation and, eventually, perceptual confusion. So jarring, in fact, is this resort to the cheap device of representing madness as witlessness that one is almost inclined to suspect the reviser of subversive intentions. Less than enamoured of his task by this stage, he may have yielded to a mischievous impulse on discovering that Lear appears not to be sure of his own age (*cf.* the equally silly half-line addition at V.ii.11, which one might be tempted to explain on the same hypothesis as covertly cynical comment).

28 V.iii.76   *[Rega.]* Dispose of them, of me, the walls is thine:

Very possibly an accidental omission from Q. There seems, at least, no reason to suspect the deliberate interference of the reviser. The reading *walls* is in error for *wall*. 'To give a person the wall' means 'to allow a person the right or privilege of walking next the wall as the cleaner and safer side of a pavement, sidewalk, etc. Similarly, *to have, take the wall'*. The expressions were frequently used figuratively from the sixteenth century onwards. Regan in telling Edmund 'the wall is thine' cedes him the position of superiority which till now has been hers.

29 V.iii.89–90   *Gon.* An enterlude.
                        Alb. [Thou art armed *Gloster*,]
                        Let the Trmpet sound:

It is Edmund who later suggests *Call by thy trumpet* (line 99), a proposal which comes in somewhat pointlessly if Albany has already ordered the trumpet to sound. Albany's half-line seems likely to have been introduced to fill the metrical gap occasioned by Goneril's interruption (*An enterlude*) and the intrusion of the latter is probably explained by the fact that Albany's speech in Q changes direction very abruptly. In mid-line he turns from the subject of Edmund's matrimonial pretensions to decreeing his trial by combat: *My Lady is bespoke, thou art arm'd* Gloster. The reviser may have thought it proper to mark this break in Albany's train of ideas by breaking off his speech at the same point (i.e. after *bespoke*). It will be noticed, however, that the Q line is not only perfectly intelligible in its context, but also metrically acceptable, especially if *arm'd* is altered to *armed*, as it is in F.

30   V.iii.144   [*Bast.*] What safe, and nicely I might well delay,   247

An addition prompted by a misprint in the succeeding line. For discussion see above, pp. 68–9.

31   V.iii.282   *Lear.* This is a dull sight,

Possibly a recovery of the original. It helps neither sense nor metre (which in any case is problematical), but serves merely to emphasise what Lear has said three lines earlier: 'Mine eyes are not o'th'best, I'll tell you straight'.

32   V.iii.310–11   [*Lear.*] Do you see this? Looke on her? Looke her
                            lips,
                   Looke there, looke there.

It is difficult to see these lines as anything more than an attempt on the reviser's part to provide Lear's speech with a more dramatic ending. His final words in Q (*pray you vndo this button, thanke you sir*) certainly reach the limit of dramatic understatement (but are all the more effective for that, we may now think). The reviser, however, unable to supply anything original, reverts weakly to an idea that has already been exploited to moving effect (V.iii.265–7 and 271–2), *viz.* that Lear fancies Cordelia may still be alive. There is even reason to argue that, in doing this, he has misunderstood the drift of the scene. It appears from Q that Lear, as his vitality ebbs, loses his grasp of the reality outside him. He is just able to recognise Kent, but not to connect him with 'Caius'; he is indifferent to the sight of the dead Goneril and Regan; Albany comments: 'He knows not what he sees, and vain it is / That we present us to him'. Finally – a much-debated point, though the text of Q leaves little room for debate – Lear mistakes Cordelia for the Fool: *And my poore foole is hangd* (V.iii.305). The additional lines in F (which apply unequivocally to Cordelia) are, of course, inconsistent with this, an inconsistency which (if he noticed it) the reviser evidently did not consider important. But the problem so created has exercised editors and critics ever since.

Several additions of less than a line in length were evidently prompted by the reviser's design of repairing wherever possible the defective metre in Q. None of these supplementary words and phrases is necessary to grammar or sense. The more prominent occur at I.i.120; I.i.164; I.i.248; I.ii.18; I.iv.6; I.iv.296; II.i.99; II.iv.3; II.iv.122; III.i.53; IV.vi.207; V.i.46; V.ii.11; V.iii.155.

The addition at I.i.248 is certainly unwarranted, that at III.i.53 equally so in my opinion: in both cases it is fairly easy to see why the reviser considered the lines defective though they are not in fact in need of repair.

The addition at IV.vi.207 (*Sa, sa, sa, sa*) raises the awkward question of the interjections and nonsense-syllables in F which in general differ from those in Q, and which in one or two instances (notably III.iv.59–60, *O do, de, do de, dode,* and the half-line cited above) find no equivalents at all in the earlier text. The case of *Suum, mun, nonny* at III.iv.103 (see Appendix A6, p. 208 above) suggests

248   that the reviser was on one occasion at least readier than the Q compositor to respect the precise reading of the manuscript. Should we take this as evidence of the reviser's greater conscientiousness in such matters, assuming besides that he would not descend to inventing nonsense gratuitously? Or should we assume that, having noted the frequent irruptions of nonsense, chiefly in the part of Edgar, he would on the whole have chosen to enter into the spirit of the thing rather than observe the letter, altering and embroidering as he felt disposed? I do not, I confess, see how such speculations can lead to any clear determination of the issue. Luckily nothing of any great moment depends upon it.

APPENDIX C1
Qa/Qb/F VARIANTS

Note: It is of some practical importance to the editor to know when the F text was based on Qa, and when on Qb, copy. He will, of course, be interested in the readings of F only in so far as they represent an additional witness to the manuscript underlying Q, and that they may be irrespective of the state of the copy the reviser had before him. But an agreement with, or similarity to, a Qb variant when the copy was Qa (or *vice versa*) will be a more than usually reliable, if not infallible, index to the readings of the manuscript in a not unimportant handful of cases.

Conclusions of a reasonable degree of probability can be reached about most of the variant sheets. Greg (*Variants*, p. 145ff.) has dealt with the question, but his answers require some modification; as indeed does the method he devised for arriving at the answers, since he postulated not the manuscript copy for Q as the editor's additional resource but an independent, authoritative manuscript in the shape of an already existent prompt-book.

The method we must adopt, however, is not in essentials different, merely somewhat simpler. Any agreement between F and Qa or Qb in a correct reading is not significant of the state of the F copy, since a correct reading may have been discovered independently by the reviser in the manuscript. An agreement in error, where the other variant is correct, is obviously significant; so also, however, is an agreement with Qb in a sophistication of error in Qa, on the assumption that the reviser would not have found the sophistication in the manuscript and would be extremely unlikely to have arrived at the same reading independently. On such occasions, we must assume, he either failed to consult the manuscript or consulted it and found it wanting.

The intervention of Q2 on certain pages complicates the issue. The agreement of F with Qa or Qb on these pages is uninformative where F coincides as well with Q2, because in all such instances Q2 may itself be the source of the reading.

About sheet D Greg is certainly right that it appeared in the copy for F in its corrected state: F *at task for* at I.iv.366 obviously derives from the Qb sophistication *attaskt for*. Qa readings from sig. D4^v (*prize* at II.i.122; *best* at II.i.125) very possibly derive from Q2.

Sheet E, Greg suggests tentatively, stood in its uncorrected state, but the evidence he advances is not convincing: an F/Qa 'error' of punctuation (a full

250   stop instead of a mark of interrogation after *strike*, II.ii.45) which in fact comes
to F from Q2, and an F/Qa spelling (*woosted* for *worsted*, II.ii.17) which has very
weak, if any, significance, since *woosted* is not an unusual spelling, and since, in
any case, the spelling in Qa (*wosted*) is not identical with it. More significant, I
think, are the two or three Qb readings repeated in F which are either obviously
'bad' or unconvincing as true corrections of Qa, or both: *saw* (Qa: *say*, II.ii.167),
their (Qa: *and*, II.ii.177), *Turlygod* (Qa: *Tuelygod*, II.iii.20) and *tombe* (Qa: *fruit*,
II.iv.133). If the reviser's copy were Qa, we should have to suppose that he
found all these readings in the manuscript, which is unlikely, or that they
represent guesses on his part which happened to coincide with the conjectures of
the press-corrector, which is impossible. It is easier to believe that the reviser
found the readings in Qb copy. Two of them (*saw* and *tombe*) he possibly
overlooked, since they make perfectly good sense. The others he very probably
left standing because the manuscript could provide nothing better: *Turlygod* has
baffled conjecture to this day, while *their* occurs in textually very dubious
surroundings. One or more of these Qb readings may have been introduced into
F *via* Q2 but it is unlikely that they all were, and there is some independent
evidence that at least one of them (*tombe*) was not (see concluding paragraph of
this note).

  No variants of importance occur in sheet F.

  About sheet G no decision can be reached. Greg argues, justly, that Qa *the* for
Qb *this* at III.iv.12 must be an error. There is no significance, however, as he
was inclined to think, in the agreement here of F with Qa, since *the* was quite
possibly passed on to F from Q2, the copy at this point. The remaining variants
from this sheet are unhelpful: none shows F coinciding in error with either Qa or
Qb.

  Greg, on the other hand, must be correct about sheet H in stating that F
agreement with Qa *seemes* (Qb: *shewes*, IV.ii.60) and *Iustices* (Qb: *Iustisers*,
IV.ii.79) demonstrates its derivation here from the uncorrected state of the text.

  On sheet K occurs the well-known omission from Qa of the phrase *and
appointed guard* (V.iii.47), a phrase absent from F as well. Greg advances this
coincidence as proof not only of an uncorrected sheet K in the copy for F, but as
part of a more general proof of the derivation of F from Q1. It has since acquired
some celebrity as a model of the kind of evidence required to prove the
relationship of two editions. However, there is reason enough to think that the
phrase may have been deliberately deleted by the reviser in preparing the
prompt-book (see Appendix B2a, no. 33, p. 237 above). It was certainly
deliberately deleted in the Q2 copy used by the compositors. Another sheet K
reading in F makes it, in any case, extremely probable that the reviser was

working from the corrected state of this sheet. Both Qb and F omit Qa's phrase at IV.vi.230, *to saue thee* (substituting Qb: *to boot, to boot*, F: *To boot, and boot*). Yet the phrase in Qa cannot have been invented by the compositor. It is too apt to a context which his accompanying blunders make quite clear he has not understood (hence, would not be capable of sophisticating intentionally): *Hartie thankes, the bornet and beniz* (i.e. 'the bounty and benison') *of heauen to saue thee*. It is possible, of course, that the compositor accidentally omitted *to boot, to boot*, which may have formed an additional part of the sentence. Instructed to insert it, he may mistakenly have substituted it for the other phrase. But we should not in any case expect to find F and Qb agreeing to replace one phrase by the other, whatever the reason for the substitution, unless F were dependent on Qb. Added reason for assuming this dependence is to be found in a common reading (*alteration* for *abdication*, V.i.3) which is both 'easier' and less pointed than the original. These considerations make it very probable in my view that the phrase at V.iii.47 was intentionally removed by the reviser. (See Appendix B2, p. 237 above, for further comment on the motives for the omission.)

The list which follows excludes trivial variations in spelling and punctuation, as also all variants in Q which occur in passages omitted from the text of F.

To indicate, wherever relevant, that Q2 copy was used by the F compositor, an asterisk appears against the Q1 variant which would have appeared (unchanged, unless otherwise specified) in the Q2 text. Three variants on sig. E4ᵛ of Q1, marked with queries as well as asterisks, appear in a portion of the text supposedly set by compositor E, and therefore supposedly from Q2 copy. There is some reason to believe, however, that compositor B was responsible for it. His manuscript copy would very probably have derived here, like Q2, from the corrected state of Q1 (see above, p. 144, n. 6).

252	Q page		Qa	Qb	F
	D1	I.iv	196	learne	*learneto (Q2: learne to)	learne to
			211	*thou, thou	now thou	now thou
	D2ᵛ		322	the vntender	the vntented	Th'vntented
			323	peruse	pierce	Pierce
			363	*after	hasten	hasten
			364	*mildie	milkie	milky
			366	*alapt	attaskt for	at task for
	D4ᵛ	II.i	102	*these -- and wast of this his	the wast and spoyle of his	th'expence and wast of his
			122	*prise (Q2: prize)	poyse	prize
			125	*defences	diferences	differences
			125	*best	lest	best
			126	*hand	home	home
	E1	II.ii	1	deuen	*euen	dawning
			17	three snyted	*three shewted	three-suited
			17	wosted stocken	*worsted-stocken	woosted-stocking
	E2ᵛ		133	ausrent	*miscreant	ancient
			139	Stobing	*Stopping	Stocking
			141	set	*sit	sit
			167	say	*saw	saw
	E3		172	my rackles	*my wracke	miracles
			174	not	*most	most
			177	and	*their	their
			178	Late	*Take	Take
		II.iii	15	numb'd mortified	*numb'd and mortified	num'd and mortified
			16	Pies	*Pins	Pins
			17	frame	*from	from
			20	*Tuelygod*	*Turlygod*	*Turlygod*
	E4ᵛ	II.iv	102	fate	*father	Father
			103	with the	*with his	with his
			103	come and tends seruise	*commands her seruice	commands, tends, seruice
			105	The fierie	*Fierie (Q2: Fiery)	Fiery? The fiery
			133	deuose	?*diuorse (Q2: diuorce)	diuorce
			133	fruit	?*tombe (Q2: toombe)	Tombe
			139	deptoued	?*depriued	deprau'd

G1	III.iv	6	*crulentious	tempestious	contentious
		10	*raging	roring	roaring
		12	*the	this	the
		14	*beares	beates	beates
G2ᵛ		113	leadings	lendings	Lendings
		114	come on bee true	come on	Come, vnbutton heere
		120	*Sriberdegibit*	*fliberdegibek*	Flibbertigibbet
		122	gins	giues	giues
		122	the pin-queues the eye	& the pin, squemes the eye	and the Pin, squints the eye
		123	harte lip	hare lip	Hare-lippe
		126	a nellthu night more	he met the night mare	He met the Night-Mare
		129	with	witch	Witch
		135	tode pold	tod pole	Tod-pole
		135	wall-wort	wall-newt	wall-Neut
G4ᵛ	III.vi	102	Take vp to keepe	Take vp the King	Take vp, take vp
H1ᵛ	III.vii	58	aurynted	annoynted	Annointed
		59	of his lou'd	on his lowd	as his bare
		60	layd	bod	buoy'd
		61	steeled	stelled	Stelled
H2	IV.i	10	poorlie, leed,	parti, eyd,	poorely led?
H3ᵛ	IV.ii	12	curre	terrer	terror
		21	coward	command	command
		27	womans	a womans	a Womans
		28	My foote	A foole	My Foole
		28	body	bed	body
		29	whistle	whistling	whistle
H4		60	seemes	shewes	seemes
		79	your Iustices	you Iustisers	You Iustices
K1	IV.vi	229	bornet and beniz	bounty and the benizon	bountie, and the benizon
		230	to saue thee	to boot, to boot	To boot, and boot
		231	was framed	was first framed	was first fram'd
		245	fortnight	vortnight	vortnight
		247	battero	bat	Ballow
		256	*British*	*Brittish*	English
K3	V.i	3	abdication	*alteration	alteration
K4ᵛ	V.iii	28	And	*One	One
		46	saue	*send	send
		47	(*om.*)	*and appointed guard	(*om.*)
		49	coren	*common	common

APPENDIX C2
UNMETRICAL LINES IN F THE RESULT OF INTERPOLATION OR OMISSION

I.i.46   Q: *{Lear.}* The two great Princes *France* and *Burgundy*,
               F: *{Lear.}* May be preuented now. The Princes, *France &* *Burgundy*,

(The first half of the line in F forms the concluding phrase of an addition; the second, as is sufficiently obvious, abbreviates the corresponding line in Q.)

I.i.246–8   Q: *{Burg.}*   . . . and here I take *Cordelia*
                    By the hand, / Dutches of *Burgundie*,
                    Leir. Nothing, I haue sworne.

              F: *{Bur.}* And here I take *Cordelia* by the hand,
                    Dutchesse of *Burgundie*.
                    Lear. Nothing, I haue sworne, I am firme.

I.iv.283–4 Q: *{Lear.}* . . . then the Sea-monster, detested kite, thou list

              F: *{Lear.}* Then the Sea-monster.
                    Alb. Pray Sir be patient.
                    Lear. Detested Kite, thou lyest.

I.iv.334–7 Q: *Duke.* I cannot bee so partiall *Gonorill* / to
                    the great loue I beare you.
                    Glou. Come sir no more, / you, more knaue then foole, after you master?

              F: *Alb.* I cannot be so partiall *Gonerill*,
                    To the great loue I beare you.
                    Gon. Pray you content. What *Oswald*, hoa?
                    You Sir, more Knaue then Foole, after your Master.

II.i.80   Q: *{Glost.}* . . . would he denie his letter, I neuer got him,

              F: *{Glo.}* Would he deny his Letter, said he?

II.i.118–19   Q: [*Duke.*]   . . . you, we first seaze on.
                    Bast. I shall serue you truly, / how euer else.
                    Glost. For him I thanke your grace.

               F: [*Cor.*] You we first seize on.
                    Bast. I shall serue you Sir truely, how euer else.
                    Glo. For him I thanke your Grace.

II.iv.59–60   Q: *Kent.* With the Earle sir within.
                    Lear. Follow me not, stay there?

               F: *Kent.* Wirh the Earle Sir, here within.
                    Lear. Follow me not, stay here.

II.iv.90–1   Q: [*Lear.*] They traueled hard to night, meare Iustice,
                    I/the images of reuolt and flying off,

               F: [*Lear.*] They have trauail'd all the night? meere fetches,
                    The images of reuolt and flying off.

II.iv.170–1   Q: [*Lear. – om.*] To fall and blast her pride.
                    Reg. O the blest Gods,

               F: [*Le.*] To fall, and blister.
                    Reg, O the blest Gods!

(The omission in F of *pride* from Lear's speech was doubtless accidental.)

IV.i.54–6   Q: *Edg.* Poore *Toms* a cold, I cannot dance it farther.
                    Glost. Come hither fellow.
                    Edg. Blesse thy sweete eyes, they bleed.

               F: *Edg.* Poore Tom's a cold. I cannot daub it further.
                    Glou. Come hither fellow.
                    Edg. And yet I must:
                    Blesse thy sweete eyes, they bleede.

IV.vii.70   Q: [*Lear.*] To be my child *Cordelia. Cord.* And so I am.

               F: [*Lear.*] To be my childe *Cordelia.*
                    Cor. And so I am: I am.

256 V.iii.129   Q: [*Edg.*] Behold it is the pruiledge of my tongue,

              F: [*Edg.*] Behold it is my priuiledge,
                    The priuiledge of mine Honours,

APPENDIX D1
Q2/Q1 PUNCTUATION VARIANTS

Note: In the left-hand column are listed those Q2 marks of punctuation which were added to, or substituted for, the marks in Q1.

Intra-verbal signs (hyphens, apostrophes) are excluded, as are all marks of interrogation and periods at the close of a *speech*. Agreement in F with the two later categories of point is so nearly constant as to be non-significant. A few cases of F disagreement with question marks in Q2 are noted separately in Appendix D2, p. 268 below.

No note is taken of the punctuation in those parts of the Q text omitted from F. Sentences or parts of sentences in Q which have been so revised in F as to change their syntactical structure have also been discounted. Where, however, F merely substitutes for the reading of Q a word or phrase of equivalent syntactical function, it has been assumed that agreement or disagreement in punctuation remains significant, and the evidence is recorded accordingly.

Where a mark of punctuation in Q2 has been transferred to a position in the sentence different from the one it occupies in Q1, the transference has been recorded as a process of deletion *and* addition. This seemed the safest policy in view of the many ambiguous and complex cases (e.g. transpositions which involve conversion as well, from comma, for example, into semi-colon).

It goes without saying that F additions to the Q text are irrelevant here. But it may be worth noting that their presence in the F text accounts for the paucity of comparative data available for certain pages in F (e.g. sig. qq5b).

The right-hand column below shows the number of times that F agrees with the revisions of Q2. Beside the total of agreements for each page is given a roughly calculated percentage figure, indicating the proportion of agreements to the total number of Q2 changes. It will be seen that the percentages on compositor B's pages before quire ss are, on the average, much lower than those on compositor E's pages and on all pages of quire ss.

Two anomalies occur, which are discussed in footnotes. These apart, it is clear that the evidence divides the pages of F into (a) those which show appreciably more than a 70% level of agreement with the Q2 punctuation variants and (b) those which show appreciably less; furthermore, that these categories correspond (except on quire ss, of which all the pages fall into category (a)) with the type-setting stints of compositors E and B respectively.

258 The data have been classified according to columns in F, so as to illustrate as clearly as possible the use, or non-use, in F of Q2 copy. The change of style in Q2 punctuation referred to on p. 135 above occurs, as the data show, at a point in the text (IV.v.17, which marks the top of sig. I1 in Q2) corresponding roughly with the division between F columns rr5^{v}a and rr5^{v}b.

Oversights are bound to have occurred here and there in a work of minute and tedious collation. But every care was taken to avoid them, and the reader may rely, I believe, on the substantial accuracy of the results given below.

		Q2	F
qq2a (B)	δ,	2	1
	,	4	4
	.	1	1
		—	—
		7	6
qq2b (B)	δ,	1	1
	,	4	4
	;	2	—
	:	1	—
	.	2	1
		—	—
		10	6
qq2^{v}a (E)	,	9	9
	;	1	1
	:	1	1
		—	—
		11	11
qq2^{v}b (E)	δ,	2	2
	,	13	13
	;	4	3
	—	1	—
		—	—
		20	18

qq2 12:17 = 71%[1]

qq2^v 29:31 = 94%

---

[1] An unusually high proportion of agreements for compositor B, though not so high as to offer a convincing indication of Q2 copy.

There is clear evidence (see Appendix D4, p. 277 below) that qq2b, at least, was *not* set from Q2 copy.

qq3a (E)	δ,	2	2	
	,	6	6	
	:	1	1	
	.	3	3	
		—	—	
		12	12	

qq3b (E)	,	3	3	
	;	1	—	
	:	2	1	
	.	4	4	
		—	—	
		10	8	qq3 20:22 = 91%

qq3^{v}a (B)	δ,	1	1	
	,	8	5	
	;	2	—	
	:	1	1	
	.	1	1	
		—	—	
		13	8	

qq3^{v}b (B)	δ,	2	—	
	,	2	—	
	;	5	—	
		—	—	
		9	0	qq3^v 8:22 = 36%

qq4a (E)	δ,	2	2	
	,	3	2	
	;	4	2	
	.	1	1	
		—	—	
		10	7	

qq4b (E)	δ,	2	2	
	,	1	1	
	;	2	1	
	:	1	1	
	—	1	1	
		—	—	
		7	6	qq4 13:17 = 77%

260	qq4^{v}a (E)	δ,	1	1
		,	3	3
		;	3	2
			—	—
			7	6
	qq4^{v}b (E)	δ,	3	3
		,	1	—
		;	2	2
		:	1	1
			—	—
			7	6	qq4^v 12:14 = 86%
	qq5a (B)	δ,	2	2
		,	2	1
		;	5	1
		:	1	1
			—	—
			10	5
	qq5b (B)	,	2	1
		;	1	—
			—	—
			3	1	qq5 6:13 = 46%
	qq5^{v}a (E)	δ,	1	1
		,	3	3
		;	4	2
		—	1	1
		!	1	—
			—	—
			10	7
	qq5^{v}b(E)	δ,	3	2
		,	2	2
		;	1	1
			—	—
			6	5	qq5^v 12:16 = 75%
	qq6a (E)	δ,	6	6
		,	2	2
		;	6	6
		:	1	1
		()	1	1
			—	—
			16	16

qq6b (E)	δ,	3	2	
	,	1	—	
	;	1	—	
		—	—	
		5	2	qq6 18:21 = 86%

qq6^{v}a (E)	δ,	1	1	
	,	3	3	
	;	1	—	
	.	2	2	
		—	—	
		7	6	

qq6^{v}b (E)	δ,	1	1	
	,	5	5	
	;	2	2	
	.	2	2	
		—	—	
		10	10	qq6^v 16:17 = 94%

rr1a (E)	δ,	1	—	
	,	2	2	
	;	2	1	
		—	—	
		5	3	

rr1b (E)	δ,	1	1	
	,	3	3	
	;	4	4	
	.	1	1	
		—	—	
		9	9	rr1 12:14 = 86%

rr1^{v}a (E)	δ,	1	1	
	,	6	5	
	;	5	3	
	.	1	—	
	!	1	1	
		—	—	
		14	10	rr1^{v}a 10:14 = 71%[2]

2   These proportions are neither high enough nor low enough to count as conclusive. If I am correct in thinking that B set not only rr1^{v}b

262

rr1^{v}b (B)	δ,	4	3	
	,	4	3	
	;	1	—	
	.	1	1	
		10	7	rr1^{v}b 7:10 = 70%^{2}
rr2a (E)	δ,	2	2	
	,	4	4	
	;	3	2	
	:	1	—	
	( )	1	1	
		11	9	
rr2b (E)	δ,	3	3	
	,	7	5	
	;	5	2	
	—	1	1	
		16	11	rr2 20:27 = 74%
rr2^{v}a (B)	δ,	1	1	
	,	9	6	
	;	1	—	
	.	1	—	
		12	7	
rr2^{v}b (B)	δ,	2	1	
	,	4	4	
	;	1	—	
	.	1	1	
		8	6	rr2^v 13:20 = 65%

but a part of column a as well (from II.iv.129 onward – see above, p. 144, n. 6), the figures are distorted. In E's portion of column a F agrees seven times with the Q2 variants out of a total of nine, a proportion of 78%. For the rest of the page, set by B, the ratio is 10:15, 66%.

rr3a	(E)	δ,	1	1
		,	10	7
		;	5	5
			—	—
			16	13

rr3b	(E)	δ,	2	2	
		,	1	1	
			—	—	
			3	3	rr3 16:19 = 84%

rr3^{v}a	(B)	δ,	2	1
		,	3	3
		;	2	—
		.	1	—
			—	—
			8	4

rr3^{v}b	(B)	,	7	3	
		;	3	—	
		.	2	1	
			—	—	
			12	4	rr3^v 8:20 = 40%

rr4a	(B)	δ,	1	1
		,	6	2
		;	2	—
		.	2	—
			—	—
			11	3

rr4b	(B)	,	13	9	
		;	3	—	
		:	1	—	
		.	2	2	
			—	—	
			19	11	rr4 14:30 = 47%

rr4^{v}a	(B)	δ,	1	1
		,	8	2
		—	1	—
			—	—
			10	3

264   rr4^{v}b   (B) δ,

rr4^{v}b (B) δ,	2	1
,	6	4
;	2	—
	—	—
	10	5

rr4^v 8:20 = 40%

rr5a (B) δ.	1	1
,	11	6
;	4	—
:	2	—
.	1	1
	—	—
	19	8

rr5b (B) δ,	1	1
,	11	8
;	1	—
	—	—
	13	9

rr5   17:32 = 53%

rr5^{v}a (B) δ,	5	5
,	13	6
:	1	1
	—	—
	19	12

rr5^{v}b (B) δ,	1	—
,	6	2
;	3	—
:	8	4
.	3	3
	—	—
	21	9

rr5^v 21:40 = 52%

rr6a (B) δ,	2	1
,	15	11
;	3	—
:	10	2
.	6	4
	—	—
	36	18

rr6b	(B)	δ,	5	—		
		,	6	5		
		;	4	—		
		:	9	3		
		.	7	5		
			—	—		
			31	13	rr6	31:67 = 46%
rr6ᵛa	(B)	δ,	2	2		
		,	16	9		
		;	2	—		
		:	5	2		
		.	5	5		
			—	—		
			30	18		
rr6ᵛb	(B)	δ,	7	4		
		,	4	—		
		;	1	—		
		:	6	2		
		.	6	5		
			—	—		
			24	11	rr6ᵛ	29:54 = 54%
ss1a	(B)	δ,	4	3		
		,	12	10		
		:	3	2		
		.	3	3		
		()	1	1		
			—	—		
			23	19		
ss1b	(B)	δ,	1	1		
		,	3	3		
		;	1	1		
		:	7	7		
		.	3	3		
		!	1	—		
		()	2	2		
			—	—		
			18	17	ss1	36:41 = 88%

266 ss1^{v}a (E)

ss1^{v}a (E)	,	6	5
	;	1	—
	:	3	2
	.	3	3
		—	—
		13	10

ss1^{v}b (E)	,	10	10
	;	2	2
	:	7	6
	.	3	2
		—	—
		22	20

ss1^{v} 30:35 = 86%

ss2a (E)	δ,	3	3
	,	6	6
	;	2	2
	:	7	7
	.	3	3
		—	—
		21	21

ss2b (E)	δ,	1	—
	,	6	6
	:	4	4
	.	4	4
		—	—
		15	14

ss2 35:36 = 97%

ss2^{v}a (E)	δ,	5	4
	δ.	1	1
	,	13	11
	;	1	—
	:	5	4
	.	4	3
	( )	1	1
		—	—
		30	24

ss2^{v}b (E)	δ,	3	2	
	,	4	4	
	;	1	1	
	:	9	7	
	.	7	3	
		—	—	
		24	17	ss2^v 41:54 = 76%
ss3a (B)	δ,	1	1	
	,	2	2	
	:	3	3	
	.	4	4	
		—	—	
		10	10	
ss3b (B)	δ,	2	2	
	,	3	3	
	;	1	—	
	:	6	5	
		—	—	
		12	10	ss3 20:22 = 91%

APPENDIX D2
Q1/F AND Q2/F ANOMALIES IN PUNCTUATION

Note: Since there was quite evidently no consensus of opinion in the early seventeenth century about the principles of punctuation, it would be impossible to establish what constitutes, in the strict sense, an *error* of punctuation in a seventeenth-century text, apart from those rare occasions on which one finds, for example, a period or question mark placed in what is manifestly, and on any principles, an impermissible position. We are, however, examining a situation in which the compositors of one text (F) set out deliberately to elaborate upon and to improve the punctuation of another (Q2, or the manuscript derived from Q1, as one or another served for 'copy'). In the circumstances, it is not unreasonable to assume, when F agrees with Q1 in a punctuation clearly inferior to that which appears in Q2 (inferior by the standards elsewhere generally maintained in F), that at this point the possibility of Q2 copy is probably excluded; but that the agreement of F with Q2 in an anomaly (against a superior reading in Q1) is, on the contrary, a good index of Q2 copy. The evidence given below is, therefore, less a list of common errors than a list of common (or, in some instances, closely similar) readings which by comparison, in each case, with a third text reveal themselves as anomalous.

(a) *Q1 and F*

I.ii.124–5   Q1:   find out this villaine *Edmund*,
                F: Find out this Villain *Edmond*,

                [Q2: finde out this villaine, *Edmund*]

Edmund is not the villain: the words are addressed to him.

I.ii.178–9   Q1:   that with the mischiefe, of your parson it would scarce allay.
                F: that with the mischiefe of your person, it would scarsely alay.

                [Q2: that with the mischiefe of your person it would scarse allay.]

F has transferred Q1's comma – unnecessarily.

I.iv.357   QI   and F: What haue you writ

             {Q2: What, haue you writ}

What is an expletive, not the object of *have . . . writ*, as the rest of the sentence makes quite clear.

II.iv.131–2   QI: *Regan* I thinke you are, I know what reason
                     I haue to thinke so, if thou shouldst not be glad,
            F: *Regan*, I thinke your are. I know what reason
                     I haue to thinke so, if thou should'st not be glad,

             {Q2: *Regan*, I thinke you are, I know what reason
                     I haue to thinke so; if thou shouldst not be glad,}

F ignores the heavier stop in Q2 after *thinke so*, and thus obscures the fact that *if* begins a new sentence.

II.iv.136–9   QI: . . . she hath tyed,
                   Sharpe tooth'd vnkindnes, like a vulture heare,
                   I can scarce speake to thee, thout not beleeue,
                   Of how depriued a qualitie, O *Regan*.
            F: . . . she hath tied
                   Sharpe-tooth'd vnkindnesse, like a vulture heere,
                   I can scarce speake to thee, thou'lt not beleeue
                   With how deprau'd a quality. Oh *Regan*.

             {Q2:   . . . she hath tied
                   Sharpe tooth'd vnkindnesse, like a vulture heere.
                   I can scarse speake to thee, thou't not beleeue,
                   Of how depriued a quality, O *Regan*.}

Q2 is correct in starting a new sentence with *I can*, though a dash should appear after *speake to thee*, and again after *quality*, to show that Lear, his emotion overcoming him, leaves his sentences incomplete. The inadequate punctuation in QI has misled the reviser into an emendation in line 139 (*With* for *Of*) which produces a single, loosely articulated sentence (the phrase *With . . . quality* referring back to *she hath tied*). In the circumstances it is, perhaps, less significant than it might otherwise be that the F compositor has followed QI in a comma after *heere*, though it is still on balance likelier that he would have introduced a full stop had he found one in his copy.

II.iv.152–3   QI: Therfore I pray that to our sister, you do make
                   returne,
            F: . . . therefore I pray you,
                   That to our Sister, you do make returne,

270
[Q2: Therefore I pray, that to our sister you do make
  returne,]

The comma after *Sister*, though not erroneous according to the practice of the time, was nevertheless regarded as unnecessary by the Q2 compositor. *Cf.* the similar case above at I.ii.178.

II.iv.259   Q1 and F: wel fauor'd

               [Q2: well-fauour'd]

III.ii.47–8   Q1:   . . . such grones of
                          Roaring winde, and rayne, I ne're remember
               F: Such groanes of roaring Winde, and Raine, I neuer
                    Remember

               [Q2:   . . . such grones of
                          Roring winde and raine, I nere remember]

Another intrusive comma in Q1 and F after *winde*.

III.iv.112   Q1 and F: vnaccomodated man, is no more but such

               [Q2: vnaccomodated man is no more but such]

III.vi.68–9   Q1:   . . . auant you curs,
                          Be thy mouth, or blacke, or white,
               F: . . . Auaunt you
                          Curres, be thy mouth or blacke or white:

               [Q2:   . . . auant you curs.
                          Be thy mouth, or blacke or white,]

A full stop is absolutely necessary after *curs*, since it brings to an end a passage of prose. The next line is the first of a stanza of rhymed verse.

III.vi.74–5   Q1: *Tom* will make them weepe & waile,
                          For with throwing thus my head,
               F: Tom will make him weepe and waile,
                          For with throwing thus my head;

               [Q2: *Tom* will make them weepe and waile. For with
                    throwing thus my head,]

For begins a new sentence.

IV.i.51–2   QI: Ile bring him the best parrell that I haue
                  Come on't what will.
             F: Ile bring him the best Parrell that I haue
                  Come on't, what will.

           [Q2: Ile bring him the best parrell that I haue,
                 Come on't what will.]

IV.iv.8–9   QI: . . . what can mans wisdome
                 In the restoring his bereued sence,
             F: . . . What can mans wisedome
                 In the restoring his bereaued Sense;

           [Q2:   . . . what can mans wisedome do
                 In the restoring his bereaued sence?]

The addition of *do* in Q2 may be unwarranted, but there is no doubt that a question mark is required after *sence*.

IV.vi.52–4   QI: . . . [thou] speakest, art sound,
                 Ten masts at each, make not the altitude,
                 Which thou hast perpendicularly fell,
             F: . . . [thou] speak'st, art sound,
                 Ten Masts at each, make not the altitude
                 Which thou hast perpendicularly fell,

           [Q2:   . . . [thou] speakst, art sound:
                 Ten Masts at each make not the altitude,
                 Which thou hast perpendicularly fell,]

A heavy stop as in Q2 is preferable after *sound* to mark the division of sentences. Q2 removes as well the superfluous comma after *each*.

IV.vi.66–8   QI: This is aboue all strangenes
                 Vpon the crowne of the cliffe what thing was that
                 Which parted from you.
             F: This is aboue all strangenesse,
                 Vpon the crowne o'th'Cliffe. What thing was that
                 Which parted from you?

           [Q2: This is aboue all strangenesse:
                 Vpon the crowne of the cliffe, what thing was that
                 Which parted from you?]

The bizarre error in F could not have been suggested by Q2.

272 IV.vi.161   Q1: And the creature runne from the cur,
                 F: And the Creature run from the Cur:

                [Q2: And the creature run from the cur?]

It is obvious from the context that this is a sequel to the preceding question: *Hast thou seen a farmer's dog bark at a beggar?*

IV.vi.213   Q1: Do you heare ought of a battell toward.
             F: Do you heare ought (Sir) of a Battell toward.

             [Q2: Do you heare ought of a battell toward?]

IV.vi.264–5 Q1b:leaue gentle waxe, and manners blame vs not
                    To know our enemies minds, wee'd rip their hearts,
             F: Leaue gentle waxe, and manners: blame vs not
                    To know our enemies mindes, we rip their hearts,

             [Q2: leaue gentle wax, and manners blame vs not,
                To know our enemies minds wee'd rip their hearts,]

Q2 divides correctly, though a colon rather than a comma should appear after *not*. F mispunctuates badly, and produces an odd distortion of the sense. The absence of a point after *not* suggests derivation from Q1, and the comma after *minds* indicates, more particularly, Qb – the comma does not appear in Qa. This serves to confirm that sheet K in the reviser's copy was in its corrected state: we are here on sig. K1 of Q1.

V.iii.264   Q1 and F: Or image of that horror.

             [Q2: Or image of that horror?]

(Follows upon the question in the preceding speech: *Is this the promis'd end?*).

(b) *Q2 and F*
I.v.22   Q2: Why to keep
             F: Why to keepe

             [Q1: Why, to keep]

II.i.38   Q2 and F: no helpe?

             [Q1: no, helpe?]

See Appendix A5, p. 204 above, where it is argued that *no* is a mistake for *ho*, probably produced by foul case. If so, Q1's punctuation is not incorrect, the point of interrogation after *helpe* standing, as very frequently elsewhere in the Q1 text, for a mark of exclamation. This does not make it quite certain, however, that *no helpe?* in F derives from Q2 copy: the F reviser and Q2 editor may well have arrived independently at the same sophistication of Q1.

II.i.60–1   Q2: the Noble Duke my master, my worthy Arch and
                    Patron comes to night,
           F: . . . the Noble Duke my Master,
                  My worthy Arch and Patron comes to night,

           [Q1: the noble Duke my maister, my worthy Arch and
                  Patron, comes to night,]

V.iii.121–3   Q2: O know my name is lost by Treasons tooth:
                  Bare-gnawne and canker-bit,
                  Where is the aduersary
           F: Know my name is lost
                  By Treasons tooth: bare-gnawne, and Canker-bit,
                  Yet am I Noble as the Aduersary

           [Q1: O know my name is lost by treasons tooth.
                Bare-gnawne and canker-bitte; yet are I mou't
                Where is the aduersarie]

All three texts are wrong in omitting a comma after *lost*, and in placing a heavy stop after *tooth* where none is required at all. But only Q1 is correct in marking the beginning of a new sentence with *yet*.

V.iii.176–7   Q2:   . . . I must embrace thee,
                Let sorow split my heart if I did euer
           F: . . . I must embrace thee,
                Let sorow split my heart, if euer I

           [Q1:   . . . I must embrace thee.
                Let sorow split my heart if I did euer]

APPENDIX D3

THE EVIDENCE OF DASHES AND BRACKETS IN Q1, Q2 AND F

(a) *Dashes*

Where a dash appears in both Q1 and Q2 no inference can be drawn from its reappearance in F. It is curious, however, that this occurs only twice: at IV.v.22 and V.iii.224 (assuming that the single hyphen at the end of this line in Q1 is doing duty, because of the lack of space, for the three that normally represent a dash). Elsewhere the Q1/Q2 dash is either ignored in F:

II.i.44   Q1 and Q2: when by no meanes he could - - - {——}
                 F: when by no meanes he could.

III.iv.149   Q1: *modo* he's caled and ma hu - - -
                 Q2: *modo* hee's called, and ma hu ——
                 F: *Modo* he's call'd, and *Mahu.*

III.vii.34   Q1 and Q2: villaine thou shalt find - - - {——}
                 F: Villaine, thou shalt finde.

III.vii.52   Q1 and Q2: wast thou not charg'd at perill - - - {——}
                 F: Was't thou not charg'd at perill.

III.vii.72   Q1 and Q2: If you see vengeance - - - {——}
                 F: If you see vengeance.

or it is made redundant by the completion of the sentence:

II.i.29   Q1 and Q2: aduise your - - - {——}
                 F: Aduise your selfe.

II.iv.172   Q1 and Q2: When the rash mood - - - {——}
                 F: when the rash moode is on.

IV.i.14–15   Q1: this forescore - - -
                 Q2: this fourescore ——
                 F: these fourescore yeares.

The last four of the first group of readings were set by compositor B and may simply illustrate a perverse quirk of his, or even perhaps a temporary dearth of dashes in his case. The first comes from a line of print too long to accommodate a dash, and awkwardly placed at the foot of a page, so that adjustment would have been tiresome.

The second group of readings, however, seems to indicate the reviser's dislike of broken speeches. Compare his sophistications in equivalent circumstances (the interruptions on these occasions not marked by dashes in the Q texts) at I.iv.279 (Appendices A7 and B1, pp. 215 and 231 above), I.iv.321 (Appendix A7, p. 216 above) and II.iv.138–9 (Appendix D2, p. 269 above).

No instance occurs of a dash in Q1 not repeated in Q2. Dashes introduced for the first time in Q2 are significant of Q2 copy when repeated in F (at I.iv.49 and II.iv.283). The two instances, however, of their omission from F are both anomalous. The first (at I.i.162) has already received comment (see above, p. 152, n. 18). The second (at III.vii.69) offers another specimen of the reviser's dealings with incomplete speeches: the reading was, we may be fairly certain on other grounds, taken into F from manuscript copy, but it might in theory, so different is the sense obtained, have been transferred into Q2 as a 'correction'. Gloucester is speaking, at the moment of his blinding:

III.vii.69–70   Q1:   He that will thinke to liue till he be old
                      Giue me some helpe, O cruell, O ye Gods!

                F: He that will thinke to liue, till he be old,
                      Giue me some helpe. — O cruell! O you Gods.

                Q2:   He that will thinke to liue till he be old —
                      Giue me some helpe, ô cruell, ô ye Gods!   ·

Modern editors, unaccountably, follow F. If the reading of F is correct, it is a grim reflection on Gloucester's foolishness that the one man who springs to his aid is killed instantly.

(b) *Brackets*

All of the brackets in Q1 are repeated in Q2. Brackets introduced for the first time in Q2 are, in turn, repeated in F. The transmission to F of the latter, since they occur relatively infrequently, and since their provision is never absolutely required by the context, must be indicative of Q2 copy. Brackets appear in Q2 and F, but not in Q1, at the following points: II.i.86, II.iv.250, IV.vii.38, IV.vii.69, IV.vii.74, V.iii.184–6.

APPENDIX D4

THE DIVISION OF F 'COPY'

(A summary of the evidence showing the dependence of F on two types of 'copy':
(a) based on Q2; (b) traceable to Q1 only.)

F pages are listed in the extreme left-hand column, and against the number of
each page is noted the compositor responsible for setting it. The figure which
follows shows, as a percentage, the proportion of the punctuation marks
peculiar to Q2 which reappear in F (i.e. in the section of text corresponding to
that page).

The columns on the right cite or refer to various categories of supplementary
evidence. They comprise:

(a) *Evidence of Q2 origin*

Q2   Readings peculiar to Q2 appearing in F (see above, pp. 132–3).
Q2?   Cases of doubtfully significant agreement between Q2 and F.
Q2p   Q2/F agreements against Q1 in anomalous punctuation (see Appendix
      D2b, p. 272 above).
Q2d ⎫ Dashes and brackets appearing in Q2 and F, but not in Q1 (see
Q2b ⎭   Appendix D3, p. 274 above).

(b) *Evidence of Q1 (non-Q2) origin*

Q1   Readings peculiar to Q1 appearing in F. It is to be noted that only those
      Q1 readings are significant here which are unlikely to have been
      incorporated into Q2 as 'corrections', and so to have passed *via* Q2 into
      the F text. A pair only of spelling anomalies common to Q1 and F satisfy
      the criterion.
Q1p   Q1/F agreements against Q2 in anomalous punctuation (see Appendix
      D2a, p. 268 above).
MS   Presumptive manuscript misreadings in F (see list on pp. 100–101 above).
      (The anomalous items on the list, nos. 2–6, are excluded here. For a full
      discussion of these see above, pp. 147ff.) No significance can be
      attributed to those misreadings which may have originated at a stage
      earlier in the history of the text than the type-setting. Only those
      misreadings are significant which cannot have been caused by manu-
      script alterations to Q2 copy, or, originating earlier, have been trans-

mitted to the F compositor as 'corrections' of Q2 copy. Where Q2 agrees 277
with Q1 in the true reading the conditions are, as nearly as possible,
satisfied. It is, at least, far more probable in such cases that the F
misreading stems directly from manuscript copy, and is to be laid at the
compositor's door, than that it should originate in some misunderstanding, or perverse alteration, of what is perfectly clear, and obviously
correct, in both prints.

qq2	B	71%[1]	I.i.56	*weild*	Q1		
qq2ᵛ	E	94%	I.i.166	*Physition*		Q2	
qq3	E	91%	I.i.270	*farwell*		Q2	
qq3ᵛ	B	36%	I.ii.124–5				Q1p
			I.ii.148	*sigh(e)*			Q2?
			I.ii.178–9				Q1p
qq4	E	77%	I.iv.4	*raiz'd*		Q2	
			I.iv.33	*canst thou do?*		Q2	
			I.iv.49			Q2d	
qq4ᵛ	E	86%	I.iv.111	*ones*		Q2	
			I.iv.151	*Do'st thou know*		Q2	
qq5	B	46%	I.iv.267	*grac'd*	MS		
			I.iv.357		Q1p		
qq5ᵛ	E	75%	I.v.22			Q2p	
			II.i.38			Q2p	
qq6	E	86%	II.i.61			Q2p	
			II.i.86			Q2b	
qq6ᵛ	E	94%	II.ii.158	*Come my Lord*		Q2	
rr1	E	86%	II.iii.4	*vnusall*		Q2	

1 An anomalously high
percentage, though close to
the 70% criterion. Qq2 is a
half-page. The mis-spelling
weild (corrected in Q2)
clearly connects column
qq2b, at least, with non-Q2
copy.

278	rr1ᵛa	E	71%[2]	II.iv.132			Q1p[3]
				II.iv.137		Q1p[3]	
	rr1ᵛb	B	70%[2]	II.iv.153		Q1p	
	rr2	E	74%	II.iv.250			Q2b
				II.iv.259		Q1p[4]	
				II.iv.283			Q2d
	rr2ᵛ	B	65%	III.ii.48		Q1p	
	rr3	E	84%	III.iv.2	*tirrany*		Q2
				III.iv.83	*Iustice*	MS[5]	
	rr3ᵛ	B	40%	III.iv.112		Q1p	
	rr4	B	47%	III.vi.17	*hiszing*	Q1	
				III.vi.68		Q1p	
				III.vi.73	*tight*	MS	
					Troudle taile	MS	
				III.vi.74		Q1p	
	rr4ᵛ	B	40%	IV.i.10	*poorely led?*	Q2?	

2 On, or very close to, the 70% criterion, hence hardly significant. A calculation on the assumption that B set a part of rrl[ᵛ]a (from II.iv.129 onwards) produces more conclusive, and consistent, results. See above, p. 261, n. 2.

3 From a portion of the column very probably set by B. See above, p. 144, n. 6.

4 This at first sight striking Q/F agreement in the reading *wel fauor'd* is probably not significant. It appears to be the case that hyphens were more or less arbitrarily inserted or omitted in each of the three texts: their evidence is not trustworthy. The contracted spelling in Q and F is more interesting and may, for practical purposes, be treated here as a punctuation variant. The agreement may, however, quite easily be explained. The word occurs at the end of a long line and in neither Q nor F was space available for the expanded spelling.

5 This reading occurs in the last line of rr3b. According to Hinman (*Printing*, II. 279) the last ten lines of this column were set by B.

rr5	B	53%	IV.i.51		QIp	
			IV.i.71	*slaues*	MS	
			IV.ii.17	*names*	MS	
			IV.iv.3	*Fenitar*	MS	
			IV.iv.4	*Hardokes*	MS	
rr5ᵛ	B	52%	IV.iv.9		QIp	
			IV.iv.18	*desires*	MS	
			IV.vi.17	*walk'd*	MS	
rr6	B	46%	IV.vi.52–3		QIp	
			IV.vi.66–7		QIp	
			IV.vi.71	*enraged*	MS	
			IV.vi.83	*crying*	MS	
			IV.vi.161		QIp	
rr6ᵛ	B	54%	IV.vi.213		QIp	
			IV.vi.236	*Dar'st*		Q2⁶
			IV.vi.264–5		QIp	
ss1	B	88%	IV.vii.38			Q2b
			IV.vii.59	*mocke me*		Q2
			IV.vii.69			Q2b
			IV.vii.74			Q2b
ss1ᵛ	E	86%				
ss2	E	97%	V.iii.121–2			Q2p
ss2ᵛ	E	76%	V.iii.155	*stop*		Q2
			V.iii.159	*araign(e)*		Q2
			V.iii.176			Q2p
			V.iii.184–6			Q2b
			V.iii.250	om. *the Captaine*		Q2

6 For discussion of the significance of this apparent agreement with Q2, and of other less striking common readings on the same page, see above, pp. 145–7.

280   ss3   B   91%   V.iii.264   Q1p[7]
                         V.iii.292   *So I thinke*   Q2?[8]

7   F substitutes a full stop (as found in Q1) for the undoubtedly correct mark of interrogation in Q2. But this is unlikely to be significant since B has a habit of converting dashes, exclamation marks, etc., into full stops. Examples occur at I.ii.72, IV.ii.72 (question marks); I.iv.273, III.vii.33, 46, 82 (exclamation marks); III.iv.149, III.vii.34, 52, 72 (dashes).

8   Almost certainly a coincidental agreement. F reads: *I* (= aye) *so I thinke*, which, since it involves a reconstruction of the sentence, is as likely to represent a revision of Q1 (*So thinke I to*) as of Q2 (*So I thinke too*) – see above, p. 133. The revision in fact must have stood in the manuscript prompt-book before being incorporated into Q2, so that the F/Q2 agreement in word order (*I thinke* instead of *thinke I*) is not significant.